Secrets in His Presence

Cross House Publishing

Secrets in His Presence. Copyright ©2008, 2010 by Gina Moroney.

Protected by the copyright laws of the United States of America. All rights reserved. No other part of this book may be reproduced in any form or by any electronic or mechanical means including information storage and retrieval systems without permission in writing from the publisher, except by a review, who may quote brief passages in a review.

Library of Congress Cataloging-in-Publication Data: Moroney, Gina
LCN: 2008937233
ISBN: 978-1-934749-34-0

Published by: *Cross House Publishing, www.crosshousepublishing.org*

Book cover, design, and page production: *Blue Dot Creative, www.bluedotcreative.com*

Unless otherwise noted, all scripture quotations are taken from Nelson's New King James version Study Bible (NKJV), copyright 1997 by Thomas Nelson, Inc. Used by permission. All rights reserved.

Scripture quotations marked NLT are taken from the *Holy Bible,* New Living Translation, copyright 1996, 2004. Used by permission of Tyndale House Publishers, Inc., Wheaton, Illinois 60189.

"Scripture taken from THE AMPLIFIED BIBLE. Old Testament copyright 1965, 1987 by The Zondervan Corporation. The Amplified New Testament copyright 1958, 1987 by The Lockman Foundation. Used by permission."

"Scripture taken from the HOLY BIBLE, NEW INTERNATIONAL VERSION. Copyright 1973, 1978, 1984 International Bible Society. Used by permission of Zondervan Bible Publishers."

Prayer Poems by Gina Moroney.

This edition printed on acid-free paper.

First Edition.
Printed in the United States of America.

To God be the glory...He is forever worthy of all our praise!

With a grateful heart...
I thank my loving family and dear friends for taking leaps of faith with me.
Without your advice and encouragement, this would not have been possible.
Karen, may you be blessed immeasurably for your countless hours
of serving God through this project.

for you

Dedicated to your journey, a lifetime of intimacy with God.
May you experience His presence every moment
and grow in your relationship with your Heavenly Father.

For You have made him most blessed forever;
You have made him exceedingly glad with Your presence.
Psalm 21: 6

What a joy to pursue God and reach for a deeper level of intimacy with Him in the moment to moment of life! *Secrets in His Presence* will help you move from your desire to know God, to the place where you experience Him everyday. This study companion to *Living in His Presence* will encourage and equip you to apply Biblical principles to your life so that you can thrive in the presence of God.

Spiritual growth is a journey, very much like a long road trip. Your journey has wide interstate lanes, narrow passageways, road signs, hazards, and much more. In *Living in His Presence,* you learned to watch for them, allowing the Holy Spirit to sit in the driver's seat and guide your journey to its final destination. You also learned that the final destination is not the real goal. The goal is the journey, the process of learning to live with God everyday. This study book is like a road map to help guide you and make the best of your journey.

When the pressures of life come our way, we become entangled in a politically correct way to handle them. Oftentimes we deprive ourselves of the freedom to be transparent for fear of what others might think. Yet we need a safe place to be honest and transparent. *Secrets in His Presence* offers you freedom to be yourself and reflect upon your spiritual life. My reflections and transparency are meant to help you be more open with yourself. I think you will also enjoy getting to know others whose stories will inspire your journey.

I am excited about your journey! God will reveal Himself to you as you give yourself to Him uninhibited. Deep within the heart of God is a soft spot where He longs for you. The warmth and security of His love is welcoming as you bask in His presence moment by moment. Delight in the Lord! The God of the universe anxiously awaits you, and His Spirit is ready to escort you into His presence.

God bless your journey,
Gina

Contents

For You	iv
Before You Begin	6
Prayer of Salvation	7
Gain the Most from this Book	8
New Beginning The Secret...Uncovered Treasure	9
Ingredient One Praise and Thanksgiving...Attitude of Gratitude	21
Ingredient Two Prayer and Communication...Loving Fellowship	47
Ingredient Three Trust in God...Celebration of Dependence	81
Ingredient Four Desire for God...Heart's Desire	123
Ingredient Five Abandonment...Letting Go	171
A Blend of Ingredients Life in His Presence...The Goal	209
Personal and Group Planning Guides	233

before you begin... an invitation
From *Living in His Presence*

Who do you say that Jesus Christ is? Was He merely a great man who lived over 2000 years ago, or is He the Son of God, the Messiah, your Savior? Is Jesus the way to everlasting life? How you will experience *Secrets in His Presence* depends upon what you believe to be true about Jesus Christ. Jesus is the Son of the one true God, and Jesus is alive. His Spirit dwells in the hearts of all those who believe in Him and have invited Him to be their personal Lord and Savior. Jesus paid the price and died for your sins and mine. He rose from the dead so that we may have a right relationship with God the Father and live forever with Him in Heaven someday. Jesus is God's free gift of salvation to the world. There's nothing you can do to earn salvation; it is a gift of love.

Perhaps you have never invited Jesus to be your personal Savior, or you have felt undeserving of God's gift of salvation. Maybe you believe that Jesus is the Son of God but have never entered into a relationship with Him. You might feel like you once had a relationship with Jesus, but somehow you've distanced yourself from Him. If you are nodding your head, then I encourage you to take a step of faith; take a closer look at Jesus Christ in the Bible. The most famous scripture of the Bible reads: *"For God so loved the world that He gave His only begotten Son that whoever believes in Him should not perish but have everlasting life"* (John 3:16). When Jesus began His ministry, He said, *"The time is fulfilled, and the kingdom of God is at hand. Repent, and believe in the gospel"* (Mark 1:15). Jesus responded to a man who wanted to understand more about Him. Jesus said, *"Most assuredly, I say to you, unless one is born again, he cannot see the kingdom of God"* (John 3:3). Believe, repent, and experience spiritual rebirth; then you will be saved! This is the reality of the good news of the gospel for you and for me.

The following prayer is a first time prayer of salvation for spiritual rebirth. It is also a rededication prayer for those who have already been spiritually reborn. The prayer reminds me of who Jesus is, who I am, where I've come from, and where I am going. It is a prayer of deep conviction, of salvation. Whether it is your first time to pray this type of prayer or not, these are powerful words that need to come from your heart. The power behind this prayer opens up the flood gates of Heaven to welcome you into God's kingdom where His children will live forever one day with Jesus Christ. You will be empowered to walk with Jesus on this earth and live for Him. If you sense that Christ is drawing you near, then please join me in prayer.

prayer of salvation

Dear Heavenly Father, I know that I am a sinner

and that I've sinned many times.

Jesus, You are the Son of God, and You came to earth

to save me from the consequences of my sins.

You died on the cross for my sins, and then

You rose from the dead so that I may enter

into a right relationship with the Father

and live in Heaven with You forever.

Please forgive me of my sins, and thank you that You do.

Thank you for Your grace, that undeserved mercy

You extend to me, which covers all of my sins.

Please come into my life now, be the Lord of my life,

and please help me to be the person You want me to be.

I invite You, Jesus, to live within my heart,

and I ask You to send Your Holy Spirit to be with me.

Thank you that Your Holy Spirit will never leave me nor forsake me.

I belong to You, Jesus, and You are my Lord and Savior forever.

Thank you!

Amen

Gain The Most From This Book

Secrets in His Presence will help you experience God and equip you to live with Him moment by moment. It centers on the five ingredients from *Living in His Presence.* These ingredients are discussed at length because they are necessary for an intimate relationship with God. Like its companion, this book is very personal and reads as if you and I are having a meaningful conversation.

This book is not divided into daily assignments, allowing freedom to journey at your pace. Simply be consistent and remain committed. For a more structured study, a Planning Guide is provided to map out a twelve-week journey for personal or group study.

This study book follows its companion closely. It is helpful to read the corresponding chapter from *Living in His Presence* before you begin with each ingredient from this book.

Journey through *Secrets in His Presence* in its proper order. Then use it on a continual basis to practice the ingredients, gain fresh insights from the Lord, and embellish your journey.

The various topics we discuss are marked and easy to identify. Some days you will study an entire topic while other times you might want to stay with it a while longer. Let the Holy Spirit guide you; He knows what you need each day.

Enjoy the personal stories and word pictures; try to relate them to your life.

Take time to reflect along the way. The first few pages of the book offer frequent opportunity for reflection and transparency, in preparation for your journey. The thought provoking questions throughout the rest of the book are meant to make you more aware of your relationship with God. Journal your thoughts and feelings in the spaces provided.

The Living Applications always follow the times to reflect and help make your journey more meaningful. Be sure to apply them to your daily walk with the Lord.

The Prayer Poems from *Living in His Presence* are in a new format. Spend as much time as you need with them, and allow the Holy Spirit to touch your heart and minister to you.

Your journey is a life long process. Don't be discouraged when you feel challenged along the way. Remain prayerful, stay on the path, and allow God to work in your life while you journey through this book.

God is going to carry you to spiritual places you've never been while you journey through the pages of this book. The Holy Spirit has secrets to share with you so that you can learn to live with your Heavenly Father just as Jesus did, moment to moment. Allow yourself to be real and experience all that God has for you in *Secrets in His Presence.*

New Beginning

The Secret... Uncovered Treasure	10
Experience God and Live Like Jesus	11
God Longs for a Relationship with You	13
Intimate Road Blocks	13
Uncovering Hidden Treasure	15
The Good Shepherd	16
Living in God's Presence, Then and Now	17
Companionship or Quick Fix?	18
Great Expectations	20

> *"You have made known to me the ways of life;*
> *You will make me full in the joy of Your presence."*
> Acts 2:28

What comes to mind when you think of actually living each moment in the presence of the God of the universe?

- Do you expect a meeting in a business setting where you come with an agenda?
- Do you anticipate spontaneous "run ins" with God throughout the day?
- Is God eerie, so mysterious that you are unsure as to what to expect?

None of us has seen God in the flesh. Even though God sent His son, Jesus Christ, to us in flesh and blood over 2000 years ago, God the Father isn't flesh and blood. His Holy Spirit who now lives with us on the earth isn't flesh and blood either. We don't have someone tangible to look at. So how do you know if you are in the presence of the Holy Spirit? What is an encounter with God like?

In Living in His Presence, I talked about my first encounter with God. It was monumental, and I marked it on my time line of major events. I had heard stories about encounters with God from others who had already met Him. Now it was my turn.

My husband, Mike, and I were invited for a weekend away to a Christian retreat. Mike was there for the spiritual food, the Bible studies, and worship times. I went along for a different kind of food, the homemade dinners and desserts that everyone raved about. I didn't think I was interested in a relationship with God; I was happy just going to church most Sundays. But the spiritual food turned out to be tasty, and I became intrigued with the idea of relationship with God.

The last evening of the retreat weekend, there was a call for those who would like to meet Jesus. My heart pounded; I was compelled to go forward even though I had no idea what would happen. Have you ever "just known" you needed to do something irregardless of your thoughts and emotions? That's what it was like for me. There wasn't time for a thought process or for logic. All I had was a certainty that I wanted and needed to meet Jesus. I remember going forward; I prayed the prayer of salvation and invited Jesus to be my Lord and Savior. My eyes were half closed, but my mind was focused on Jesus. Someone told me to close my eyes because I was about to meet Him. One would think that if someone was about to meet a special person, both eyes should be wide open. Not knowing any better, I did what I was told with the expectation of meeting my Savior. The next thing I remember was falling to the floor in tears. Someone proclaimed, "You see Jesus, don't you?" I nodded in agreement. This is who I "saw," and what my heart "just knew."

I knew I was in the presence of God, but I wasn't looking through my natural eyes. "Exactly what do you see?" someone asked.

At that moment, I didn't have the words to express what I saw through my heart. Now many years later, I can articulate it somewhat for you.

I "saw" myself lying down and knew that Jesus was there bending over me. Jesus was smiling, and He was removing two sets of rusted iron cuffs that were locked onto my wrists and ankles. I felt His love and a sense of freedom at that moment like never before. There was also an incredible peace that swept throughout my body manifested by a warm, physical sensation. Who says God doesn't reveal Himself to us anymore or that we cannot experience Him? Even though my physical eyes could not see God, my spiritual eyes looked right at Him. I was never the same after that moment, and the experience changed the way I view God. I had to press in and find out more about what it is like to follow Jesus Christ. I'd like to think that I was following Jesus because I believed in Him and went to church. However, that "born again" experience was really the beginning of a spiritual journey for me. I had a fresh, real encounter with the God of the universe!

An encounter with God isn't eerie; it isn't a formal meeting or a "run in" with Him. It is an amazing feeling, a certainty that you are on holy ground with the Almighty. Your spiritual eyes focus on Him, and you know that you are in the presence of God. It is similar to knowing when you love someone. You "just know," don't you?

Time to Reflect

- Can you think of a time when you felt like you had an encounter with God?
- Recall that moment. How did it impact you?
- Are you wondering if you've ever really had a personal experience with God?
- Would you like to experience Him and feel His love as never before?

_____
_____
_____
_____
_____

Living Application: Begin to pray and ask the Holy Spirit to reveal Himself to you personally so that you won't mistake His presence. Sometimes God is revealing Himself, but we are so busy that we don't recognize Him. Set aside short quiet times alone with God; close your eyes to the distractions of life, and focus on Jesus. Read Scripture and listen to music that draws you closer to God. Take time to journal how you feel and what you "see." Start to notice even the slightest inclinations of His presence. Be persistent!

Experience God and Live Like Jesus

There is danger in operating exclusively out of feeling without applying Biblical principles to life. Yet the flawless example of the lifestyle of Jesus is still our inspiration.

Jesus experienced the presence of God; He knew the Father. Everything Jesus did was out of relationship with the Father.

"All things have been delivered to Me by My Father, and no one knows the Son except the Father. Nor does anyone know the Father except the Son, and the one to whom the Son wills to reveal Him" (Matthew 11: 27). Out of His relationship with the Father, Jesus accomplished all that was planned for Him.

The timeless words of the Bible guide us as we pursue our relationship with God so that we will remain on track and not operate solely out of feeling. Everything you experience from God and all that you hear from the Holy Spirit should be confirmed by the Bible. The Holy Spirit will never manifest Himself to you or speak anything to you that goes against the Word of God in the Bible.

There is also danger in ignoring the manifestation of the Holy Spirit, being unwilling to allow yourself to experience God on a personal level. Unfortunately we can limit the beautiful ways that the Lord wants to reveal Himself to us if we are too cautious. The danger mostly comes from missing out on the relationship we were created for. I believe it saddens the Lord when His children choose to live only with intellectual knowledge of Him.

Jesus was quite clear about his dependency upon His relationship with His Father. He said that He could not operate without knowing the will of God. Knowing the will of God comes from relationship. And out of relationship comes transformation.

Time to Reflect

- Do you have a relationship with God?
- What is your relationship with God like?
- Do you tend to relate to God through feeling and experience?
- Do you tend to relate to God through your intellect?

_____
_____
_____
_____
_____

Living Application: Do some real soul searching, and be honest with yourself about your relationship with the Father. In relationship there is a connection, one to another. Even though you love Jesus, perhaps you are feeling disconnected from Him and His Holy Spirit right now. Press in and establish a great rapport with our Lord by spending time with Him. Go for a walk and talk to God, but don't bombard Him with needs and prayer requests only. Simply enjoy being with God; you will sense His presence in time. Pursue relationship.

God Longs for a Relationship with You

Perhaps you have lived most of your life loving God, but you never really understood that God longs for a loving relationship with you. Jeremiah 31:3 says, *"...Yes, I have loved you with an everlasting love; therefore with loving kindness I have drawn you."* Being drawn with loving kindness indicates desire on God's part. The Lord's desire is real enough to allow us to explore His deepest nature with true intimacy. We are talking about the Creator of the Universe here; this is powerful!

Time to Reflect

- Are you convinced that God loves you enough to draw you in with loving kindness?
- Have you ever sensed the Holy Spirit drawing you closer? What was it like?
- Do you watch for times when the Spirit of God could be drawing you in?
- Are you still unsure, not convinced that God is drawing you near?

_____
_____
_____
_____
_____

Living Application: Write the scripture, Jeremiah 31:3, on a piece of paper. Keep that scripture with you at all times. Read it aloud as many times in a day as you can. Think about it, and meditate upon those words. Ask the Holy Spirit to burnish this scripture deep within your heart and bring the words to life for you. Ask that it would be as if God is appearing to you in the flesh.

Intimate Road Blocks

I wish I could say that every moment is heavenly bliss with God. That just isn't the way it is all the time. It is what I strive for, but I fall short. There are constant road blocks that keep me from entering a sweet state of intimacy with God as often as I desire. Sometimes it is a struggle to get past them. Road blocks come in all sizes, and they can be disguised so that we won't notice them. They can be subtle, yet plentiful.

The most obvious road block for me came as a surprise once I identified it. I used to entertain the thought that I needed a perfect attitude about everything in order to have intimacy with God. I thought God wouldn't desire to be with me if I wasn't just right in all areas. What a lie that was! Do you know anyone who displays a perfect attitude moment by moment? If you think you do, then that person probably has a pretty good outer cover.

"For all have sinned and fall short of the glory of God." Romans 3:23

None of us is without faults. If that was the case, then we wouldn't need a Savior. Heaven would be a slam dunk all on our own. By now we agree that without Jesus Christ, Heaven is unattainable.

What about that bad attitude day? Does the Holy Spirit leave your heart and visit someone else on that day? That probably sounds like a silly question. Of course the Holy Spirit doesn't leave your heart! But I am telling you that even though we know that, we don't act that way. Oftentimes when we sin or have a poor attitude, we tend to run from God instead of embracing Him. We shy away from prayer. Praising God is almost impossible because we can't see beyond our road block.

I used to try my hardest to obtain a perfect attitude before the Lord. I would work at it daily, but to no avail. Then one day I realized that in the same way that I needed Jesus because I could not earn my salvation, I also needed Him to get past the road block of my mind and emotions. It was not something I could do on my own. Now whenever I am having a bad day, I ask Jesus to lift me over the miry muck on the road and take me to my sweet destination for the day.

Here are a few other road blocks that will try to stop you from having intimacy with God. You might be surprised to learn of some of them.

- An arrogant mind…nothing will get in **my** way; I can do this myself!
- Distractions…too busy today for intimacy!
- Selfishness… not going to share **my** time with God today!
- Legalism…didn't read my Bible or have a quiet time today, so no intimacy!

Time to Reflect

▸ Have you ever allowed a bad attitude day to keep you from intimacy with God?

▸ What other road blocks have you stumbled upon on your journey?

▸ Be honest! Are you willing to let go of your road blocks?

▸ Will you give Jesus access to your mind and heart to overcome the road blocks?

_____
_____
_____
_____
_____

Living Application: Identify your road blocks and write them down, but do not allow them to stop you. Don't be intimidated by them or try to skirt your way around them. Pray and ask the Holy Spirit to help you get past them every time they attempt to hinder the progress of your journey. Always remember that Jesus Christ is there for you and that His Holy Spirit never leaves the sweet spot of your heart. You **can** go deeper in intimacy with the Father no matter what. Choose intimacy with God, and allow Him to draw you in. You will watch the roadblocks diminish as you establish your intimacy with God.

Uncovering Hidden Treasure

In *Living in His Presence,* we talked about discovering the hidden treasure. When I learned that God actually speaks to His children, I felt like I had uncovered a hidden chest filled with treasures. Actually, I was pretty upset that I had lived my life without knowing that God speaks through the Holy Spirit. I felt like I wanted to make up for lost time with God.

> **Picture this!**
>
> A precious part of the uncovered treasure is the knowledge that Jesus is alive and well and that He is ever present by His Holy Spirit. This tells me that all the benefits to those who knew Jesus Christ when He walked on the earth are now available to you and to me. If you and I were living then and knew that Jesus was in the vicinity, wouldn't we race to find him? I have a word picture to help you visualize this.
>
> Picture a long avenue with shops and cafés lined up and down on both sides of the street. You hear the news that the most powerful man who will ever live is somewhere on that avenue with no body guards or attendants. You **have** to check it out! You run frantically from shops to cafés, looking everywhere for this person. Out of breath, you drop your belongings and shopping bags along the avenue in hopes of sprinting in and out of stores to find him faster. When you find him, you want to catch a glimpse or even shake his hand. You even push your way out in front of everyone on that busy avenue because you want the prestigious privilege of being associated with this famous, powerful man. Alas, you find him in a café sitting with a group of children, eating an ice-cream cone, waiting for you. Exhausted, you inch up and introduce yourself to this amazing person. Not only does he shake your hand, but he stands up to embrace you. He gives you his contact information and offers you his personal assistance for whatever you need. Then this generous man buys you all the ice-cream you can eat for the rest of your life!

Jesus is even more tangible and available than the man you just pursued in the picture. The words of the Bible are true; you are being drawn to Him, and the benefits are too numerous to count.

Sometimes doubt and unworthiness slip in through the cracks. This makes it difficult for you to believe that the person of Jesus Christ desires **you** enough that His Spirit would draw you in. When you look into the spiritual mirror on the wall, I hope that you see who you really are. You are saved by grace through Jesus Christ, and you are highly valued simply because you belong to **Him**. You are the first person He would invite, not the next to the last one. Now uncover the treasure and take hold of your great privilege!

Time to Reflect

▸ Who would you run frantically to meet? Would you do the same for Jesus?

▸ What would you want to discover inside of a hidden treasure chest?

▸ Are you comfortable in your salvation alone, or do you want more?

▸ How important to you is an intimate relationship with God?

_____
_____
_____
_____
_____

Living Application: Take some time and revisit that word picture. Is your heart pounding at the thought of racing to find Jesus on the avenues of life? Decide how much effort you are willing to put forth in order to pursue your treasure. Now close your eyes and imagine finding your treasure chest. Open it up and discover all that the chest holds for you. Pray to the Father, and ask Him to establish the sound of His voice into your spiritual ears so that you will recognize Him. Anticipate your conversations with God. List your expectations and anxieties about listening for the voice of the Holy Spirit. This will prepare you for our discussions on prayer and communication later on.

The Good Shepherd

"…the sheep hear his voice; and he calls his own sheep by name and leads them out. And when he brings out his own sheep, he goes before them; and the sheep follow him, for they know his voice" (John 10:3, 4).

I've read a really good book, *A Shepherd Looks at Psalm 23.* It was written by a modern day shepherd, Phillip Keller. It studies our beloved 23rd Psalm from the Bible one verse at a time. It is an allegory about the similarities between a real shepherd and Jesus, the Good Shepherd. You will be surprised to read of how our lives and character parallel that of sheep. Without the sound of our Shepherd's voice, the perilous journey we face everyday can only bring harm; we are as directionally challenged and unprotected as wandering sheep. You will be even more amazed to discover the great lengths Jesus goes to in order to give us constant care and attention, just like sheep. The Good Shepherd is meticulous about the way He cares for His own sheep and draws them in.

Throughout the book, as I read about real sheep, I was struck with awe at how the Good Shepherd knows every detail about His sheep and about how closely they follow Him to know and depend upon Him. Prior to reading the book on the 23rd Psalm, I never paid much attention to the scriptures where we are compared to sheep. Now I think about them and the beautiful word picture often as I focus on my pursuit of God.

Time to Reflect

▸ Does it bother you to be compared to a sheep?

▸ Do you **know** that you need the Good Shepherd's voice in your life?

▸ Have you ever felt directionally challenged, in need of a Shepherd?

▸ Are you ready to pursue a genuine relationship with God and get to know Him better?

_____
_____
_____
_____
_____

Living Application: Try to obtain a copy of *A Shepherd looks at Psalm 23* by Phillip Keller. It is well worth your effort to read this small book; you will enjoy every chapter. In the mean time, meditate upon the 23rd Psalm and ask the Holy Spirit to give you a greater desire to know God and hear His voice. Below is the 23rd Psalm from the Amplified Bible. It will give you good clarity and understanding of this beloved passage of Scripture. Read it aloud often, with the expectation of being drawn in to know God and live in His presence.

Psalm 23, A Psalm of David

"The Lord is my Shepherd (to feed, guide and shield me), I shall not lack. He makes me lie down in (fresh tender) green pastures; He leads me beside the still and restful waters."

"He refreshes and restores my life (my self); He leads me in the paths of righteousness (uprightness and right standing with Him-not for my earning it, but) for His name's sake. Yes, though I walk through the (deep, sunless) valley of the shadow of death, I will fear or dread no evil, for You are with me: Your rod (to protect) and Your staff (to guide), they comfort me."

"You prepare a table before me in the presence of my enemies. You anoint my head with oil; my (brimming) cup runs over."

"Surely or only goodness, mercy, and unfailing love shall follow me all the days of my life, and through the length of my days the house of the Lord (and His presence) shall be my dwelling place."

Living in the Presence of God, Then and Now

I have spent quite a bit of time thinking about my spiritual heroes of the past and their intense relationships with God. I admire the way they were able to get to that place of abundance in His presence moment by moment. Because they lived long ago, I imagined that life was not as hectic as it is now. After all, they didn't drive car pools, coach soccer games, or volunteer at school. Those who pursued God didn't spend hours in traffic jams, go to the gym and the spa, or keep various appointments. But then again, maybe they did keep schedules similar to ours.

They had to walk miles to their destinations, and they spent a great deal of time teaching and training their children. My spiritual heroes of long ago had to repair broken, wooden wheels on their wagons and carts, they scrubbed the grime out of their clothes with their bare hands, and they probably grew or raised most of what they ate. Why would I think they had more time to pursue God? Perhaps it's because there was mostly candle light, and they couldn't burn the late night oil to do their chores. They probably kept an earlier bedtime.

It is easy for me to come up with excuses for why I don't have time to pursue my Maker. There will never be enough time to give God all He desires of me if I am putting boundaries around my time with Him. God is on every avenue of life, in every inch of space around me, and He is calling me to live with Him moment to moment.

Those who lived long ago were every bit as busy as you and me; they met as many needs as we do. Yet they pursued God and lived in His sweet presence. Life is never too hectic to pursue an intimate relationship with God. Perhaps the Lord will meet some of those daily needs, and we won't have to work as hard. Now there's a thought! We will have to talk more about that later on.

Time to Reflect

- Does it seem unrealistic to live with God every moment…if so, why?
- Do you tend to place boundaries around your relationship with God? What are they?
- Does your day become so busy and focused that you forget about the presence of God?
- What keeps you from pursuing an intimate relationship with God, moment by moment?

_____
_____
_____
_____
_____

Living Application: Try to get in touch with your feelings about living with God. Since the Holy Spirit lives in your heart, perhaps you have imagined God coming and going like a roommate would do. Instead, close your eyes and imagine what your life might be like if you lived in the continual awareness of His Spirit within you. List your concerns about allowing God to occupy that kind of time in your life. List the benefits for living with God moment by moment.

Companionship or Quick Fix?

When I talk about living in God's presence and hearing His voice, some might want to go directly to the "hearing" part without cultivating a love relationship with God as well.

We must guard against an instantaneous "hear-His-voice" fix.

> **Picture This!**
>
> My friend, Deanne, once gave me a word picture about listening for the voice of the Holy Spirit. Thinking about it helps me guard against my tendency to listen solely for the next thing God might have to say. Deanne told me it is much like being a news reporter with a microphone in hand to catch every word that is said in an interview. Keeping my conversation at arms length, I ask a question and then point the microphone toward the Holy Spirit, expecting Him to answer. The microphone goes back and forth until I get my information from God. Sometimes I set aside my loving relationship and run off to report what I thought God said to me. Then there are the times when I take His precious words for granted, as in a quick fix, and run merrily on my way until I need to interview Him again. When I stop and catch myself, I am so sorry for allowing my time with the most powerful One in the world to be like an impersonal interview.

Perhaps you have never thought of your relationship with God this way, but it is important that you understand how easily that can happen. We all have the tendency to leave companionship on the back porch. We enter the relationship with a quick-fix mentality without intending to.

Jesus is our most faithful and loyal companion, waiting to share life with us through His Holy Spirit. Once in a while, there is such great need that we have to throw out an "SOS" prayer to God in hopes of a quick answer. That is just fine, and it happens to all of us on occasion. We have many other times to enjoy fellowship with God, so we don't have to feel guilty when those desperate needs arise. He understands!

"God is faithful, by whom you were called into the fellowship of His Son, Jesus Christ our Lord" (1Corinthians 1:9). Here's what comes to mind when I think of relationship and companionship. In relationship we relate one to another, yet we can also be related to one another as in kinship. Companionship has a warm feeling about it, as in intimate fellowship. Our relationship with Christ is one of fellowship, relating one to another as kin, and the warmth of His presence is continual.

We shouldn't be an arm's length from Jesus; we are **His** kin and His Holy Spirit is closer than close! We can touch the Living God, not just stand at a distance hoping to get a glimpse. This world of instantaneous fixes goes up in smoke for each one of us as we fix our eyes on Jesus and press in for lasting fellowship with Him.

Time to Reflect

- Is your relationship with God about tender fellowship or more about a quick fix?
- When have you stretched the microphone out just to hear a word from the Lord?
- How do you relate to God?
- In what way is God becoming your constant companion?

_____
_____
_____

Living Application: Take some time to evaluate your relationship with God. Be totally honest with yourself. Are you satisfied with the relationship? How would you like it to change? If you could imagine yourself having intimate fellowship with the Holy Spirit, what do you think it might look like? Pray and ask the Holy Spirit to draw you closer so that you would feel His presence and have fresh encounters with God.

Great Expectations

Secrets in His Presence is going to help you achieve your goal to live in the sweet presence of God. Fix your eyes upon your Savior, and you will move forward on your journey with determination. What a great privilege to cultivate and nurture the relationship you have with God! If you are just beginning your relationship with God, then you are about to embark on the greatest adventure you have ever taken.

We must all remember that it takes time, patience, and some pruning to cultivate and grow our relationship with God. You are in this for a lifetime, so be ready for the journey. Always keep in mind that the journey is your goal.

Together we will dig into the five ingredients that help us learn to live with God moment by moment. I will share stories, and you can glance at word pictures that bring simple concepts to life. There is plenty of time to reflect, pray, and then use the living applications to help on your journey. Before long, you will have milestones that will highlight your time line of life's events with God.

Let's pray!

Dear Lord, I thank you that you are drawing me into intimate fellowship and lasting relationship with You. I can hardly wait to embrace my journey with You. Thank you for a lifetime of living with You in genuine intimacy. Help me to see You with my spiritual eyes and experience all that You have for me. I desire to know and love You more than anything else. I want my life to be a reflection of You and Your ways, so I give You **my** life and **my** ways so that I can become more like You.

First Ingredient

Praise and Thanksgiving...
Attitude of Gratitude 22
A Praiseworthy God 22
A Healthy Reverence of God 24
Living in the Kingdom 26
To Know Him is To Love Him 27
Praise in the Midst of Tribulation 29
Ways to Praise 31
No Guilt 33
From the Shallow End to the Deeper Waters 35
Ponder God 37
Surprising Benefits 40
Restful Praise 43
Unattractive Risks 44
Soaring on the Interstate 46

*"You are worthy, O Lord, to receive glory and honor and power;
for You created all things, and by Your will they exist and were created."*
Revelation 4:11

The first major ingredient that we must add to our lives in order to live in the presence of God is praise and thanksgiving. What comes to your mind when you think of praise and thanksgiving?

- Do you think of two separate ingredients, each with a different meaning?
- Does a feeling come to your mind, or do you sense an action?
- How well do you correlate these two words with an attitude of gratitude?

In *Living in His Presence*, I listed praise and thanksgiving as one ingredient; yet they are two separate words with different meanings. But the Holy Spirit showed me that they operate together as one ingredient, one attitude of the heart for learning to live in His presence moment by moment. Thanksgiving unto the Lord might come for a specific reason, but praise is usually a natural by-product. Likewise, when we praise God, gratitude stretches out to reach Him at the same time. Living with the Lord calls for praise and thanksgiving, and they are one ingredient.

The dictionary shows us that each word indicates an action. Praise requires an action because it is an expression of admiration. Thanksgiving also requires an action; it is an expression of gratitude. For the longest time, I thought that an attitude of gratitude was mostly a feeling. But it needs to be an expression of the heart, and it requires an action. We can "feel" all that we want, but without acting on that feeling through expression, nothing happens. Praise and thanksgiving are part of an action of the heart, an outflow of what is taking place inside. Together, and they are meant to **express** our utmost worship of the One True God.

Choosing to operate with praise and thanksgiving unto the Lord opens the door for an attitude of gratitude to waltz into your life. It isn't a state of mind; it is an active lifestyle of worship for God. It means that whatever your circumstance, you fix your eyes on God's goodness and establish your lifestyle of gratitude toward Him. You will automatically be drawn closer to God and the awareness of His precious presence. The awareness of His presence changes everything about your outlook and perspective on life.

A Praiseworthy God

When you woke up this morning, were you able to see the time on the alarm clock? Did you look out the window and see the beauty of daylight? Could you hear the birds singing? Perhaps you heard the laughter of your children as they awakened to a new day. How did the warm water feel across your back when you slipped into the shower?

When you received a hug to wish you a good day, how did that feel? The smell of freshly brewed coffee or your favorite muffins baking in a warm oven... was that a welcome whiff? Perhaps the fragrance of last night's rain lingers in today's crisp morning air for you to enjoy. That first sip of coffee or tea is always the best one, isn't it? On your way out the door, you grabbed a cookie to enjoy in the car; how did it taste?

Even though we vary in what we enjoy and appreciate, we should be abundantly grateful for the five senses that we have. I only appealed to a few of the simple pleasures you might have as you begin your day. The rest of your pleasures throughout the day continue because of God's gracious gift to you through your senses. They are too numerous to count, aren't they? We haven't even begun to list all the reasons to express praise and thanksgiving to God, but through our five senses, we already have enough to last until we go to bed tonight. What a praise-worthy God!

The Bible is full of verses expressing praise and thanksgiving for God's creation... the beauty of nature, and for the beauty of you. Here are a few verses from The New Living Translation of the Bible that paint a picture of a praiseworthy God:

"Let the godly sing with joy to the Lord for it is fitting to praise him. The Lord merely spoke, and the heavens were created. He breathed the word, and all the stars were born. He gave the sea its boundaries and locked the oceans in vast reservoirs. Let everyone in the world fear the Lord, and let everyone stand in awe of him. For when he spoke, the world began! It appeared at his command." (Psalm 33:1, 6-9 NLT)

"You take care of the earth and water it, making it rich and fertile. The rivers of God will not run dry; they provide a bountiful harvest of grain, for you have ordered it so. You drench the plowed ground with rain, melting the clods and leveling the ridges. You soften the earth with showers and bless its abundant crops. You crown the year with a bountiful harvest; even the hard pathways overflow with abundance. The wilderness becomes a lush pasture, and the hillsides blossom with joy. The meadows are clothed with flocks of sheep, and the valleys are carpeted with grain. They all shout and sing for joy." (Psalm 65:9-13 NLT)

"O Lord, you have examined my heart and know me. You know when I sit down or stand up. You know my every thought when far away. You chart the path ahead of me and tell me where to stop and rest. Every moment you know where I am. You know what I am going to say even before I say it, Lord. You both precede and follow me. You place your hand of blessing on my head. Such knowledge is too wonderful for me, too great for me to know! You made all the delicate, inner parts of my body and knit me together in my mother's womb. Thank you for making me so wonderfully complex! Your workmanship is marvelous...and how well I know it. You watched me as I was being formed in utter seclusion, as I was woven together in the dark of the womb. You saw me before I was born. Every day of my life was recorded in your book. Every moment was laid out before a single day had passed. How precious are your thoughts about me, O God! They are innumerable! I can't even count them; they outnumber the grains of sand! And when I wake up in the morning, you are still with me!" (Psalm 139:1-6, 13-18 NLT)

PERSONAL NOTES

We know, love, and serve an awesome God. There are not enough words or examples that I can bring to you that would express His grandeur, His praiseworthiness. Surely you have your own unending list of reasons why God is praiseworthy, and you can add to it daily if your mind is focused upon the greatness of our God.

A Healthy Reverence of God

Just recently, I decided to read the entire Old Testament from its beginning in Genesis to the last book of Malachi. I was reacquainted with the God of the Old Testament even though I know Him under the New Covenant today. It helped me reestablish a healthy reverence for God, and I came away more in awe of Him than I was before. His power and sovereignty became unmistakably real, and I wondered if my reverence for God was as sincere as it should be. Have I kept God Almighty on the throne where He belongs, or have I treated Him more like a peer?

As I read, a few Old Testament passages were really impressed on my heart. I will share some of them with you. Perhaps they will help to keep your healthy reverence of God alive.

There were times in the Old Testament when the earth shook and trembled at the sound of God's voice. The people couldn't even look upon the face of God for fear of death. "*Now all the people witnessed the thunderings, the lightning flashes, the sound of the trumpet, and the mountain smoking; and when the people saw it, they trembled and stood afar off*" (Exodus 20:18).

God knows that when we hold Him in proper esteem it is to our benefit; He will make us holy. "*You shall not profane My holy name, but I will be hallowed among the children of Israel. I am the Lord who sanctifies you*" (Leviticus 22:32).

A healthy reverence for God brings blessing to me and to my family. "*Oh, that they had such a heart in them that they would fear Me and always keep all My commandments, that it might be well with them and with their children forever*" (Deuteronomy 5:29).

We live with the tangible signs of God's power "*Let all the earth fear the Lord; let all the inhabitants of the world stand in awe of Him. For He spoke, and it was done; He commanded, and it stood fast*" (Psalm 33:8,9).

God is God, and I am not! "*Be still, and know that I am God; I will be exalted among the nations, I will be exalted in the earth*" (Psalm 46:10).

Pause a Moment

Do you keep God Almighty on the throne where He belongs, or is He more like a peer to you?

Under the New Covenant we access our Heavenly Father through our relationship with Jesus Christ. Perhaps that is why some tend to embrace a more casual view of God. While we relate to the humanity of Christ, sometimes we overlook His deity. In His humanity, Jesus relates to us perfectly and understands every feeling and emotion we have. Our relationship with Him is close, tangible, and candid. If we aren't careful, it could alter our view of who God really is and the way we relate to Him.

The scriptures in the New Testament also make it perfectly clear that we are to have a genuine reverence for God. Those who have a healthy fear of God are walking in obedience to His command. This awesome God we fear is reigning in victory.

Jesus said, "*And do not fear those who kill the body but cannot kill the soul. But rather fear Him who is able to destroy both soul and body in hell*" (Matthew 10: 28).

God is fair and just; no one will fool Him. "*Then Peter opened his mouth and said, 'In truth I perceive that God shows no partiality. But in every nation, whoever fears Him and works righteousness is accepted by Him'*" (Acts 10: 34,35).

Learning to live with God in an attitude of gratitude fosters a healthy reverence for Him. "*...but be filled with the Spirit, speaking to one another in psalms and hymns and spiritual songs, singing and making melody in your heart to the Lord, giving thanks always for all things to God the Father in the name of our Lord Jesus Christ, submitting to one another in the fear of God*" (Ephesians 5: 18-21).

The Kingdom of Heaven is our inheritance, and we must serve out of reverence to God. "*Therefore, since we are receiving a kingdom which cannot be shaken, let us have grace, by which we may serve God acceptably with reverence and godly fear. For our God is a consuming fire*" (Hebrews 12: 28, 29).

We want to be on God's side because in the end, God still reigns! "*We give You thanks, O Lord God Almighty, the One who is and who was and who is to come, because You have taken Your great power and reigned. The nations were angry, and Your wrath has come, and the time of the dead, that they should be judged, and that You should reward Your servants the prophets and the saints, and those who fear Your name, small and great*" (Revelation 11: 17, 18).

Those who have a close relationship with the Lord are challenged to relate to a loving God who is also the most powerful being. The God of the Old Testament is the same today as He was then. Nothing about God changes; He simply is. The Bible is filled with stories, passages, and verses that give praise and glory to the Almighty. We must keep God on the throne at all times, revere Him with a holy fear, and praise Him with our lives.

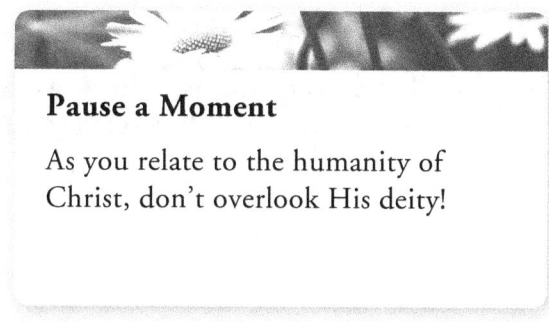

Pause a Moment

As you relate to the humanity of Christ, don't overlook His deity!

Living in the Kingdom

Sometimes when I think of the Kingdom of God, I think about earthly kingdoms that existed long ago. They had well-defined, physical boundaries that were meant to keep outsiders from entering. Those who lived in the kingdom were forced to live under the rule of the king and his magistrates. There was severe punishment for anyone who went against the king, perhaps even death. In fact, there were those whose sole purpose in life was to protect the king.

Remember the Musketeers and how much of an honor it was to be an appointed member? They put their lives on the line in order to protect the king; they were sold out to his service. People bowed before the king and held him in highest esteem. There was an unspoken, patriotic love for the king and his kingdom. Those kingdoms were filled with flaws and evil deception, yet people revered and honored their king even though most of them would never have a glimpse of him.

Today we have the utmost privilege of living in the Kingdom of God, and that is incredibly good news! There are no physical boundaries in God's kingdom. It is everywhere; it is in the air all around us. In *Living in His Presence* we talked about how our God doesn't rule with an iron fist. He is a loving God, and His Holy Spirit guides and directs as each one yields himself unto His leadership.

Jesus is our king, but no one is forced to succumb to His leadership. Yet, for those who choose not to accept Jesus as their personal Savior, there is the promise of a painful eternity without God. Each follower of Jesus is appointed to be like a Musketeer; to protect and defend the Kingdom of God.

As a follower of Christ, we have the distinct honor of getting to know the King on a personal level. Therefore we should be sold out to Jesus Christ, enough to put our lives on the line for God and for His kingdom. Here is where praise and thanksgiving come in. Instead of an automatic bow before the Lord, wouldn't an attitude of gratitude be the perfect posture before Him? Your heart should be overflowing with all the good and perfect things that come from God, enough to live each moment in a posture of praise.

Your love for the King doesn't have to be unspoken. It should be expressed in shouts of praise and thanksgiving on every avenue and corner of life. *"Shout joyfully to the Lord, all the earth; break forth in song, rejoice, and sing praises"* (Psalm 98: 4). Here is the best part: you are loved by the King, and you have an invitation and the means to know Him personally because you are one of His very own.

Not only are you living in God's kingdom, but you have access to the throne room where He sits in loving admiration of you. God beams with joy when you live in an attitude of gratitude in His presence. I cannot emphasize this enough.

The King of all the other kings is longing for moment by moment fellowship with you.

God is ready and willing to reveal the treasures of the kingdom to you through His Spirit. Doesn't that make you want to enter in and praise Him more and more?

Time to Reflect

- How well do you esteem God the Father?
- Are you truly sold out to Jesus Christ, your King? What makes you think so?
- Would you give your life for your King and His kingdom? How do you know?
- Does your life radiate an attitude of gratitude toward God?

_____
_____
_____
_____
_____

Living Application: List the things that appeal to your five senses for which you are very grateful, and be sure to think through your entire day. Praise Him and thank Him for those blessings, then watch for God to inhabit your attempts to honor Him. Begin to picture the Kingdom of God all around you. Be mindful of God's presence in your heart as well as in every molecule of air and space. Start to get a feel for the grandeur of God while you realize your place in His arms.

To Know Him is to Love Him

When we were talking about living in God's kingdom, I mentioned that we have the distinct honor of getting to know our King. I think of how the people long ago loved their king out of respect, but most of them didn't know the king personally. I have often wondered how someone can love another if he doesn't know that person. Perhaps some equate respect and reverence with love. I am not sure, but I do think that most people tend to fall in love after getting to know someone.

Those who have spent a good deal of time with God are the ones that I'd expect to know Him well. If you are spending time with the Holy Spirit, you will get to know Him and understand the heart of God much better. I know that I don't feel very close to God when I haven't invested much time into our relationship. Yet when I spend time reading my Bible, and focus on my relationship with the Lord, I seem to draw near to Him and hear His voice more clearly. It is in that time of getting to know God that we fall in love with Him.

Love for God isn't merely a warm, fuzzy feeling that coats the lining of your heart when He does something grand for you. Love for God is an intentional act of your will. It says that no matter what it seems like God does or doesn't do for me, I choose to love Him even more because I know Him and understand His heart.

Your love for God should be unconditional. I hope that you can grasp this concept and take it straight to your heart. This is a simple revelation that will change your life forever. You no longer worship or praise the Lord because of how you feel about Him at the moment. You will praise Him because of who you **know** Him to be, through your relationship with Him. Then a life of praise and thanksgiving unto the Lord comes naturally.

But God demonstrates His own love toward us, in that while we were still sinners, Christ died for us (Romans 5:8). It wouldn't seem right if I went on and didn't spend some time discussing God's love for **us**. If God hadn't loved us enough to send Jesus to ransom us from our deadly fate, we wouldn't be capable of knowing **or** loving Him. God gave His first fruits, His Finest so that we could live with Him forever in Heaven some day. That alone is enough to bring us into a lifestyle of praise and thanksgiving for God. Just when you think it doesn't get any better, God tops it all off with wonderful, gracious gifts for each of us.

You can't look anywhere and not see the goodness of God. Yes, He is praiseworthy!

God is the picture of unconditional love. It doesn't matter what you do or don't do, His matchless love for you will never waver. God's love isn't based on your mistakes or sins, and it doesn't hinge on your success or good deeds. God's love sees who you are and how much you mean to Him, no matter what. Take that thought and run with it; run straight into the arms of your Father with an attitude of praise and thanksgiving!

Prayer Poem Ministry
"THOUGHTS OF EXCELLENCE"

When you cast your eyes upon the Lord and not on this world, then you will see things as He sees them. First you must contemplate His love. Fix your eyes on His truth, His nobility, His righteousness, purity and loveliness…He is admirable! Is that not excellent and worthy of praise? Think about such a thing. And as you think and contemplate, the Holy Spirit shall transpire your mind, that the goodness of God will infuse your memory cells. What you remember and what you feel will be filtered by the love of God and His goodness. For in your strength you cannot think this way, but in His strength and love, you will always think this way. Your life is all about God's love, so allow His love to be reflected in your life.

See the world and those around you through the eyes of your Savior. It isn't difficult when you fathom His love for you! All that He is…is for you, all that He has…is for you. Allow the Lord to surround you with His presence so that your mind will be changed and your very being will be about His will and His love. But you must think about the Lord first, and He will inhabit your thoughts and your life, so that Jesus is reflected in you.

Praise in the Midst of Tribulation

In *Living in His Presence*, we talked about Paul and Silas and the powerful display of God's power and presence in their midst when they acted out their feelings for Him. It wasn't enough to feel, they had to express their attitude of praise toward God. I would like to tell you a powerful story about a friend of mine who had an experience much like Paul and Silas.

> Claudia had been battling clinical depression for quite some time. She was a lover and follower of Jesus Christ, and she was very serious about her faith. It is a long story, but Claudia slipped into a darkened state of mind much like being chained in a deep pit, unable to climb out. Claudia did all of the right things. She sought wise counsel and was diligent about doing all the things she was told to do. She found a very capable physician who made every medical effort to lift her out of the depression. She took walks and exercised just as she was told. She also had the love and support of her family and friends. For months, many prayed around the clock for Claudia, yet she still felt chained and bound. Unable to sleep or eat well, Claudia still pressed in to maintain normalcy for her husband and family. I watched her with great respect and awe as she pursued her relationship with Christ the best she could. Claudia had a beautiful voice and loved to sing unto the Lord. But her joy and ability to reach out to her Savior in song was snatched from her. It felt as if the chains would never fall. She wasn't able to feel the presence of the Lord, and that was one of her biggest frustrations.
>
> One day, Claudia received a note from a friend. The friend had been praying and felt like the Holy Spirit gave her a specific directive for Claudia. God wanted Claudia to go for a walk with a distinct purpose. He wanted her to make a sacrifice of praise unto Him. This required Claudia to praise God out of sheer will, even though she couldn't muster up the feelings in her heart that she had prior to her depression. This was difficult for her because the heaviness of a single day was more than enough for her to bear. How could God ask even more of her? But Claudia took that note and its directive quite seriously. She went for a walk and praised God on the walkway in a neighborhood green-belt. A very powerful thing happened because of her willingness to obey God. Claudia was instantly and supernaturally set free of clinical depression as she walked and praised. Claudia describes that moment as the day when the chains that bound her were broken and fell to the ground. She called me and told me that she left the chains on the sidewalk where she had been walking. There was great rejoicing in what God had done for His child who was obedient and praised Him in the midst of darkness. Immediately, I relived the story of Paul and Silas and the rousing display of God's power. In my very midst, God did the same thing for Claudia. It felt like a story from the Bible!

It's easy to love God and praise Him when life feels good. But I find it very difficult to praise God when I am down in the dumps of despair. That is when I have to ask myself two important questions: "Gina, is God merely a part of **your** life, or is your life a part of **God's** life?" "Am I going to live life on my terms or on God's terms?"

If God is only a part of my life, then He is "hit or miss" throughout the day. It's okay not to praise God or miss out on Him here and there because I can pick and choose how much of God I want in my life. But if I am a part of God's life, then every moment is "a hit" as I partake in His life for me. If things aren't going well, I still need to make a sacrifice of praise because my life should be about **Him**. The way you live your life reflects your relationship with God.

I hope you are nodding in agreement with me because this will help you. Life is filled with ups and downs, but living in an attitude of gratitude unto the Lord will give you joy and help you keep a right perspective on things.

Long before I met Claudia, I went through a very difficult period of time that lasted three years. I was fairly new as a follower of Jesus Christ. I remember one Christmas when I was so distraught that I couldn't even listen to Christmas carols or sing; I had no joy. Life was only about going through the motions, and that is how I handled Christmas. I couldn't praise God for my Savior's birth; I barely survived each day. I wasn't angry with God, but I wasn't willing to celebrate the birth of His Son on His terms either. I was learning to hear the voice of the Holy Spirit, but my despair overshadowed my ability to listen objectively. How I wish I had been more of a part of God's life and made a sacrifice of praise that tearful Christmas. Even though my circumstances might not have changed, perhaps the despair would have lifted, and there could have been Christmas joy for me. Perhaps my story could have been much like that of Paul and Silas or my friend, Claudia.

When you don't feel like praising God because you are too tired or because you are angry with someone, pray and ask the Holy Spirit to empower you and draw you into an attitude of gratitude toward God. In your attitude of praise, you might find that your fatigue or anger lifts from you. If you think God has forgotten you, passed you by, or ignored you, then make a sacrifice of praise. You might be able to see things more clearly and give thanks instead of allowing anger or bitterness to bombard you.

Time to Reflect

- When times are tough, what is your relationship with God like?
- Do you feel like praising God for who He is, thanking Him for your blessings?
- Have you ever made a true sacrifice of praise unto the Lord? Recall one of those times?
- Be honest. Is your life a part of God's life, or is God a part of your life?

_____
_____
_____
_____
_____

Living Application: Determine whether you want to be a part of God's life or if you'd rather have God be a part of your life. Think this through, and don't be too quick to answer. That might sound like an easy question, but whenever any kind of sacrifice is involved, many decide to live life on their own terms and give God only a part of it. If you desire genuine intimacy with God, then list the areas where you have made Him only a part of your life. What changes do you need to make in these areas so that you can live more in an attitude of gratitude? Pray and ask God to help you play a vital role in His life within you.

Ways to Praise

In *Living in His Presence*, you read about how I began my day listening to praise songs as a way to worship God and thank Him for who He is. That worked very well for me for a long time. Even now, when I have trouble with that first ingredient, I go back to praise songs first thing in the morning and go from there. It is my favorite way to express praise and thanksgiving to God. Eventually God helped me worship in other ways that I can share with you.

I have grown to love the psalms in the Bible. They've become melodies to me. I can almost hear music as I read and pray them aloud. I have my favorites, but it is really fun when I ask the Holy Spirit to lead me to a psalm where I could express my love for God that day. It is interesting when sometimes God leads me to an unfamiliar psalm, perhaps one I wouldn't normally choose on my own. Later in the day, something would happen to remind me of the psalm, and I'd realize why the Holy Spirit wanted me to praise God with that particular one that morning. When you are being led by the Spirit, it is always interesting!

There are times when I go for a short, morning walk or drive and choose to praise God for all I see. Before bed, you can make a list of the blessings from that day so that in the morning you can start with a prayer of praise to God for all He has done and will do for the new day. It is shocking to see your anticipation for a good day grow to new heights! For those times when I need to get out the door in a hurry, I simply take God with me. In the car, I put on good music or just praise Him for who He is and for the blessings and joys of my life. You will be amazed at the ways you will discover to praise and thank God. Before long you will discover yourself living with a sweet attitude of praise.

Those are a few of the typical things you can do to praise God. There are also the atypical ways to express praise and thanksgiving to the Lord. Do you remember the sacrifice of praise we talked about? Here is something else to consider. *"Therefore, whether you eat or drink, or whatever you do, do all to the glory of God"* (1Corinthians 10: 31).

Sometimes we have the opportunity to come out of our comfort zones and be of help to others in areas that stretch us. Perhaps it is someone you dislike.

You are still stewing over an argument with your spouse who now needs your undivided attention and help. Your friend only calls you when she needs you; will you call and invite her to lunch? You are planning a lazy day, but your neighbor across the street needs help with a garage sale. You are concentrating on a project and someone asks you a question that requires more than a simple yes or no.

Can you see how people and situations come along everyday that would test your willingness to stop and treat them as you would treat the Lord? When you have to make a sacrifice and treat others to the glory of God, it is an act of worship in fine form.

In whatever way you choose to praise God, don't hold anything back. Belt it out! Make a fool of yourself if you want to. *"Shout joyfully to the Lord, all the earth; break forth in song, rejoice, and sing praises"* (Psalm 98: 4). Let God know how much you love Him. Find someplace where you can be yourself. When you are real with yourself, then you are more likely to be real with God as well. Alone with God, there is freedom to reach out to Him in any fashion.

I can tell you that any act of praise and thanksgiving to God is ever so pleasing in His sight. When you experience true worship with no distractions, you will crave the presence of God more and more. His presence and the freedom to praise Him will change you. Your heart will soften, and you will know you are in His presence. You **will** draw closer to God.

Your very life and existence can be an act of praise and thanksgiving to God. The ways to practice praise and thanksgiving unto the Lord are too numerous to count. How you choose to look at life and see God is up to you. Whether or not you make the best of every opportunity to worship God through your words and actions, is your choice. How quickly you will grow in your relationship with God is determined by your willingness to embrace His world and His kingdom.

Be a part of God's world; don't ask Him to take part in yours. You will see that both worlds soon become one, and they belong to God.

Picture this!

I have a word picture to help you see the benefits of coming out of your comfort zone and allowing God to stretch you in praise and thanksgiving. In a small town in the Rocky Mountains, there is a salt water taffy shop. In the window, is a large, metal "figure eight" machine that pulls and stretches the homemade taffy in different directions before it is ready for sale. Whenever I watch the taffy being stretched, I think of how the Lord wants me to be like that taffy in the window. If I allow the Holy Spirit to stretch me in areas where I can please Him, then I am closer to learning to live in His presence. The stretching process might not be comfortable, but the end product is soft, pliable, sweet, and pleasing to God.

Time to Reflect

▸ What is your favorite way to express praise and thanksgiving to God?

▸ Which method of praising God is most uncomfortable for you?

▸ Name a situation that came across your path when you had the opportunity to worship God.

▸ Are you really ready to be stretched, so you can grow in your relationship with God?

_____
_____
_____
_____
_____

Living Application: Make it your lifestyle to take a few minutes each day to practice using the first ingredient, praise and thanksgiving. Try to use the same method for at least a week so that you become comfortable enough to be yourself before God. It is okay if you use the same method of praise for long periods of time. Ask the Holy Spirit to lead you and prompt you in ways that are pleasing to God each day. Pray and ask the Father to inhabit your lifestyle of praise and thanksgiving and draw you closer so that you will be able to live in His presence moment by moment.

No Guilt

It was easy for guilt to settle in when my quiet time in the morning consisted mostly of praise and thanksgiving. Shouldn't I do more or turn spiritual somersaults for God? But I've learned that being a follower of Jesus Christ is about being, not doing. When you are living in an attitude of gratitude, **being** in true praise and thanksgiving, then you are drawing close to God which is a very good thing. You might feel like you are not accomplishing anything, but you are! You are experiencing the journey, your goal. You are simply being with God.

The Holy Spirit is doing the work; He is drawing you in. This is only the beginning; more will come later. Your quiet times will become more involved with the Bible and prayer as you draw in. While you are trying to focus on the first ingredient, the Lord will prompt you to make time for Bible study sometime in your day. It seems that Jesus was most intimate with those who spent time with Him. Spend time with your Savior, bask in His presence, and don't feel guilty.

The presence of God is quite irresistible, but there are still circumstances that interfere with your intimate times together. While you need to have some disciplines in order to keep your appointments with the Lord, you will also need to be somewhat flexible.

Occasionally, you might need to change your appointment time with the Lord in order to accommodate an unusual schedule.

There's freedom to make changes as long as you don't slip into neglectful patterns that keep you from praise and thanksgiving on a regular basis. If you choose to sleep in or do something else instead of meeting with God, don't let guilt keep you from seeking Him the next day. It's not as if you are sinning because you spent your time in a different way. The Lord knows your heart, and He will draw you back in.

> **Once you have become accustomed to His sweet presence in your praise times, you will do your best to keep your appointments with God.**

God doesn't want you to come to him out of obligation or to avoid guilt; He wants you to come because you want to be with Him, trust Him, and live in an attitude of gratitude toward Him. *"But it is good for me to draw near to God; I have put my trust in the Lord God, that I may declare all Your works"* (Psalm 73: 28).

Your learning curve about God is going to show dramatic growth. Your attitude of praise in those quiet moments with God will spill over into the rest of your day; you will even rest and sleep with a heart of praise. When you spend time in worship and live in an attitude of gratitude, you open the doors for the Holy Spirit to teach you and reveal the treasures of God's kingdom. Your spirit becomes sensitive to the leading and promptings of the Spirit. We will talk more about that when we discuss the next ingredient.

The combination of your spiritual encounters with God and the knowledge you receive from the Bible, creates the perfect learning environment for anyone who wants to live with God moment by moment. Your posture of praise draws you deeper into intimacy with God and makes you much more aware of His precious presence.

Prayer Poem Ministry
"ANOINTING"

"…You anoint my head with oil; my cup overflows." Psalm 23:5 (NIV)

While you meditate on these words, you will come to realize the power in them. As the Lord pours forth His anointing upon your head, your very life…you will indeed overflow with everything He has for you. You will utter words of praise and thanksgiving; they shall be on your tongue always. You will give freely, all that He has given to you. You will be a blessing, a messenger of hope and of love…a true ambassador on the Lord's behalf. It is written: you will overflow! Indeed you will not ever be empty as long as you walk in God's anointing; it is endless. Yes, truly only goodness and love will follow you all the days of your life!

Desire the greater things in life, the Lord's sacred oil of approval and His presence within. His presence will draw you close, and you can't help but utter lovely words of praise unto your King. Give God all of your praise, freely and without reservation, and see yourself dripping with the oil of His anointing, in His presence forever.

From the Shallow End to the Deeper Waters

When you allow the Holy Spirit to draw you into intimacy with God, you will see yourself making progress on your journey. You will go from testing the water in the shallow end to making strides, taking beautiful strokes in the deeper waters of praise and thanksgiving. This is different from making a single sacrifice of praise upon occasion. Moving into the deeper waters is a **lifestyle** of praise regardless of how smooth or turbulent the waters of life seem to be. It is ongoing, moment by moment.

You will have opportunities throughout the day to choose to praise God when you don't feel like it. The Holy Spirit might lead you to indulge in a painful act of worship, and you will have to make a choice whether or not to obey. A painful act of worship could mean praising God in whatever way He desires, perhaps in the midst of a temporary hardship as we discussed earlier. It might also require you to live in an attitude of praise for the duration of a season or even during long term tribulation. Yes, living in an attitude of gratitude does require obedience to the Father.

We talked about how this lifestyle is not always about how you feel or what you want to do. There are times when you are tempted to live on your own terms and satisfy your fleshly desires instead of tilting your head heavenward in praise and obedience to God. Don't be afraid of these times because your relationship with God grows in proportion to His requirements of you. The Bible says that the Lord will never ask more of you than He knows you can handle. *"…but God is faithful, who will not allow you to be tempted beyond what you are able, but with the temptation will also make the way of escape, that you may be able to bear it"* (1 Corinthians 10:13).

My friend, Coreen, has learned to praise God in the deeper waters of obedience. Her family endured many years of hardship. Most would not have survived the intense difficulties or disappointments they faced, but they learned to tread in the deep waters and stayed afloat. It was during those years that I became friends with Coreen. She shared the details of their ordeal with me, so I knew what her family was going through.

She loved to praise God and was an integral part of the worship team at my church. Each Sunday, I watched Coreen with sheer amazement. With all the trials that she faced, she was up on the stage praising God in the most genuine spirit of joy that I had ever seen. I recall a specific time when I knew her pain was almost too great to bear, yet she radiated joy in the most beautiful posture of praise imaginable. You see, Coreen became a part of God's world, and when He called her to be a part of the worship team at our church, she was obedient regardless of the circumstances or her pain. She had already practiced living in an attitude of gratitude so that when the hard times came, Coreen could swim in the turbulent waters with grace and dignity. The joy of the Lord became her strength. Her obedient heart to praise and thank God in every situation was an incredible testimony to me and to my family. Even now, regardless of the circumstance, Coreen's eyes still radiate joy!

Your heart of praise will soon lend itself to obedience in whatever lifestyle of praise the Holy Spirit directs. Soon **you** will radiate the joy of the Lord in every act of praise unto God.

Perhaps you have had to endure a difficult period of time. How well did you do? If life's pleasures are taken from you, how will you react? What if you have to sell your nice car and drive an older model? If you lose your house today; will you still praise God tomorrow? Can you respond with the joy of the Lord, or will you crumble when much is lost?

It's easy to love God and praise Him when we have everything we need and want. But when testing comes, how well will you do?

Will you still radiate the joy of the Lord? Will you allow His joy to penetrate your world if it is shattered hopelessly? *"Do not sorrow, for the joy of the Lord is your strength"* (Nehemiah 8: 10).

The joy of the Lord even permeates your thoughts. It is how you move from the way the world defines self-control to something more like thought control. You don't have to work at thought control; you simply abide in the joy of the Lord and come under the sweet power of the Holy Spirit to overcome every thought. You don't even have to think about having thought control; it just happens. You operate within a new realm of faith when you don't have to muster up joy everyday.

Because of your attitude of gratitude before God and your heart of praise unto Him, He deposits joy where you least expect to find it. You find yourself functioning, even thriving when you could have been crippled by despair.

Time to Reflect

- Are you swimming in the shallow end or in the deep waters of obedience unto God?

- What situations make it difficult to tilt your head heavenward and praise God anyway?

- Note a time when you entered the deeper waters with praise and obedience to God.

- In your roughest times, do you radiate the joy of the Lord to others?

_____
_____
_____
_____

Living Application: Not many welcome the opportunity to swim deeper in praise and obedience to God. It usually requires giving of one's self to praise God however He directs. Pray about your life and ask the Holy Spirit to provide small opportunities to grow deeper with God in a lifestyle of praise and thanksgiving in the moment to moment of your day.

Identify areas in your praise life where you need to grow in order to go with God, and then ask the Holy Spirit to help you step out of the shallow end and reach for the deep.

Ponder God

"Bless the Lord, O my soul; And all that is within me, bless His holy name."

Psalm 103:1

Have you ever wondered what it might be like to ponder God? Whenever I ponder something, I think quite deeply about it; I turn it inside and out. When I truly ponder, I become single minded. It is almost impossible to think about anything else, unless I become distracted. It's almost like daydreaming; I give it my undivided attention. Oftentimes, I ponder things for days. Can you imagine the emotion that would be stirred up if you pondered God that way? Your world would look differently.

When we really ponder God, we will come to terms with who we are and just who He is. We would keep God up on the throne where He belongs. The self-righteous attitude that we tend to acquire would be blown to bits and then swept away by the wind of the Holy Spirit. Life would become more about the Lord and less about us. We might see ourselves living a life of praise toward God just as we should. Pondering God lays a firm foundation for living in His presence moment by moment.

In the Bible, Job needs to be reminded of who God really is. This passage of Scripture always puts me in awe of God. It gives me a great deal to ponder. God challenges Job with these words: *"Then the Lord answered Job from the whirlwind: 'Who is this that questions my wisdom with such ignorant words? Brace yourself, because I have some questions for you, and you must answer them.'"*

"'Where were you when I laid the foundations of the earth? Tell me, if you know so much. Do you know how its dimensions were determined and who did the surveying? What supports its foundations, and who laid its cornerstone as the morning stars sang together and all the angels shouted for joy? Who defined the boundaries of the sea as it burst from the womb, and as I clothed it with clouds and thick darkness? For I locked it behind barred gates, limiting its shores. I said, thus far and no farther will you come, Here your proud waves must stop!'"

"'Have you ever commanded the morning to appear and caused the dawn to rise in the east? Have you ever told the daylight to spread to the ends of the earth, to bring an end to the night's wickedness? For the features of the earth take shape as the light approaches, and the dawn is robed in red. The light disturbs the haunts of the wicked, and it stops the arm that is raised in violence.'"

"'Have you explored the springs from which the seas come? Have you walked about and explored their depths? Do you know where the gates of death are located? Have you seen the gates of utter gloom? Do you realize the extent of the earth? Tell me if you know! Where does the light come from, and where does the darkness go? Can you take it to its home? Do you know how to get there? But of course you know all this! For you were born before it was all created, and you are so very experienced!'"

"*Have you visited the treasuries of the snow? Have you seen where the hail is made and stored? I have reserved it for the time of trouble, for the day of battle and war. Where is the path to the origin of light? Where is the home of the east wind? Who created a channel for the torrents of rain? Who laid out the path for the lightning? Who makes the rain that satisfies the parched ground and makes the tender grass spring up? Does the rain have a father? Where does dew come from? Who is the mother of the ice? Who gives birth to the frost from the heavens?*"

"*For the water turns to ice as hard as rock, and the surface of the water freezes. Can you hold back the movements of the stars? Are you able to restrain the Pleiades or Orion? Can you ensure the proper sequence of seasons or guide the constellation of the Bear with her cubs across the heavens? Do you know the laws of the universe and how God rules the earth?*"

"*Can you shout to the clouds and make it rain? Can you make lightning appear and cause it to strike as you direct it? Who gives intuition and instinct? Who is wise enough to count all the clouds? Who can tilt the water jars of heaven, turning the dry dust to clumps of mud?*" (Job 38: 1-38 NLT)

The Lord had more to say to Job. It would be good for you to read the rest of God's challenge to Job in chapters 38 and 39.

Pondering God doesn't come naturally; it is a choice, and it means that you are no longer swallowed up by self focus. You find yourself consumed with the power of God and the ways of His kingdom instead of the ways of the world in which you live. You see how small you are in comparison to how big God is, and you realize that it is only by His grace that you can draw near to Him.

This is true humility. You will esteem God highly and realize that He is the one responsible for all the good around you. Suddenly, you **know** that all good things come from God. Your acts of kindness, mercy, or love materialize out of the character of Christ, and you are moved by the presence of the Holy Spirit within you. That really goes against the grain of life, doesn't it?

We like to feel good about what **we** have done. Self-satisfaction is self-motivating. Who we are or what we do drives us down the highways of life. But that isn't the way the Lord intended it to be.

Pause a Moment

Be consumed with the power of God and the ways of His kingdom instead of the pull of the world and its ways.

In James 1:17, the Bible says that every good and perfect gift comes from the Father. I hope that you can understand this because if you do, then you will naturally live in an attitude of gratitude toward God as He works in you according to the great pleasure of His will.

This is how you fall in love with God. You see Him for who He is, and you recognize that all good comes from Him. It isn't only about forcing yourself to respect and revere God because you should; it means you have feelings of love for Him as you come to experience the "person of God." Songs of love for God will fill your head and infiltrate your being.

In *Living in His Presence* we talked about how any love song can become a praise song unto the Lord. You are in the wonderful place where you ponder and express your feelings toward God in day to day life. Soon the Holy Spirit will lead you to be an expression of God's love to others, talking about God more and more as the Bible tells us to do.

"…be filled with the Spirit, speaking to one another in psalms and hymns and spiritual songs, singing and making melody in your heart to the Lord, giving thanks always for all things to God the Father in the name of our Lord Jesus Christ" (Ephesians 5:19,20).

This is living in the presence of God at its finest. Your attitude of praise overflows and enables you to enter into worship no matter what is going on around you. You are taking God with you wherever you go, always in His presence.

Prayer Poem Ministry
"EXPRESSIONS OF LOVE"

"Praise be to the Lord God, the God of Israel, who alone does marvelous deeds." Psalm 72:18 NIV

Marvelous is only a word to express God's wonderful works, but there is no word that truly expresses the wonder of God's works, the majesty of His character, the splendor of His divinity, or the depth of His love. Such wonder, such majesty, such splendor, and such love are not only expressed in words but in heartfelt gratitude and open expressions of God's love from His loved ones. To love God is to express that love in a spirit of gratitude among all those around you. For the very character of the Lord is best described in actions, not in words…in true love and humility, and in great gratitude.

Be an expression of God's love all around you! Feel the presence of God when He holds you near and fills you with a thankful heart. Express your love to Him. He alone is worthy of your obedient praise. Give your heart of praise to the Lord, and know that His character becomes your character in all that you do, say, think, and feel.

Suprising Benefits

Your demeanor of praise before the Lord changes your life and can win others to Christ. Sometimes you don't have to say a word because your Christ-like spirit quietly draws the attention of others around you, and the presence of God within you attracts them. Sometimes when I am out and about, I get a feeling that strangers want to talk to me. Perhaps you have had that happen as well.

Once I was at a drive-thru window, and my eyes connected with the person who gave me my food. It was as if that person was in great need and wanted to jump in through my window to drive off with me. There are times when I pass people on the street, and it feels like they want to connect. If I am attentive enough, in my spirit I can even sense certain needs they have. Sometimes I see a quick flash of loneliness, anguish, or despair when my eyes connect with those of men, women, and children who happen to cross my path. Some have even tried to talk to me. When I am in a safe environment, like a store or somewhere public, I'll say hello only to find myself in a brief chat with someone I have never met before.

You will never know what hidden, godly affect you might have on someone else. Your kind hello or "God bless your day" could be a subtle seed that someone else will water down the road, and that person just might become a follower of Jesus Christ someday!

Because you radiate the love of Christ, it doesn't matter what or how little you say; others are simply drawn to you because of the presence of God.

I don't take that lightly because Jesus didn't take it lightly when He lived on the earth. In the Bible, people wanted to connect with Jesus and His disciples, as well as with the apostles and saints who were filled with the presence and power of God. I think that is the way it is supposed to be now.

People don't know anything about you, nor do they understand why they want to connect with you, but I do. It is the presence of God within you that they are drawn to. This might happen more than you realize, but you might not have been aware of it. Pay attention to what is going on around you, and always be willing to be a loving witness for Christ.

There are times when you are seated by someone you don't know. If conversation starts up, then don't hesitate to be anything less than who you are. Most people are pretty bold about who they are and what they believe, so be like Jesus and share as He would do. It isn't odd or unnatural to others, nor does it turn them away; rather... it attracts them. You might not realize it, but many want to talk about spiritual matters.

When you share about Jesus Christ, you will find that many are interested. "*...and for me, that utterance may be given to me, that I may open my mouth boldly to make known the mystery of the gospel*" (Ephesians 6: 19).

Needless to say, you must be very careful. There are also those on your path who might try to connect with you, with dangerous intentions. You have to be led by the Holy Spirit, and we will discuss more about that later. I only want you to know that the presence of God within you attracts many. Never assume that you are the main attraction. As wonderful of a person as you probably are, it is God's presence that is irresistible, not you!

There is another benefit about living in an attitude of praise and thanksgiving unto the Lord. An attitude of praise finds it easier to resist temptation and sin. The more your mind is on God, and the more you draw near to Him, the less likely you will sin when you are tempted.

As long as you are living in this fallen world, temptations will come screaming down your street and barge in on your heart uninvited. A thankful heart is more aware of the Lord and the ways of His kingdom; it steers clear of evil with the help of the Holy Spirit. There is great freedom in this. Everyone struggles with temptation and with sin. Yet the closer you are to God, the more likely you are to naturally overcome the sinful tendencies of the flesh.

As you draw near to God, He will draw near to you.

"Therefore submit to God. Resist the devil and he will flee from you. Draw near to God and He will draw near to you" (James 4 :7, 8).

By the grace of God and with the presence of the Holy Spirit, you will make steady progress overcoming sin. Please don't think that you will ever make enough progress to live a sinless life. The Bible makes it very clear that we are all sinners and that we will blow it.

This is why we need our Savior, Jesus Christ; our only hope is through our faith in Him. As you submit to promptings and leading of the Holy Spirit, you will avoid a great deal of evil. You have everything to gain when you draw near to God.

When you live with an attitude of gratitude, your outlook on life is better. It doesn't matter if you are an optimist or more pessimistic. Living with a heart of praise for God helps you to see the brighter side of things. When you seat God on the throne of life, you become increasingly aware of His power and His capability to overcome even the most difficult trials. As you learn to live in His amazing presence, you begin to see life as God sees it, and the challenges you face are easier to overcome.

There are times when things look bleak, and defeat is on the horizon. But a thankful heart and an optimistic mind see the possibility of victory through the power of the Holy Spirit. Isn't that a better way to live? Wouldn't you rather hope for the best with your head above water than wallow in doubt and sink into the depths of despair?

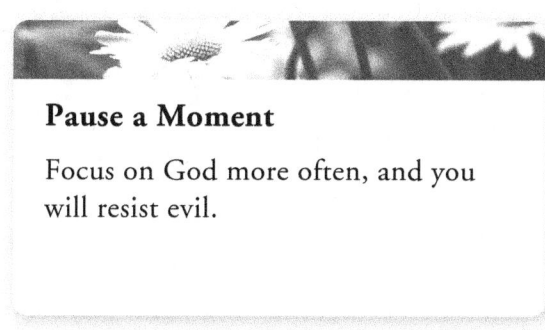

Pause a Moment

Focus on God more often, and you will resist evil.

A lifestyle of praise and thanksgiving trusts that God is in loving control. It sees the positive instead of the negative. An attitude of gratitude builds faith and confidence in Jesus Christ. *"Blessed is that man who makes the Lord his trust"* (Psalm 40: 4).

In *Living in His Presence* I mentioned that my husband, Mike, is more of a realistic optimist. He almost always sees the glass of water half full, sometimes nearly full. His mother, Loretta, was very much like that too. Perhaps some of her optimism influenced Mike when he was growing up. Loretta loved God and lived with an attitude of gratitude toward Him and everyone else. We spent a great many years together, and I don't recall a time when she didn't have a positive attitude about the Lord or about life.

Loretta endured one of life's most intense challenges; she had brain cancer. Without going into great detail, I want you to know that the pain she endured was rated off the medical charts. The treatment she completed was one of the most brutal for the human body to endure. Yet she never complained; instead she pictured herself praising God, sitting in the arms of Jesus. Until the day that Loretta went to Heaven, she hoped for the best, tackled the most grueling therapy, and continued to give of herself to her family and friends. Just days before she passed away, she made an elaborate basket of our favorite things to eat as a way of thanking us for taking care of her. She made a deliberate sacrifice of praise every moment.

How does anyone accomplish such a daring feat? Looking back, I see a woman sold out to Jesus who practiced a lifestyle of gratitude toward Him. When her toughest challenge came, she was ready because she was already living in a posture of praise.

Whether we face challenges or experience the good times, living in an attitude of gratitude unto the Lord can only embellish your time on this earth. There are no red flags when it comes to having a thankful heart. No one snickers at the one who fought the good fight or lived the good life with the right attitude.

The one who practices an attitude of gratitude toward God naturally treats others with loving kindness and respect, another great benefit or side effect. This is not someone with a phony outer shell, and it isn't about being politically correct or loving with a motive. It is about treating others the way Jesus did. It is also about choosing to think the best about others rather than being critical or judgmental.

"Be kind to one another, tenderhearted, forgiving one another, even as God in Christ forgave you." (Ephesians 4: 32)

Because all fall short, it is only natural that others will let you down from time to time. How you respond to harsh words and actions is influenced by your relationship with God. If you have been living in a posture of praise, you will choose to respond to others just as Jesus did.

Nobody really wants to mistreat others, yet it happens without thinking about it. Wouldn't it be nice if we treated others the way Jesus taught us, without having to think about that either? An attitude of praise and a thankful heart for the Lord naturally behaves well toward others.

Time to Reflect

- Think of a time when the presence of God within you could have attracted someone.
- How can an attitude of praise help you resist the temptation to sin?
- Are you more optimistic or pessimistic? How can an attitude of gratitude affect that?
- How do you treat others? What are your thoughts and actions toward them like?

_____
_____
_____
_____
_____

Living Application: Watch for opportunities to see how others respond to you. Do you attract other people? Practice a lifestyle of gratitude unto the Lord and notice how you treat others and how they respond to you. Pray and ask the Holy Spirit to draw you into a deeper attitude of praise and thanksgiving so that you will be able to resist the temptations that come along your path. Make it your purpose to take notice of the positive instead of the negative in your life. Praise the Lord for the good that you see, and you will see yourself overcome hurdles with a right attitude. Allow the Holy Spirit to bring to mind the relationships that need to be improved. Investigate the motives of your heart, and begin to improve those relationships.

Restful Praise

"It is good to give thanks to the Lord, and to sing praises to Your name, O Most High; to declare Your loving kindness in the morning, and your faithfulness every night (Psalm 92:1, 2).

You will be surprised to discover how much better you sleep when you go to bed with a few words of praise on your lips. When I go to sleep mindful of the Lord and His faithfulness for that day, I generally sleep well. Many don't cultivate their relationship with God through the slumbering hours of the night and early morning. That is when we are off duty, right? Actually, we are never off duty when it comes to God.

We have a relationship with God that should consistently abide in Him. I wouldn't like it if God went to bed and rested away from **me**! I know I need Him even when I am asleep. In Psalm 121: 3 the Bible says *"He who watches over you will not slumber."*

I am so happy to know that God stays with me while I sleep. Who knows what goes on when my eyes are closed and my mind is at rest?

When I go to bed at night, I try to read a few words of Scripture to bring me into an attitude of praise. It had to become a discipline for me because otherwise I jump into bed and fall asleep before I know it. It is almost impossible for me to lie down and read **anything**; I have to sit up to stay awake.

It's good to make a brief declaration of God's faithfulness as is talks about in Psalm 92. Sometimes I pray, and other times I am asleep too quickly. I can tell you that my sleep is much more peaceful when I make the effort to end my day in a posture of praise.

"When I remember You on my bed, I meditate on You in the night watches."
(Psalm 63: 6)

Perhaps you are different than I am; I hope so! If you have the ability to stay awake for a while and read and pray, then I applaud you. You can give the Lord more of your time, and that is wonderful. I encourage you to make the effort to spend a few moments with God praising Him before you sleep. I know that He will honor your efforts to end your day with a heart of praise.

If you wake up at any time during the night or the wee hours of the morning, talk to God. Tell Him you love Him before you drift off once again. You might be thinking that is impossible for you. You are delirious and can't even recall being awake for a moment in the dark. Actually, when you go to sleep with God on your mind, He might still be there when you crack your eyes open momentarily. Just tell God that you love Him, and be grateful for more time to sleep.

Perhaps you'll wake up in an attitude of praise as if you had thought about God all night. You might even still have the verses from the Bible in your head. Oftentimes I wake up with a praise song in my head; I love it when that happens! It makes me feel like I was in the presence of God while I was asleep.

"I remember your name in the night, O Lord." (Psalm 119: 55)

Unattractive Risks

Why do you think there are so many scriptures in the Bible about being thankful? A grateful heart is truly a merry one. Much of your happiness will spill from your attitude of gratitude. You can avoid those darkened days of gloom with your attitude. When we choose to allow the negative to crowd out the positive, there are unattractive risks that threaten life's little pleasures.

Sleepless nights, oppression, depression, and even illness can plague those who have lost a thankful heart. The list of unattractive risks goes on. We cannot have unsurpassed peace if we are negative or run the race looking behind, or even slightly over our shoulders.

**We must live with the peace of Christ and the joy of the Lord
so that our hearts and minds will always be protected.**

Without God's peace and joy we risk turmoil, and that leads to dangerous pathways and walls of destruction. We don't slip into turmoil willingly or even consciously. It is a very subtle slide downhill, and we wonder how we got there.

Be careful; always be mindful of your state of mind and attitude, and you won't be at risk. Invite the joy of the Lord and peace of Christ to reign supreme in your mind and heart. You will stay afloat no matter what is going on in your world. "*The things which you learned and received and heard and saw in me, these do, and the God of peace will be with you*" (Philippians 4:9).

Prayer Poem Ministry
"EYES UPON YOU"

As you give Him your worship and your praise, as you lift your eyes to His throne, you shall see God and God alone. With your eyes upon God, there is nothing too big or impossible for you…no mountain too high, no valley too low. You will soar and overcome your weakness. Yes, you will even overcome your own strength!

Lord, I will give you all of my worship, all of my praise.

I will lift my eyes to your throne, for there I will see You.

I will follow You and You alone, and I trust in You alone.

Picture yourself on that mountain top praising God. You have crossed various terrains in order to get to the top of your mountain. The air is crisp, the sky is blue, and the ground is soft and warm. Your arms are outstretched in holy surrender and praise unto the Lord because His Spirit enabled you to climb and reach your precious goal. Now you feel the presence of God, and His unfailing love surrounds you. There is no weakness, only strength in Him. Now you give God your worship, your praise, and your life. You are ready to come down from your mountain and follow the Lord once again and trust in Him alone.

*"My praise shall be continually of You.
Let my mouth be filled with Your praise
and with Your glory all the day.
And I will praise You yet, more and more."*

Psalm 71: 6,8,14

Soaring on the Interstate

"I can do all things through Christ who strengthens me."
Philippians 4: 13

Even though your journey is well underway, you have only explored the first ingredient that will help you learn to live in the presence of God moment by moment. Practice praise and thanksgiving throughout the day and night.

The Holy Spirit lives inside of you, and He will guide and direct you on your journey. Next, you will learn to enjoy the companionship of the Holy Spirit as the second ingredient for your journey. Before long, you will be ready to step off of your path and soar on the interstate of living in His presence. Your self-confidence will rest solely in Jesus Christ, where your true strength lies. Soon you will find that you are living with God moment by moment.

Let's pray!

Dear Father God, I only want to praise You. I want to give you all of my heart each moment of every day, and I want to grow closer to understanding Yours. You deserve all the praise and glory that life can bring, and I give all that I have and all that I am to You. Thank you for loving me so. And thank you for sending your Son, Lord Jesus, to rescue me from my sinful ways. That act of selfless love itself is enough to keep me in an attitude of praise toward You always. I want to live in an attitude of gratitude toward You every moment of my life. Please help me to focus upon You, Your splendor, and majesty. You are awesome, and I give You all of my worship and all of my praise.

Second Ingredient

Prayer and Communication...
Loving Fellowship 48
The Value of Fellowship 50
Conversing with God, Renewing Your Mind 54
Newfound Prayer Life 56
Exhausting Prayer Life and Endless Prayer List 58
Ask, Seek, and Knock 61
Enjoy God 62
Appointments with God 64
Daily Nuts and Bolts 67
Practice Makes Better 73
The Highs and Lows 77
Fine Tuning 78

> *"God is faithful, by whom you were called into the fellowship of His Son, Jesus Christ our Lord."*
> 1 Corinthians 1:9

Fellowship with God...this is not to be taken for granted; that is for sure! It is the greatest privilege you have as a believer and follower of Jesus Christ and should be valued higher than your most prized possession. Best of all, God has called you to this esteemed place of honor. Think of what it means for you to have fellowship with God.

- Perhaps you air-mail prayer requests up to the heavens hoping to reach the Father.
- Maybe it equates with knowledge of God and acts of service to Him and others.
- Fellowship with God might mean that you strive for companionship with Him.

Many attempt to reach God in various ways, but they don't understand what it means to have genuine fellowship. We live in a fast paced world, and we don't take time to cultivate relationships. We tend to associate with those who cross our paths on a regular basis. We go to social gatherings and talk about superficial issues that don't expose who we really are. It is much easier to stay under cover at home and focus on self than it is to invite others over for a meal and a deep conversation.

If you are going to have close fellowship with your loving Lord, you must first understand what fellowship really is. Fellowship is togetherness; it involves companionship, sharing interests and experiences. It lends itself to sincere, close relationships. Fellowship is warm and inviting. It finds itself on a personal pathway to friendship and accountability.

Genuine fellowship starts with a willingness or desire to be whom you really are and allow others to get to know you. It takes time and commitment. Fellowship with God through Jesus Christ is much the same. It is a loving togetherness beyond your expectations where you find yourself accepted and loved, no matter what. *"...having predestined us to adoption as sons by Jesus Christ to Himself, according to the good pleasure of His will, to the praise of the glory of His grace, by which He made us accepted in the Beloved"* (Ephesians 1: 5,6).

When you fellowship with God, His Holy Spirit becomes your most loyal companion, and you share about everything in life. You establish trust and intimacy second to no other relationship you will ever have. Fellowship with God is a never ending awareness of His presence that warms you when the thermometer of life reads so cold that you can't warm up on your own. It is more than an association with God; it is really being with Him in sweet conversation and in quiet rest.

Your time with God travels on a pathway that leads to a respectful friendship where you can't wait to establish accountability with the Living God. Nothing competes with fellowship with God; it stands alone in peaceful contentment amidst this world of uncertainties. Loving fellowship with God is your highest calling and greatest privilege.

While living in an attitude of gratitude toward God, you naturally grow closer and desire to communicate with the Person you praise. You won't be satisfied with a mere prayer request or two. You will desire a personal encounter with God, a moment to moment experience listening for His voice. "*My sheep hear My voice, and I know them, and they follow Me*" (John 10: 27).

> **Picture this!**
>
> Let me paint my word picture of our personal God for you so that you can see what He looks like to me. God has a warm and inviting look about Him. He doesn't stand at a distance; He is up close and personal as He breathes life upon me every moment. His eyes of attentive love see my true identity, and they filter out the harmful rays of the world that attempt to burn and disfigure who I really am. God's nose catches every scent that He's created, and He enjoys the sweet fragrance that flows from my very being. His mouth speaks words of wisdom and faithful instruction, and it whispers love and encouragement moment by moment. The ears of God hear my prayers, and they fine tune to my every thought. The hair on His head is full, and it blows as a cool breeze to freshen and restore me. God's arms are muscular, and they are ready to bear the burdensome loads that tend to pile upon my shoulders and force imbalance. His legs are stronger than strong, and they sprint while He carries me upon His mighty shoulders when I call for help. Even though God is supernatural, His picture is very real to me, and I try to carry it with me wherever I go.

Perhaps you have a picture of the Lord that you carry around as well. I hope it is a clear close-up shot of all His features, so clear that His eyes draw you near when you look at them. Every time you look at your photo of God, it should convince you of how much He longs for you and wants to share in the details of your life.

> I would like to share a powerful story about a detail in my life which convinced me that God is attentive and highly interested in what is important to each of us. This story recalls the day when I first learned that God speaks to each of us. I believe it pin points the exact moment in time when the Holy Spirit began to capture my attention and instigate the greatest passion of my life, to know God and hear His voice.
>
> Mike and I were planning to sell our first house and move to one that would accommodate our family better. We had just signed a contract to put it up for sale, and we were waiting for the sign to go up in the front yard. A young pastor and his wife, Chuck and Deb, offered to come over, pray, and ask God to help sell our house quickly so that we could make our move before the Christmas season. We agreed that prayer might be a good idea; it certainly would do no harm. They were praying in our front yard with us when Chuck suddenly opened his eyes and told us that God had said to put our sign in a specific spot, that we would sell our house in twenty-one days. "What do you mean, God said?" I asked. Chuck and Deb explained, and I was shocked to learn that it is possible to communicate with God and hear His voice through the Holy Spirit. I was enraged; why had no one ever told me that before?

I believed in Jesus Christ and went to church all of my life, yet it appeared that I had missed out on a fundamental, spiritual principle. Mike and I couldn't hear what God had said to Chuck and Deb, but we believed that what this godly couple told us was true. We placed our sign strategically according to God's will, and we planned for a quick sale in twenty-one days. Our house sold on the twenty-first day! It was like living in Bible days when Jesus did great things so that all would see and believe. What an amazing faith booster!

It is a long story, but I want you to know that the 21st day turned out to be the day that my husband and I gave our lives to Jesus Christ and became born again while at the Christian retreat that I talked about earlier. From that "born again" moment on, my quest to listen for His voice began. My desire to have loving fellowship with God grew into an unquenchable thirst and a passion that continues today.

Time to Reflect

▸ What do you think it means to have close fellowship with God?

▸ Is God up close and personal, or is He more at a distance from you?

▸ Do you have a picture of God that you can carry with you?
   What does He look like?

▸ What seems most challenging about your journey of fellowship with God?

_____
_____
_____
_____
_____

Living Application: Paint your word picture of God with a similar technique that I painted mine for you. Reflect upon your picture, and pray for God's help to determine if He might want you to make some changes so that it looks more like Him. Then take your picture with you and begin to look for your personal God on every avenue where you walk. Ask the Father to make you passionate about hearing His voice through the power of the Holy Spirit, just as Jesus did.

The Value of Fellowship

It is important to remember that fellowship isn't only about asking questions and getting answers from God. There are hidden treasures waiting to be discovered in your relationship with God through Jesus Christ. Who you can become is determined by your relationship with the Father. Jesus is your perfect role model. As a follower of Jesus Christ, you naturally want to become more like Him.

The Bible says that we are to become like Jesus and think more like He did when He was on the earth. *"Let this mind be in you which was also in Christ Jesus* (Philippians 2: 5).

That sounds like a tall order, doesn't it? Don't be overwhelmed; you have plenty of time. Know that the Bible is not talking about your intellect. You will not think like Jesus by getting smarter or learning more about Him. It is a life long process of getting to know Him by praising Him, spending time with Him in prayer, and reading your Bible.

In His human form, Jesus had to pray and spend time with the Father in order to accomplish His mission, and He knew the scriptures very well. He was one with the Father, and we can be one with Him in fellowship as well. We know that we will never **be** God, or even be **a** god, but when we come in close proximity to the Father, we are transformed moment by moment. *"But we all, with unveiled face, beholding as in a mirror the glory of the Lord, are being transformed into the same image from glory to glory, just as by the Spirit of the Lord"* (2Corinthians 3: 18).

You might be wondering what you will be transformed into. You'll become what you really desire, more Christ-like in every way. Your thoughts and ways can become more like that of your Savior when you spend time listening for the voice of the Holy Spirit to guide you through the day to day happenings of life.

You won't have to bow to the sinful ways of the world when you live in the presence of God, listening for His voice continually.

"And do not be conformed to this world, but be transformed by the renewing of your mind, that you may prove what is that good and acceptable and perfect will of God" (Romans 12:2). There is great value in hearing God's voice concerning His will for your life. The choice to live as Jesus did is easier to make knowing you have the same access to the Father that He did.

Every one of us has needs, and we have voids that we want filled. Sometimes our culture lends itself to loneliness and emptiness which results in deep, emotional pain. Many are homeless; widows, orphans, and single parents are everywhere. All are looking for answers and solutions to fill their voids and make life more fulfilling. Even those who seem to have stable lives are seeking worldly ways to satisfy themselves when fellowship with God is the real answer.

A weekend getaway, an extended vacation, or some expensive treat to yourself will bring a quick smile, but never satisfies the longings of the heart like a good conversation with the Holy Spirit can. Just as a good conversation with a close friend can be encouraging, a sweet conversation with the Lord can lift your spirit out of the miry muck.

Even one word from the Lord can bring healing and comfort to a needy heart.

In the midst of tribulation where there is uncertainty or fear, a few loving words from the Lord will calm a worried mind and heart. Have you ever had a situation when you tried everything in your means to overcome worry or fear about something, to no avail? If you are like me, then that has probably happened more than you would like to admit.

Sometimes we worry, and we don't even know it. Perhaps there is an unsettling or a nagging concern about someone, and you just can't find peace. The Bible says to *"Be anxious for nothing, but in everything by prayer and supplication, with thanksgiving, let your requests be made known to God, and the peace of God, which surpasses all understanding, will guard your hearts and minds through Christ Jesus* (Philippians 4:6).

In your prayer time when you hear from the Holy Spirit, incredible peace comes. It doesn't mean that your circumstance will change, but it does mean that you won't be crippled by fear in the midst of it.

My cousin, Stacy, is like me in that when she learned it is possible to hear the voice of the Holy Spirit, she had a great desire to hear from Him. She had been hoping and praying that she would soon be able to hear the voice of God in the midst of her everyday life. Her first encounter with the Holy Spirit came in the midst of a painful time. Without going into the details, Stacy was emotionally distraught about a situation. She was in deep unrest, and feelings of doubt and regret hit her so hard that she even experienced physical pain. Nothing could alleviate her physical or emotional distress. One afternoon, Stacy was folding laundry in tears as she prayed, and suddenly heard the voice of the Holy Spirit. God spoke something so profound to her that she could never imagine on her own, and it immediately calmed her anxious heart. Then she said it was as if the Holy Spirit started at the top of her head and went all the way to her toes and whispered… "Peace, peace, peace!" Instantly, Stacy felt the emotional distress lift, and noticed that the physical pain was gone as well. In the midst of tribulation, Stacy couldn't overcome her feelings on her own, but at the sound of the Lord's voice everything lifted, and incredible peace penetrated her being.

Stacy's story is inspirational. It is a powerful account of God's grace and mercy providing peace beyond all understanding when there was no other remedy for distress. But it is also a sweet display of God's faithfulness to answer Stacy's prayer to hear His voice.

You don't have to be a veteran at this; it wasn't long after Stacy asked to hear the voice of God that He satisfied the desire of her heart. Isn't it just like the Lord to give Stacy a personal, first encounter with Him just when she needed it the most?

"Peace I leave you, My peace I give to you; not as the world gives do I give to you. Let not your heart be troubled, neither let it be afraid" (John 14:27). Don't you love these calming words of Jesus? There is great power in those words. I recall a time when those words stood up in three dimensional formations for me.

About twenty years ago, when Amber and Ryan were very young, we rented a cabin in the mountains of Colorado near a large fishing lake. Mike's parents joined us and were thrilled to spend some time with their grandchildren. It was early evening when Mike and his dad took the car, planning to fish on the lake until dark.

I stayed at the cabin with his mother and our children. Mike's mom decided to take Amber and Ryan for a short walk in the woods to burn off some of their energy before bed, giving me some restful time alone. They were gone longer than I anticipated, and dusk settled in. I went outside hoping to see them coming down the path, but there was no sign of them. I began to worry that something had happened to them, but because it was almost dark, I knew it would not be wise to go out and search for them alone. Twenty years ago we didn't have cell phones, and there was no telephone in the rustic cabin. Without a phone or a car, I was stuck and had to wait hoping and praying that my precious family would return unharmed. Worry turned into a gripping fear, and I could hardly think or pray. I had been on the initial training ground of learning to hear God's voice and suddenly thought to ask the Holy Spirit what to do about this potentially dangerous situation. I heard the Holy Spirit tell me to wait and not go out. Then He said that my children and mother-in-law would return in ten minutes. It was as if the words of Jesus came to me straight from the Bible and stood tall in three dimensional formations all around me! Supernatural peace engulfed my spirit, and my heart was no longer troubled, nor was I afraid. It was just about dark when Mike's mom came waltzing in the door ten minutes later with Amber and Ryan at each hand! I don't know if I was happier to see my children and their grandmother or if I was most thrilled about hearing the comforting voice of the Holy Spirit in the midst of fear and trembling. There is no price that can be put on the lives of my family, but the presence of God with His peaceful voice is priceless as well.

You can have that same kind of experience with the Lord if you desire it. You are His precious creation, and He anxiously awaits you in loving fellowship. It doesn't matter if you are a new Christian or if you have followed Jesus Christ for many years, God is waiting for you just the same. It never matters where you have been or how little your devotion to God has been until now.

> **You can't earn the right to come into communion with God.
> It is simply a benefit when you give your life to Jesus Christ.**

If you feel unworthy of such generosity, remember that the throne room of God has been opened to you because of what Jesus has done for you, not because you've earned it or deserve it. Enter in; His very presence awaits you and holds the key to your heart.

Time to Reflect

- How important to you is personal fellowship with the Holy Spirit?
- In what ways would you like to be transformed through your relationship with God?
- What voids do you have that could be filled and satisfied by the presence of God?
- Think of a worrisome time when God's voice could have brought peace to your heart.

Living Application: If you desire greater intimacy with your King, then begin to pray and ask the Holy Spirit to speak to you in ways that you will understand. Spend a good deal of time in prayer and in your Bible, so that your spirit will be strong yet sensitive to the voice of God. Start to renew your mind in Christ Jesus everyday by keeping your focus on God and living in an attitude of praise and thanksgiving.

Prayer Poem Ministry
"THE POWER WITHIN"

The Power within you is pure. The floodgates of Heaven open up, and the Power that is with you tramples over the adversaries of your life. The Power that is within you shall go before you and prepare the path so that you will not stumble and fall. The Power that is within you knows all things and prepares you for all things. The Power that is within you loves you in the purest fashion, a most precious fashion, and the most everlasting fashion. The Power that is within you shall rise up to protect, defend, and keep you safe. The Power that is within you is the presence of the Prince of Peace, the only Power and force in your life.

May the Holy Spirit reveal His power within you, and may His power seem so real that you can hardly believe it has happened to you! May the floodgates of Heaven storm your heart and carry you into the throne room of God where you have lasting communion with your loving Creator. May you experience His pure love in every possible fashion. And may the gentle Power within you protect, defend, and keep you in His presence forever.

Conversing with God and Renewing Your Mind

Wonderful conversations with God can happen every day if you are willing to spend time with Him and if you have a desire for genuine intimacy. We already know that it is His desire to have meaningful conversations with each of us. The Holy Spirit stands at the threshold of your heart waiting to carry you across the doorway of doubt and apprehension, into the throne room of God where intimacy takes place.

If you want to know God's will for your life and hear His voice on a regular basis, your roots must go deeper into Christ and His ways.

The Holy Spirit will help you let go so that you are rooted in your Savior. You will be transformed into what the Father had in mind for you all along, and you will hear the voice of His Holy Spirit. Then you will know His will for you. *"And do not be conformed to this world, but be transformed by the renewing of your mind, that you may prove what is that good and acceptable and perfect will of God"* (Romans 12: 2).

You might be wondering what it might be like to have a real conversation with God.

- How will I know if I am hearing His voice, you might be asking?
- Do I have to do something to make it happen?
- How long will it take before I can hear the voice of the Holy Spirit?
- Is God's voice audible?

I asked myself these same questions over and again. I desperately wanted to hear the voice of God in my prayer life, and I wanted it to happen in a flash. But first, I needed to learn to cultivate my relationship with God through one-way prayer. The two-way communication system would come as my spirit grew stronger and as I consciously engaged in a continual process to renew my mind.

It isn't difficult to pursue the things that will strengthen your spirit so that it will become sensitive to the Holy Spirit. It mostly takes discipline to keep praising God, reading your Bible, and spend time praying. Renewing your mind can be a bit more challenging. In renewing your mind, you will have thoughts and distractions to contend with. They can keep you from spiritual transformation because they consume and mold you into the patterns of this world without noticing it. Sinful patterns and tendencies act like leaches, and they are tough to get rid of on your own.

Here is what you can do to help renew your mind so that you are more likely to engage in a loving conversation with your Father.

- Focus on whatever is truly important in life and put less emphasis on those worldly goals that will never give you lasting fulfillment.
- Go back to living with an attitude of gratitude, and ponder the majesty of God.

In *Living in His Presence*, I mentioned that my favorite Bible scripture is Philippians 4:8. *"Finally brethren, whatever things are true, whatever things are noble, whatever things are just, whatever things are pure, whatever things are lovely, whatever things are of good report, if there is any virtue and if there is anything praiseworthy... meditate on these things."* If you train yourself to dwell on the right things, it would make a significant difference. Certainly Jesus Christ is all of the above, so think about Him, ponder Him, and watch for the initial stages of renewal to unfold!

Then refresh your faith on a continual basis, and you will grow in your spirit as well as within the body of Christ. Read literature that will encourage spiritual growth. Listen to music that is spiritually edifying. Be willing to step out of your comfort zone and reach out to others. Pray for others, be outward focused realizing that life isn't only about you. If you practice these things, your soul will be refreshed.

Lastly, exercise your faith and start to anticipate your close relationship with God. Practice listening with spiritual ears for the sweet voice of the Holy Spirit, and be ready to step out in your renewed faith when you hear Him call.

Who would not enjoy a continual splash of refreshment? Wouldn't you drive miles for a free box of quiet contentment? You might even trade your quick fix for happiness for one day of genuine peace for your soul. Perhaps you would drop off your burdens and frustrations in exchange for words of lasting comfort. The meaningful by-products of the voice of the Holy Spirit are too numerous to count. Yet they come freely to those who will listen and obey God.

Time to Reflect

- Do you have reservations about conversing with God through prayer? What are they?
- Are you willing to take the time needed to cultivate your relationship with God?
- What are you doing now to strengthen your spirit, and in what ways can you improve?
- Where will you need to focus the most in order to renew your mind?

_____
_____
_____
_____
_____

Living Application: If you are apprehensive about your two-way prayer life, pray and ask the Holy Spirit to quiet your anxious heart. Share your feelings openly with someone and have them pray for you. Try to be disciplined about your quiet times and about spending time in the Bible. Feed on the things that are spiritually edifying. Practice renewing your mind a little each day, and expect positive results. Have a prayer journal ready to go so that you can keep an account of all you experience in prayer.

Newfound Prayer Life

"Now this is the confidence that we have in Him, that if we ask anything according to His will, He hears us" (1 John 5:14). Doesn't that scripture just give you the boost you need to encourage your new prayer life? I get excited about that because it changes the way I pray and relate to God. Everyone wants their prayers to be heard by God, or else they wouldn't bother to pray. Knowing that it's a guarantee, gives us an even greater desire to pursue God through a deeper prayer life.

We can boldly approach the throne and ask the Father what He thinks in regards to everything. Is someone on your mind? Did you know that you can go to the Father and ask Him why a certain someone continues to be in your thoughts? Chances are good that the same person is on God's mind as well and that He wants to share something with you so that you will pray for that person. Then you can pray in good faith, according to what you believe to be God's will. That is powerful because you know that whatever you pray according to His will, is heard by the Father. You are operating as Jesus did when He walked on the earth.

Oftentimes, we tend to pray according to the way we feel instead of the way we should. When I stop and ask the Holy Spirit to show me how to pray for someone or for a certain situation, I find that God's will is sometimes different from mine. God always sees a bigger picture and looks deeper than I do.

One time I was getting ready to spend some time with someone, and I really wasn't looking forward to it. That person was always a frustration to me and behaved in ways that really aggravated me and others. Yet I needed to see this person, and I had to make the best of it. I decided to pray prior to our meeting as I usually do. I was praying for patience and tolerance when the Holy Spirit suddenly revealed something about that person and told me to pray accordingly. I prayed specifically in agreement with God's will and was surprised to see the results. My meeting went great, and that person's issues will no longer be a concern for me. It turned out better for both of us! Can you begin to see how powerful and effective Holy Spirit led prayer is? Yet it was no more than a brief dialogue with God.

Many of us struggle with issues daily. I can't begin to name all of the things we deal with on a regular basis. Sometimes we are aware of our struggles, but oftentimes we are unaware of what is going on deep inside. We can't figure out why we act certain ways or why various circumstances frustrate us. "Lord, why can't I get rid of this thought and jump over the hurdle" you ask? Stop and ask the Holy Spirit to bring revelation concerning each individual issue, and He will do just that.

Just recently I realized how much I was bothered by negative thoughts about someone, and I was very upset about it. I asked the Lord to show me why I was struggling all of a sudden. He told me that I have resentment toward that person. I was shocked! I asked how that could be.

The Holy Spirit helped me to see that I had stuffed many hurts over the years and that I was building resentment toward that person and one of their family members. I was saddened by this, yet I didn't know what to do about it. I chose to embrace the truth and asked God to bring healing to my hurtful heart so that there would be no feelings of resentment. If I hadn't heard from the Holy Spirit, I would still be harboring resentment instead of welcoming restoration.

> **Picture this!**
>
> You discover a cozy, little colony of ants at your back door. You spray them with a smelly, home-made concoction and hope they will go away. Early the next morning, they are out there in greater numbers, so you make your remedy a bit more powerful and spray it again, drowning the ants. The next day, the ant colony has quadrupled, so you go out and get a good bug spray. You spray the ant colony with the toxic formula, confident that you have the proper solution this time. But the next day, there are even more ants. You spray a heavier dose on them in hopes of killing them for good. However… the next morning the ants are not only on the cement, but they are now crawling onto your house.

You panic and call the bug control people for a consultation. The experts instruct you to stop treating what you see and go deeper to "the queen." They recommend setting out a product that the ants will eat and take down into their farm, eventually killing the queen ant. You find the product to be odorless and effortless, and you solve your ant problem. If only you had thought to contact the experts, you would have saved time, money, and frustration. When you call upon the Holy Spirit, He will guide your prayer time with less effort, and it will be much more effective.

 Prayer Poem Ministry
"THE WHISPER"

In the midst of the mighty rumble and the clanging noises is the soft, sweet whisper of the One who loves you the most. It is the sound of the One who knows all about the noises and the rumbles. But the sweet soft whisper is more powerful than the noises and the interferences. Yes, dear child of God, the whisper is what will guide you through the noises. The whisper is what will still and quiet the noise. The whisper is what will bring peace to your soul like nothing else can. You must look and listen for the whisper, for it is soft. But when you find it, listen, and then follow it… the whisper becomes louder and more powerful than the rumbles and noises. The whisper will blow over the mightiest of rumbles. There is no power in the mighty rumbles; there is only power in the whisper. The whisper calls out to you and says, "Come and find peace."

Look and listen for the whisper, the still small voice of the Holy Spirit that dwells within. May the whisper guide, instruct, and keep you safe when the mighty rumbles of life roar past you. Never fear the noises because they are nothing compared to the whisper. The noise you hear is only a distraction to keep you from listening to the whisper of the Holy Spirit. By-pass the interferences, and go straight for the whisper. Truly you will find everlasting peace.

Exhausting Prayer Life and the Endless List

If we are honest with each other, then we would probably agree that prayer can be tiring when we have to get through the endless prayer list of needs. Our intentions are good, but oftentimes we become bored with repetitive prayer.

We run out of ways to pray and things to say to God as we petition Him daily. We even wonder if He is listening or if He will eventually answer our prayers. Sometimes we pass over a specific name or need because we have prayed about that so many times that we just can't do it again. Then guilt comes knocking at the door, and we fear that if we don't repeat the prayer, God will ignore the need. So we labor over our prayer lists each day in hopes of reaching the heart of God. Are you nodding in agreement with me? I know these things happen to me.

"And if we know that He hears us, whatever we ask, we know that we have the petitions that we have asked of Him" (1 John 5:15).

How did Jesus manage His prayer list? I'm sure He had quite an extensive one! He prayed for the multitudes and ministered to thousands of needs. How did He do it? Jesus' prayer life was led by the Father in Heaven.

The Bible tells us that Jesus went away to be alone with the Father and pray. He listened to the voice of His Father and always knew what to pray according to the will of God. Jesus even said, *"For I have not often spoken on My own authority; but the Father who sent Me gave Me a command, what I should say and what I should speak. And I know that His command is everlasting life. Therefore whatever I speak, just as the Father has told me, so I speak"* (John 12:49, 50).

Jesus set an example for us to follow when He consulted the Father for everything. Whatever the Father told Him to pray, Jesus prayed, and His prayers were powerfully answered.

Prayer can become mechanical, or it can be Holy Spirit led. You can repeat the same prayers day after day, or you can ask the Holy Spirit to give you the words to pray according to the will of God the Father. You can actually pray the way that Jesus prayed and accomplish more than you ever thought through your prayer life. You can feel life in your prayers, or you can feel like they are dry and dull. You can know that you have been answered, or you can wonder if you will ever be heard.

There is a difference between knowing your prayer is heard according to the will of God, and hoping your prayer is heard.

When you know your prayer is heard, you can move on; it is done and you don't have to labor over it again and again. You can simply thank God for hearing and answering your prayer. The way you decide to pray really matters. Decide to make your prayer time come alive through the power of the Holy Spirit that speaks within you. And the Holy Spirit helps us in our weakness. *"For example, we don't know what God wants us to pray for. But the Holy Spirit prays for us with groanings that cannot be expressed in words. And the Father who knows all hearts knows what the Spirit is saying, for the Spirit pleads for us believers in harmony with God's own will"* (Romans 8: 26, 27 NLT).

When I talk about the prayer list, I am mostly referring to the needs and prayer requests that come your way on a regular basis. Some of the needs might be for those you don't even know, yet you want to be available to pray accordingly. That's when it is nice to have the Lord's leading so that you will know what to pray for whom.

My prayer list doesn't include my family or close loved ones for whom I lift up prayers of protection and provision on a regular basis. I'm sure I will always pray for them continually.

Yet there are times when I start to pray for my husband or children and the Holy Spirit reassures me that all is well. Then I just thank Him wholeheartedly for all He is doing.

Sometimes I think that all God wants is a little sweet fellowship or perhaps some alone time in praise. The Holy Spirit lets me know when I can rest in God's provision over my prayer list so that I can just spend some intimate time with Him. You will find this happening to you as well.

Let's take a practical look at this. Perhaps you have a prayer list consisting of ten different people that you are praying for on a daily basis. Bring your list to the Father and ask Him who is on His heart that day. Who needs prayer now? Then ask the Holy Spirit to speak to you and tell you how to pray specifically for each one that the Lord puts on your heart to pray for.

Some days you will feel like you need to pray for everyone, and sometimes only a few or just one. Just because the Holy Spirit doesn't mention certain ones doesn't mean that God has forgotten them. God doesn't forget anyone, and He will prompt you with the right timing for prayer. Perhaps someone else is praying for others on your list that day. Maybe today God only wants you to pray for your aunt who is on your list. You really feel like you are to pray for a good measure of encouragement for her today. So as you pray, thank God for sharing His heart with you and for the encouragement that He will bring to your aunt. Later on you learn that your aunt was tremendously encouraged by a visit from an old friend, and is now feeling much better about her lonely life.

When you start to see the powerful effects of your Spirit led prayer life, you will be encouraged the most! Answered prayer brings fulfillment and always builds your faith.

Your prayers have life and meaning again, and you can accomplish much more when you know the heart of God. This kind of prayer opens the two-way communication system between you and God sending you merrily on your way to learning to live in His presence moment by moment.

This might sound like a good idea, but impossible for you. You must remember that you are on a journey, and much of your life takes place on the training ground. Step out in your faith and practice what you have learned, expecting the Holy Spirit to meet you where you are and take you to unexpected places of fellowship and prayer with God.

There will be times when you hear correctly and times when you miss it. But I can assure you that if your heart is right before God and you genuinely desire to pray the way Jesus did, then the Holy Spirit will coach you every step of the way. Don't expect perfection, and don't ever feel like this is a performance thing with God. You are not responsible for the result of your good intentions through your prayer life, so never take the credit or the blame for the outcome of your prayers. It is God's responsibility to act upon your prayers.

Remember that God is God and that you are not; it is only by His grace and mercy that you are even alive and able to pray. But… when you know you've heard the voice of the Holy Spirit correctly, then rejoice and record what it was like.

There are random times when the Holy Spirit will bring someone to mind that you are to pray for. Perhaps that someone was on your prayer list but God chose a later time for you to pray. Suddenly the Holy Spirit causes you to **feel** what that person is feeling at the time. Perhaps it is a state of despair, or anger, or hurt. Because you **feel** for the person, you are moved with such compassion that you are compelled to pray accordingly. That is how it was with Jesus.

The Bible says that Jesus was moved with compassion. *"But when He saw the multitudes, He was moved with compassion for them, because they were weary and scattered like sheep having no shepherd. Then He said to His disciples, 'The harvest truly is plentiful, but the laborers are few. Therefore pray the Lord of the harvest to send out laborers into His harvest'"* (Matthew 9:36-38). Feeling compassion is different than feeling sorry for someone. Compassion causes you to move and do something about it, oftentimes through prayer. We'll discuss compassion in more detail later on.

Time to Reflect

- Are you content in your prayer life, or do you need more intimacy with God in prayer?

- Is your prayer list exhaustive with the same prayer requests day after day?

- Name a time when you knew your prayer was heard and a time when you wondered.

- When have you been moved with compassion instead of feeling sorry for someone?

_____
_____
_____
_____

Living Application: Pray and ask God to reveal His heart to you concerning prayer and fellowship with Him through the Holy Spirit. Keep your prayer list and requests just as they are, but begin to ask the Lord to put certain ones on your heart just as they are on His. Be faithful to pray even if you are not sure you heard God's voice correctly. Always thank God for sharing His heart with you and for accomplishing His will through your prayers. Tune in on your training ground and practice listening for the voice of the Holy Spirit in your prayer life.

Ask, Seek, and Knock

Be persistent in your prayer and fellowship with God so that He will pour all of Himself into you and accomplish everything that He has for you, just as He did with Jesus.

Ask God to supply you with all the good and perfect gifts that you will need to accomplish His purpose. **Seek** God in the quiet, still moments and watch for Him because you will most definitely find Him and understand His way more and more. And **knock** on the doors of the floodgates of Heaven so that they will open and you can better live according to His will within the kingdom.

Jesus said *"Ask and it will be given to you; seek, and you will find; knock, and it will be opened to you. For everyone who asks receives, and he who seeks finds, and to him who knocks it will be opened. Or what man is there among you who if his son asks for bread, will give him a stone? If you then, being evil, know how to give good gifts to your children, how much more will your Father who is in heaven give good things to those who ask Him!"* (Matthew 7:7-11)

Be assured that when you approach the Father in prayer this way, you will be given an abundance of all that He has in store for you so that you can thrive in His kingdom. God is waiting for us to approach Him this way!

Enjoy God

"Because your loving kindness is better than life, my lips shall praise you" (Psalm 63:3).

My favorite part about prayer and fellowship with God is simply enjoying Him. You will really enjoy being with Him as well. The nature and character of a perfectly loving God is what you will begin to crave throughout your day and night.

The Holy Spirit is calling you.

- Is there something God wants you to enjoy?
- Is there something God wants you to do that will bring fulfillment to you?

When you hear the Holy Spirit whisper sweet words of love to you unexpectedly, it will stop you in your tracks and put a proud smile upon your face. Remember these words are not just idle words of fluff; these are powerful words coming from the heart of the King of all other kings. This King, just spoke kindness into your spirit, and you are touched beyond measure! You will find yourself echoing God's words of love right back to Him in loving adoration.

Pause a Moment

Allow yourself to slow down enough to enjoy the sweet presence of God and find refreshment for your soul.

Hearing from the Holy Spirit is so grand that I decided if I had to choose between one way prayer **to** God and one way communication **from** God, I would go with only hearing from God. The Bible says that God already knows what I need without saying a word to Him. He knows my every thought. *"For your Father knows the things you have need of before you ask Him"* (Matthew 6:8). But I can't say that I know **His** every thought, so communication from God is life to my very being. I couldn't go back to that one way system again. I need to hear from the Lord on a regular basis.

The times when you've blown it and feel badly about yourself are overcome by a few loving words from God, like…"That's okay, I still really love you" or "Don't worry about it; you will do better next time" or "I know how you feel; let me hold you and make you feel better." *"I have called you by your name; you are Mine"* (Isaiah 43: 1b). Can you imagine hearing those kinds of words from your King?

For many, this personal side of God is really hard to grasp. How could the God of the universe, the Alpha and Omega, the Beginning and the End, stoop so low as to whisper words of love and comfort to little me? Are you wondering about that too? I am talking about the same God who also sent His only Son, Jesus Christ, to earth in a humble posture to take on the sins of the world so that we wouldn't have to. Because Jesus became lowly, we can have the loving fellowship with God that we were created for.

- Do you have self esteem issues?
- Are you insecure in some areas of life?
- Have you been rejected and passed over time and again?
- Have you been betrayed, and have you had trouble trusting others?
- Is there still pain whenever you recall the loss of a loved one?

Jesus knows about each challenge you face, and He understands how you feel. That is why He sent the Holy Spirit to comfort and love you as if He was still walking on the earth. It is the heart of God that lives within you, and it is His presence that fulfills every need you have. Remember that He is your constant companion.

With all of the twists and turns in life, it is difficult to sort through the piles of confusion that blow across the path. Your mind can only handle so much before everything begins to blend together. Instead of wandering aimlessly in a state of confusion, your relationship with your Father entitles you to access the spirit of wisdom that He has for you. *"…that the God of our Lord Jesus Christ, the Father of glory, may give you the spirit of wisdom and revelation in the knowledge of Him"* (Ephesians 1:17).

You don't have to live with confusion or figure anything out for yourself! All you have to do is get to that place where you are comfortable in your relationship with God and ask for wisdom and revelation in your circumstances. God won't turn you down because He loves to give good things to His children. *"Or what man is there among you who, if his son asks for bread, will give him a stone?"* (Matthew 7:9)

Part of your enjoyment of God is simply being his child and asking Him for whatever you need. As you fine tune to the voice of the Holy Spirit, you will recognize His words of wisdom even in the midst of difficult times.

Remember that the Holy Spirit is your constant companion. Everywhere you go, whatever you do, God is with you.

You have the incredible opportunity to enjoy His companionship moment by moment. *"For He Himself has said, 'I will never leave you nor forsake you'"* (Hebrews 13: 5).

You can enjoy His presence and everything that goes along with the companionship of God as much as you want. Don't wait until you go to your quiet corner before you talk to God. Take Him with you all day long and visit with Him. Tell God what a beautiful day it is. Let Him know that you are glad to be in His kingdom today. Ask God which restaurant He thinks you might enjoy for dinner tonight. When you marvel at some part of His creation, tell Him what you are thinking and thank Him for such beauty. When you arrive on time for work after a hectic rush hour, be sure to let God know how grateful you are.

Picture the Lord standing beside you every moment. I assure you He is right there and waits for you to engage in loving fellowship with Him. Sometimes the Holy Spirit initiates the loving fellowship. Practice listening so that you will be sure to recognize His voice and respond to Him.

Prayer Poem Ministry
"POUR FORTH"

You are blessed because you may sit in His presence and bask in the light of His glory. For if you come and seek His presence, you will not go home empty handed. You will carry home box loads and crates filled with the light of God's glory. Seek the Lord earnestly, seek Him honestly and truthfully, and you will find Him. He will lift you up and fill your vessels with everything He is about. You are His child, and the Lord has more to give you than you have even asked for. Don't limit yourself. Tell those around you that there is more, much more of God that they can have. Ask for all that you may have, and see that God is willing to pour forth the light of His glory if you desire it so.

May the Holy Spirit draw you close and cause you to live and breathe in the sweet awareness of the Lord's presence. You will shine for all to see the light of God's glory in you, and He will fill you up, that you will pour forth all the goodness of God. The Lord will draw you in honesty and truthfulness so that nothing will keep you away from Him and His goodness. Remember that you belong to Jesus and that you have access to everything He has. May you walk in your true heritage and bask in the light of God's glory on every avenue of life.

Appointments with God

I hope that you are really excited about growing your relationship with God through loving fellowship and prayer. I know that the Lord is excited about having that kind of intimacy with you! He wants you to pursue Him as He draws you in, and He waits patiently for you.

"Therefore the Lord will wait, that He may be gracious to you" (Isaiah 30: 18). You already know it's God's will, but how do you get there? How do you recognize the voice of the Holy Spirit in the midst of the rumbles of life? What does the voice of God sound like?

Sometimes I still ask myself those same questions. There are times when I feel like a veteran and times when I find myself back on the initial training field. I will never have it all figured out, but that is okay because the journey is well worth every step.

When I first decided to step onto the training field, I went for it with everything I had. I have always liked the quiet of the early morning hours, so it was easy for me to set aside a few minutes early each day to practice listening for the voice of the Holy Spirit. At first, after reading my Bible and praising God, I sat quietly for about five minutes and just waited on the Lord. Sometimes those five minutes seemed like five hours. I wanted to say something to God or read more, but I did my best to be silent. There were times when I fell asleep in those few, quiet moments. I'd wake up, embarrassed that I had allowed myself to sleep instead of listening intently for the voice of God. Yet I didn't know how to be anything other than myself before my Father. I don't think God was upset with me because He knew I was trying my hardest. Then throughout the day, I would tell God that I loved Him and waited to hear something back. As you know from *Living in His Presence*, it wasn't long before I heard the voice of the Holy Spirit, as I sat quietly before Him one evening.

Thinking back, those deliberate times of complete quiet prepared me and really helped me tune in to God.

When prayer and loving fellowship with God become your priority, it's your great advantage to set aside time to sit and wait on Him. *"But those who wait on the Lord shall renew their strength; they shall mount up with wings like eagles, they shall run and not be weary, they shall walk and not faint"* (Isaiah 40: 31).

We are all pretty good at making appointments and keeping them, so why not make one with the Lord each day. If you can't set aside the same time each day, then look at your calendar and make your daily appointments with God according to your schedule.

- Make your time with God a priority.
- Be committed...keep your scheduled time with God.

You will be tempted to cancel your scheduled time with the Lord when the busyness of your day becomes overwhelming. In fact, you can be almost certain that you will have a very hard time keeping your appointment with God at first. But press in and make it a real priority to meet with God. If you want to learn to live with the Lord moment by moment, then you must first quiet yourself enough to learn to recognize His voice and precious presence. Then you can move along in your continuous pursuit of God.

When you are trying to establish a two way communication system with God, one of the hardest obstacles to overcome is doubt. Doubt can weaken your faith. At first you wonder if hearing the voice of God is possible, or you find yourself unworthy and doubt that God would speak directly to you.

When you think you have heard from God, you will wonder if that was really Him or just a good thought. Then doubt steps in and answers the question for you. Sometimes when you pray and stop to listen for a reply, the Holy Spirit might be silent for a little while. Doubt says that God wasn't listening. When you struggle with sin or temptation, you will automatically think that you have not been good enough that day to have loving fellowship with the King.

It's amazing how many circumstances come your way that cause you to wonder or doubt if God is listening or intends to answer your prayer.

The rebuttal to doubt lies within your faith.
You must exercise your faith.

I hope that I didn't just burst your bubble. It's just that everything we do is hinged upon our faith. *"But without faith it is impossible to please God, for he who comes to God must believe that He is, and that He is a rewarder of those who diligently seek Him"* (Hebrews 11:6).

Oftentimes I think of those in the Bible who heard the voice of God. I have wondered if it was audible for them or if God spoke to them the same way He speaks to us today. If the latter is the case, then it had to take great faith to step out in obedience in order to accomplish the will of God. In Hebrews chapter eleven, the Bible lists a few whose faith was tested. By faith…Abel, Enoch, Noah, Abraham, Sarah, Isaac, Jacob, Joseph, Moses, and more…all stepped out and obeyed God. It might not have been easy, but they trusted God and believed. These Biblical characters are role models for us today.

When you trust in the Son of God, seek Him, and practice living in Him…you will automatically receive more faith than you thought you could ever have. On your journey you learn to comply with God and conform to His will, and faith builds. Spend time reading your Bible, and be in prayer; you will watch your faith grow.

The Bible says, *"So then faith comes by hearing, and hearing by the word of God"* (Romans 10:17). Then you can exercise your faith and take steps toward learning to live in the presence of God through loving fellowship. The more you exercise your faith, the stronger it will become. But don't be thinking that you do all of this yourself. You can only do your part; it is up to the Holy Spirit to take it from there and multiply your faith as you take steps to grow in Him.

The Holy Spirit will also give you patience while you wait on God in those quiet moments. You can't make yourself believe, be patient, or overcome doubt. You must simply practice living in Christ, and His Holy Spirit will be there for you.

Time to Reflect

▸ Are you willing to set aside time in your prayer life each day to wait patiently on God?

▸ What hinders your fervent pursuit of God through prayer and loving fellowship?

▸ Have you identified the quiet place where you'll keep your appointments with God?

▸ In what ways does doubt knock on the door of your personal prayer life?

_____
_____
_____
_____
_____

Living Application: Take a serious look at the things that hinder your intimate relationship with God. Then ask the Holy Spirit to change your heart in those areas so that you can better pursue the Lord. Begin to make appointments with God, and be sure to pray about your best time together so that you won't have to cancel. Spend time in praise and thanksgiving and read your Bible every day. Start with five minutes and practice listening for the voice of the Holy Spirit in your quiet place. Be sure to keep a journal of what happens when you are quiet before the Lord. Pray and ask the Holy Spirit to excite you, increase your faith and level of patience, and help you to turn your back on doubt.

Daily Nuts and Bolts

The daily training ground is crucial. Most don't automatically hear from the Lord on a regular basis without putting in some time on the training field. The Holy Spirit is calling you into an intimate relationship with God, but you have to cooperate and that takes an action. *"As the deer longs for streams of water, so I long for you, O God"* (Psalm 42: 1).

Remember that you are pursuing God, so chase after Him feverishly and you will get the results you are hoping and praying for. Practice and patience will help you hear the voice of the Holy Spirit moment by moment in the everyday circumstances of life.

But what does the voice of God sound like and how will I recognize it, you might ask? You are unique in the way that God created you. The Holy Spirit will speak to you in a way that best suits your nature, personality, and gender. Then you can rest, assured that you will grow in your relationship and two-way communication system with God.

I will recount that first time when God spoke to me and told me that He loved me. Here is what happened: God's voice wasn't audible; it was Spirit to spirit. It seemed as if the words I heard in my spirit were spelled out across my mind, and I was silently reading them as I would in a book. Some call that the still, small voice. I really don't think I would have recognized God's voice for the first time if it hadn't been a quiet moment. However, that doesn't mean you have to be still when you hear from the Lord.

You might recall that it wasn't a quiet moment when my cousin, Stacy, heard God's voice for the first time.

It is always up to God to decide how and when He will speak to His children.

Never think that you can manipulate the ways of the Holy Spirit; God is always in control. Remember my softball story from *Living in His Presence*? That wasn't a quiet moment. There was a lot of commotion going on, but the Holy Spirit sent me into the quiet of the forest and directed me to the missing softball.

There are numerous ways to recognize the voice of God through His Holy Spirit. I just mentioned the "still small voice" which is how I would describe my first experience and what it is like for me most of the time. When God speaks, I generally hear His voice as if I was talking. For example, my verbal vocabulary is pretty simple. Therefore, the Holy Spirit speaks to me in a similar vocabulary so that I can understand Him without going to the dictionary.

The Holy Spirit once spoke to my sister in an audible voice. It was a time when Marilyn was resisting dramatic change, and she desperately needed to hear from God beyond a shadow of a doubt.

There are times when you might receive a revelation from the Lord and "just know something" deep inside. You can't explain it because there were no words spoken, but you have a real certainty about something. This is how my husband hears from God most often. Mike calls it a "gut feeling."

"…I will pour out My Spirit on all flesh; your sons and your daughters shall prophesy, your old men shall dream dreams, your young men shall see visions and also on My menservants and on My maidservants" (Joel 2:28).

God also speaks through dreams. Generally, you will recognize a dream from God because you "just know" that it was profound enough to remember. Sometimes dreams don't make sense. Pray and ask the Holy Spirit to reveal the meaning, but be patient because it could take a while for you to understand the full meaning. My children hear from God in dreams. One night Amber and Ryan had an identical, profound dream at the same time. That really got our attention!

My son-in-law senses the voice of the Holy Spirit when he has specific thoughts that are not like the norm. Jim says those thoughts are not like his own, and they really stand out. He tries to press in when that happens and take note in case God wants his attention.

There are the times when you might be reading in your Bible and the "light bulb comes on" pertaining to a specific issue you have been praying about. Suddenly, you know what to do about it.

Pause a Moment

God loves to speak to you through His written Word. Take time to read it, meditate, and listen.

God also speaks through others. There are times when words come from a friend, a family member, or even a total stranger, and you have a sense that God was speaking to you through that person. The Lord uses my friend, Terri, in this way. She calls, unsolicited, with helpful suggestions or a solution to a dilemma that I had been laboring in prayer about.

Perhaps you know of other ways that God speaks. God's ways are multi-faceted; there is no cookie cutter methodology when it comes to learning to hear the voice of the Holy Spirit. That is why the practice field is essential training ground for those who follow Jesus Christ and desire intimacy with Him day to day and moment by moment.

Your Holy Spirit led life can flow with God without even being conscious of it.

It is a lifestyle that naturally evolves with time. You might be out shopping for something specific, notice a store, and know to stop in. You go right to what you were looking for, find it at a great price, and you're out of there in hardly any time. You didn't hear a voice or have a deep gut feeling; you simply walked in what the Lord was doing at the time.

Once, I was stopped at a traffic light on a busy street. Quite suddenly, I thought to inch forward, very close to the car in front of me. Just as I pulled up, I heard a crashing sound, saw smoke, and noticed that the car behind me had just been hit from behind and was jolted forward. If I hadn't moved up a few feet, I would have been involved in that accident as well. My heart pounded, but I knew the Holy Spirit had directed me.

That day everywhere I went I sensed God's leading and provision, but I never really "heard" anything specific. Later on, I recalled my prayer to God. I had prayed that the Lord would be a part of everything I did, make each moment count, and help me to accomplish all I needed to do in a short time. It was a different experience for me because the Holy Spirit chose to speak and lead me in unexpected ways.

You will find that to be the case more often as you move along on your journey. Try to remember that God is in control and that you are not. Just when you think you are comfortable with the way your relationship is going with God, He might choose to take you out of that comfort zone so that you will grow more in Him. God also knows where you are needed in His kingdom, so He will make sure you have the proper training.

It's up to God to lead, and it's your responsibility to follow His lead. It can be quite the adventuresome journey, but it is also a joy when you live, move, and have your being in Christ!

Don't be intimidated by your training ground. The practice field is where you run and play with God. You can ask God questions and wait for His Holy Spirit to answer. It is much easier to start out asking God simple questions about things that won't have a serious impact on your life while you are learning to listen.

You can exercise your faith practically as you step out in areas that are not crucial or that don't have significant life consequences when you make a mistake. You **will** make mistakes, but you have to work through them so that you will learn from them.

A Few Red Lights

Beware of a few red lights that can hinder your genuine pursuit of God. Some of my biggest mistakes come when I make assumptions about what I think I just heard from God. I tend to run with the information before asking the Holy Spirit exactly what He wants me to do with it. Sometimes I let my mind and emotions carry me off in the wrong direction instead of using spiritual wisdom to stay the course.

There are times when the Holy Spirit speaks to me concerning something that is yet to come. When I assume it is simply for today and go merrily on my way, it feels like I hit a brick wall, and I wonder what went wrong. Did I misunderstand what God said? Maybe I missed it. Doubt and confusion settle in, and I start to second guess God. That is why we must pray for great measures of wisdom so that we will operate in His will, His timing, and with His understanding.

Sometimes I think I've heard from God, yet I also have a deep feeling that is in direct conflict with the thought. It is like I "know" differently and then realize that what I think I heard might not have been from the Holy Spirit. It is a safeguard that helps me fine tune my prayer life.

Beware of treating God like a psychic. God is not a magician or a crystal ball, and neither are we! In Acts 8:20, Peter rebuked Simon the sorcerer. Simon became a believer in Jesus Christ and had just been baptized, but he was intrigued with the power that the Holy Spirit had given to the apostles. Simon's motives were wrong; he focused on the power and what he could do rather than what God was all about. We have to be careful not to fall into Simon's trap.

Test the sincerity of your heart.

- What is **your** motive for wanting to hear God's voice?
- If no one else knew you heard from God, would you be alright with that?

Our relationship with God should never be a manipulative act in order to get Him to perform. We can't control God through prayer; we must submit to Him instead. It is a mistake that proves costly because then hearing from God becomes a mystical thing. We risk stealing the glory that only belongs to God, and that takes away sweet intimacy leaving a sour residue to contend with. Manipulation is a danger for anyone who gets used to hearing from God on a regular basis.

Getting used to hearing from God could become a problem; it can be a bit like taking Him for granted. We must remember that communication through the Holy Spirit is God's idea, and it's never less than a privilege.

"Enter into His gates with thanksgiving, and into His courts with praise. Be thankful to Him, and bless His name." (Psalm 100:4)

Always approach God with praise and a heart of gratitude. None of us would like it if our children barged in, hurled requests at us, and gave us orders to perform without a greeting or expression of love. That might sound dramatic, but I assure you that it happens to God. Anyone can stumble and approach God with such insensitivity if they are not careful.

Whenever I'm not as connected to God as I should be, I stumble into an insensitive mode. I forget to express my love and affection. I fall into selfish expectations that seem more like "God on demand." I think it saddens His heart. That is why it is important to learn to live in God's presence and remain connected through a loving, mutual, relationship. Then the relationship is ongoing, and we learn to pray without ceasing instead of meeting and greeting God every time we choose to connect with Him.

The power of pride is one of the deepest pitfalls that can hinder your relationship with God. It is difficult not to be arrogant in areas where you excel or have strengths, even if your strength is in your relationship with God. You must always remember that all good things come from God. Even the relationship that you have worked so hard to cultivate wouldn't exist if God wasn't in charge.

Do your best to avoid every prideful avenue because danger lurks on both sides of the street. Pride puffs us up and tells us that we are something special because we connect with God. Don't be fooled because "*God resists the proud, but gives grace to the humble*" (James 4: 6). If we are not careful, an arrogant aroma emits from the heart and lures us away from true intimacy with God. We start to feel good about what we can do in the name of Jesus, and we like being "in the know" with God. It doesn't matter if others sense that or not; God knows the attitudes of the heart.

**Be satisfied with your sweet intimacy with God,
as if no one else even knows about it.
Then your relationship with Him will remain pure and holy.**

A prideful attitude will damage your relationship with God. None of us wants that to happen or even think it might happen. Pride is subtle and occurs while we are not aware of it. If undetected, that kind of arrogance will put you on the outskirts before you know it. So don't go there; it is simply not worth taking the risk.

Remember that your new found prayer life is a privilege, an honor, a high calling, and always about glorifying God. Then you won't be tempted to explore prideful avenues that bring mayhem directly to your humble spirit before the Lord.

Your intellect is a gift, a true blessing from God. But your intellect can also make you stumble in your relationship with God if you allow that to happen. You were saved by grace and through faith in Jesus Christ. You didn't think your way through your salvation; you simply believed. It was an act of your faith.

A powerful prayer life doesn't come from the intellect; it comes from the heart, and it is Spirit to spirit.

If you try to reason your way through your relationship with God, you will miss Him. You can't come up with a formula or equation that will determine if, or to what degree, you just heard from the Holy Spirit. Many feel left out; they are unable to hear from God because they rely on the mind instead of the heart. If you are nodding your head, then thankfully you know that about yourself, and you can go from there. You are not doomed to fail in your two-way communication system with the Holy Spirit. God always meets you right where you are, and He will help you take Spirit-led steps in His direction.

Time to Reflect

- Considering your personality, how can you best recognize the voice of the Holy Spirit?
- Name a time when you sense God was speaking to you. What was it like?
- Which red lights hinder the success of your journey to live with God each moment?
- How do you respond to your mistakes? Do you learn from them, or do they stifle you?

_____
_____
_____
_____
_____

Living Application: Take note of your personality traits… Are you more figurative or literal? Perhaps you are more visual than audio. Are you more of a bottom line person? Do you tend to reason through most of life? Are you a deep thinker? What captures your attention most easily? Pray about your personality so that you might be more likely to recognize the voice of the Holy Spirit more readily. Journal the times when you feel like God is speaking to you, be sure to jot down how you felt, and then date it. Try to keep your prayer journal current so that you will be more accurate about recording spiritual matters with the Lord. Don't be afraid to admit your red light zones.

Consider this:

You will overcome your spiritual stumbling blocks easier when you are aware of them. Be sure to remember that we all make mistakes when it comes to following the lead of the Holy Spirit. Practice giving yourself a little slack, room for error on your journey. Identify an accountability person who will pray with you and help to confirm the promptings of the Holy Spirit. Always practice the first ingredient and live a life of praise and thanksgiving unto the Lord. Try to start your day with some form of praise, even if it is in the car. If necessary, plan it out so that you can build it into your lifestyle. Rejoice in your awesome privilege to know God intimately!

Practice Makes Better

The practice field is also the place to be quiet and still before God. Your quiet reverence before the Lord as you wait on Him is excellent training ground and teaches patience.

Don't forget that scripture reading is essential on the practice field. It will feel like spiritual vitamins and supplements that give you the power boost you need to chase after God. Keep your head above ground with an attitude of praise and thanksgiving in everything you think and do.

God knows how much you desire to get to know Him intimately, so His Spirit will meet you and carry you down the field. I always remind myself that God initiated this two-way communication system and that I am simply blessed to be able to join in with Him. What a privilege!

There are a few things I always keep in mind that help me recognize the voice of the Holy Spirit. God's voice always brings peace or comfort, never fear or condemnation. If I think I have heard a word from God but I am gripped with fear, then I am sure I am listening to something other than the voice of God.

Whatever I feel like I have heard from God must always agree with what is in the Bible. For example, the Bible says that God will never leave or forsake us. If I feel like God is responding to me in anger and tells me that He is not going to be with me wherever I am going, then I have not heard from God.

One of the Ten Commandments says, *"You shall not murder"* (Exodus 20: 13). No one can ever justify murder by saying that God told them to do it. Whenever you sense the Holy Spirit speaking, always test what you've heard with this scripture: *"But the fruit of the Spirit is love, joy, peace, long suffering, kindness, goodness, faithfulness, gentleness, and self-control"* (Galatians 5:22).

Remember that God will never speak anything to you that contradicts His Word in the Bible.

In *Living in His Presence*, I mentioned the time when the Holy Spirit told me to begin to desire a quiet life for my family. I made the mistake of assuming God wanted us to live a life of seclusion far from the land I loved, my suburban neighborhood. I wasn't happy about the implications of the word from God, so I didn't tell my husband. I was afraid Mike would push for a move westward to live off the land. Those feelings should have clued me in to realize that I had misinterpreted what the Holy Spirit was really saying to me. My incorrect assumptions caused me to react with fear and deceit. Remember earlier when I mentioned that we have to test what we think we hear from God and sample the fruit of it? The Bible doesn't teach to be fearful or withhold from your husband. I ran with "the word" and made an assumption that was contrary to what the Bible teaches. Later on, my husband and I prayed for clarity. The Holy Spirit redirected our thoughts, and we had great peace together.

The quiet lifestyle that God had intended for us provided some of the best years for our family! The word was right on, but the wrong interpretation could have prevented the blessing and journey that God had for our family.

▸ Do you wonder what kinds of questions are appropriate to ask God?
▸ Is it difficult for you to be personal with the God of the universe, Creator of all things?

Don't be concerned if you just answered "yes." You are in good company because everyone struggles at first. You have to deal with your thoughts of doubt and operate in faith. You already know it is the will of God to have loving fellowship with His beloved ones who follow His Son, Jesus. You have to get personal with God without taking the awe or any reverence away from Him. How do you do that?

You must first give God total authority over everything concerning your training ground. That means He has the right to do anything with you that He feels is necessary on the practice field.

Keep an attitude of gratitude as much as possible toward the Lord. Give Him the praise and thanksgiving He deserves... every moment if needed. You aren't settling anything with God; but you **are** establishing His sovereignty in your own heart. By keeping God on the throne, while inviting Him to become more personal and intimate, you are setting yourself up for great success in pursuing the God of the Universe. His Holy Spirit will put you at ease and lead you every step of the way, and you won't even realize it. You will simply start moving by the Spirit naturally.

Once you have established God's authority in your heart and you are comfortable with your pursuit of Him in loving fellowship and prayer, you are ready for the training ground. You can start to exercise your faith on the practice field. In your pursuit of God you might have to initiate the conversation at first. Start by asking simple questions. Here are a few suggestions, but you can think of countless questions on your own.

- Ask God to give you creative dinner ideas that would please your family.
- Ask the Holy Spirit for a great idea for a family outing or date with your spouse.
- Give the Lord permission to orchestrate your day or your work schedule.
- Ask the Holy Spirit to point out good qualities in others that you have not noticed.
- Allow the Lord to show you simple, specific ways to pray for others.
- Ask God to bring someone to mind who needs encouragement, and then step out in faith and contact that person.
- Ask the Holy Spirit to help you find scriptures in the Bible without having to look them up in the concordance.

When your children are young, practice listening for God's voice concerning them. Ask questions about them and wait for the answer. It is an excellent practice field when they are young because their issues are small.

As your children grow up, you will want to be familiar with the way the Holy Spirit speaks to you about them. Then you can follow His leading when they are older and issues become more critical.

Remember my story about Amber and Ryan's hike at dusk when they were very young? Imagine your peaceful feeling instead of worry, when your teenager is frightfully late getting home!

While you are busy asking the Holy Spirit specific questions, remember to continue to ask for the most important thing…"Dear God, please help me to be passionate about my relationship with you, and help me to learn to listen for your wonderful voice moment by moment every day." The Bible says, *"Ask and it will be given to you; seek, and you will find; knock and it will be opened to you. For everyone who asks receives, and he who seeks finds, and to him who knocks it will be opened"* (Matthew 7:7, 8).

Remember that it is God's will for you to know Him intimately. Never stop asking, seeking, or knocking!

When I first started to pursue God in prayer and loving fellowship, I asked the Holy Spirit some of those same questions and involved Him in my day to day activities. One day, I was out to buy a present for Ryan's birthday in January. Because it was shortly after Christmas, it felt like everything I wanted was already sold out. I was sad about that because I wanted something our little toddler would really enjoy. I remember going to one last toy store and praying that they would have his special toy. Suddenly, I "just knew" that I was going to find it. Yet in my search up and down the toy isles, I came up short. "Sure Gina," I said to myself, "that wasn't God; you just had a good thought." Doubt was knocking on the door, but I had to resist letting it in. Then a sweet peace came over me and I heard the "still small voice." "Look up high," the Holy Spirit said. When I looked high above the normal shelves, I saw **the** toy. Ryan was going to have his fun present!

I rejoiced in what God had done, yet it seemed like such a casual thing for Him to do for me. Later on, I realized that there was a valuable, spiritual lesson to be learned on my training ground. Sometimes we are up against the odds and it seems hopeless. But you have to look **up high,** above the normal or the natural, to experience the supernatural. In Matthew 19:26 Jesus said, *"With men this is impossible, but with God all things are possible."* And I say, "Amen to that!"

Times when I misplaced something, I asked God to show me where it was. Then I would sit still, wait, and listen. Sometimes I could hear correctly and sometimes not. It mostly depended upon my spiritual attitude and posture of praise at the time. Whenever I operated out of doubt or fear, I usually came up short. But when I exercised my faith, trusting and praising God, I generally heard His voice correctly.

Pause a Moment

What does your spiritual attitude and posture of praise look like right now?

Emotions can affect your ability to hear God's voice clearly. That is why it is valuable to make the most of your training ground and work hard on the practice field to recognize the voice of God. Remember to listen for the voice of the Holy Spirit in simple circumstances when there is nothing critical involved. Then when emotional issues arise, you will be more apt to discern the voice of God and follow His leading.

Imagine how much more effective you will be in prayer when you can hear the voice of the Holy Spirit prompting you to pray a certain way. There is no limit to the ways that the Lord will use you in His kingdom when you are tuned in to Him.

Try not to allow yourself to become discouraged on the practice field. At first it might seem like you are only going to be able to operate in a one way communication system with God, especially if you are having trouble listening for Him. But pursue the Lord and continue to practice listening for His voice. I can assure you that once you hear His voice and know you have had a personal encounter with God, you will become passionate about your pursuit of Him in loving fellowship and prayer.

Allow the scope of your training ground to become vast, and try very hard not to place boundaries around it. God will call the plays and prompt you to operate by His Spirit moment by moment; cooperate and be obedient.

A great, personal relationship requires time, patience, and constant nurturing. But you won't be the only one to nurture the relationship; the Holy Spirit will lavish you with the wealth of His presence as His part of the commitment.

Prayer Poem Ministry
"LIVING WATER"

Living water, isn't it refreshing to you? Don't you simply delight in watching fresh, living water flowing down the mountainside? Won't you pull over and stop to listen to the gushing waters, the purity of the sound, and then watch the glistening of the water as the sun shines upon it? The sprinkle that touches you from the gushing of the waters, yes even those few droplets... are they not refreshing to your dry, parched skin and lips? And oh the beauty and the growth of the living plants that settle near the water! It is so green and fertile there; the soil is soft and moist. Be like living water, and be the one whom many will see as pure, alive, glistening by the Son of God, and refreshing to be around. Encourage others to be like living water and set an example for them to follow. Always remember where the living water comes from, and be all you are called to be.

May there be refreshment in your life as you become like living water in the presence of God. The Father will draw you near and help you to flow in loving fellowship with His Spirit. There on the mountainside of His sweet presence, you will glisten in the light of His Son, Lord Jesus. May you be a sprinkling of refreshment to those around you who are dry and parched from their journeys!

They will grow from the rich, fertile soil of your life and become like living water flowing in the presence of God. May the Holy Spirit lead you and guide you in your pursuit of God through tender, loving fellowship and prayer so that you will become all that you were created to be.

The Highs and Lows

When I first pictured my practice field, I envisioned it to be like a flat plain of green grass, freshly mowed and well manicured. I thought I would be able to run and frolic upon my field of green and never grow weary. I could take giant leaps forward and do perfect cartwheels on the soft, spongy turf. The wind would be still, and it would never rain upon my precious field. After all, this is where I would meet God every day, and it would be picture perfect.

The practice field upon my training ground **was** picture perfect because the Lord met me there every day. However, it didn't turn out to look the way I had envisioned it many years ago when I was suiting up and raring to go. My practice field wasn't smooth and level at all; it had hills and valleys. There were peaks, plateaus, and pot holes. The curves and bends in the road came unexpectedly. Sometimes the wind howled and blew hard enough to tip me over, and I was drenched in the rain more than once.

It was still my perfect practice field because the Holy Spirit was there with me every step of the way.

I grew to like the terrain of my practice field, and I learned to acclimate to the weather conditions quickly. It became my special place because I learned so much there.

Today, my practice field looks somewhat like it did when I first stepped out many years ago. Thankfully, the terrain and the weather conditions continue to improve as I grow in my relationship with God. Sometimes I feel like I am on top of the mountain having loving fellowship with God; my prayers are being answered and His sweet voice is so comforting. Even one loving word or impression from God is enough to send me to the top of the mountain.

"But let him ask in faith, with no doubting, for he who doubts is like a wave of the sea driven and tossed by the wind" (James 1: 6). There are still times when doubt chases after me, and it seems I am sliding down the mountainside. If I don't stand my ground, then doubt will cause my faith to quiver and shake, and I'll stumble into a deep pothole. The climb out and upward is tough but rewarding as my eyes are fixed on the peak once again.

When I am not pursuing God as much as I should, I feel like I am standing still on a plateau, not growing in intimacy with Him. I have grown to like the curves and bends in the road because great learning takes place there as long as I keep my eyes on Jesus.

Now adverse weather doesn't bother me as much because I know how to find shelter in the shadow of His wings and wait out the storms. *"Because You have been my help, therefore in the shadow of Your wings I will rejoice"* (Psalm 63: 7).

Growing in intimacy with God will never take place on flat, green, spongy turf. We won't grow to have loving fellowship with God if we don't have the same terrain and weather conditions that many have had to experience. Those who have gone before us had to plow some serious ground. I can't imagine how many highs and lows that came their way, yet they braved the elements to pursue intimacy with God.

Let the lives of those who have lived to tell their stories and those in the Bible inspire and encourage you to step out on your practice field so that you can learn to live with God moment by moment each day.

Time to Reflect

- Are you ready to explore your training ground and step out on the practice field?
- Is there anything hindering you from moving out onto the field? Identify your obstacles.
- How do you envision your practice field?
- Is there anything in your heart that would keep you away from your field? Name it.

_____
_____
_____
_____
_____

Living Application: Take your first steps on the practice field by spending some time in prayer asking God to meet you there. Settle any issues you discover in your heart that might prevent you from living in an attitude of gratitude toward the Lord. Ask God a few, simple questions and practice listening for the voice of the Holy Spirit moment to moment. Keep your eyes on Jesus, and stay grounded in the Word of God everyday. Be mindful of the terrain and the weather conditions on your field so that you won't become discouraged as you journey and learn to enter into loving fellowship and prayer with God.

Fine Tuning

You will become quite good at fine tuning your prayer life with God. Even though encountering God through loving fellowship is the most wonderful experience, it takes commitment and concentration. The unexpected can happen, and you will have choices to make. But when you are trying your best to enter into loving fellowship with God, you will get there for sure.

Remember that God speaks in many ways, and He might even speak to you in more than one way. Try to journal what you felt like the Holy Spirit said to you so that you can compare from time to time. If you become confused, stop and pray, and spend some time reading your Bible. Then you will know how to go back to the spot where things were most clear so you can proceed from there.

Never act upon or change anything if you are confused because God will not stir up confusion when you are seeking direction from Him. The Bible says *"For God is not the author of confusion but of peace"* (1Corinthians 14: 33).

If you are seeking God's will and listening for His voice in a critical situation, be sure to spend lots of time in prayer and in your Bible. You will need to be strong in your spirit to discern the will of God in the midst of turbulent times. Keep in mind that your emotions can sometimes speak louder than you think, and they mask the voice of God. It is always best to ask someone you trust spiritually to confirm the promptings in your heart when your circumstances are critical.

When the Holy Spirit is silent and hasn't answered your question or prayer request, what will you do?

- Will you still trust Him for your circumstance?
- Will you keep the Lord on the throne where He belongs?
- Will you remember that God is in charge and can be quiet whenever He desires?

God might want to use those silent times to build patience in you. He might also choose to be silent so that when He does speak, you will recognize His voice in easy or difficult circumstances.

The distractions of life will always try to crowd your relationship with God. It is like being tangled within a love triangle. You will have to make a choice to ward them off. You might be distracted by the busyness of life with work and family. Special events and activities can be distractions, and you will have to learn to build in time with the Lord.

Remember that you are to be a part of **God's** life…God should not have to be a part of **your** life. The influences of the world are serious distractions that make it difficult to hear the voice of God. They will rumble, so be sure to fine tune and follow the Whisper. You are spending time on the training ground so that even if there are distractions, your spirit is strong and you can recognize the promptings of the Holy Spirit anytime.

It is easier to fine tune when you keep your spirit strong in the Lord. It is important to fortify your spirit by reading your Bible and spiritually edifying literature on a regular basis. Remember that you need to keep the Word of God close to your heart everyday, even if you just meditate on a scripture or two in the midst of a consuming time. *"I will meditate on Your precepts, and contemplate Your ways"* (Psalm 119: 15).

Don't be too busy to pray, even if it feels like it is only one-way for a while. You will still grow stronger in your spirit and in your relationship with God. God hears all prayers, and you must not cease prayer in any form.

You are a follower of Jesus Christ, so never stop thinking about Him. Jesus is your Savior, your ultimate role model, and He deserves all of your attention and praise. Somewhere I read that if you want to know the Father, then get to know Jesus because He is the visible image of an invisible God.

When you live with a proper praise posture before God, your spirit is strengthened. You will fine tune and discern the will of God much easier.

Learning to live in the presence of God in loving fellowship is not a crash course. It is a process, and there are no short cuts. There will be no cliff notes to read or memorize. In *Living in His Presence* we talked about the journey and the goal. This is between God and you. The Holy Spirit will never force Himself upon you, but He desires sweet intimacy with you every moment. He will draw you, but you must respond. The more passionate you become about your pursuit of God, the more progress you will make on your journey.

Don't be afraid of your practice field. It is a custom fit, designed by God specifically for you, so step out on it and give it your best. Some never step out because they are waiting for the perfect timing that doesn't seem to come around. Many are afraid of acting upon what they feel the Lord has told them to do because it seems foolish. *"Let no one deceive himself. If anyone among you seems to be wise in this age, let him become a fool that he may become wise"* (1Corinthians 3:18).

My husband once asked me how I know that the light will come on when I flip the switch. I told him that I know it will come on because it always comes on when I flip the switch. "Exactly," Mike responded. "The more you flip the switch, the more the light comes on, and the more you will expect it to turn on whenever you flip the switch."

I encourage you to step out, flip the switch, and act wisely upon whatever God tells you to do. As you see progress in your new prayer life, you will trust God for more. You will feel more confident each time you act on behalf of God's will and flip the switch.

Let's pray!

Father, thank you that you are real and that I can live in Your presence. I know I am never alone; You are with me! Draw me near in loving fellowship and prayer. Please help me hear Your voice, see You every moment, and know it is You when You speak. Make me wise to act upon Your will. Please strengthen me to exercise my faith and pursue You. I want to live with You every moment and make a difference in the Kingdom of God, just as Jesus did. Thank you that I belong to Jesus, and please protect me as I follow in His footsteps. May I truly learn to live in Your presence moment by moment, every day.

Third Ingredient

Trust in God...
Celebration of Dependence — 82
Trusting God — 86
Viewing Your Dependence — 87
Roadside Perks — 89
Drawing Close — 93
Identify with Your Foundation — 95
More or Less — 98
Three Hidden Benefits — 100
Watch Out! — 105
Faith or Fear? — 108
Stumbling Blocks — 110
The Look of Trust — 114
The Great Artist — 115
Precious Patience — 116
God's Faithfulness — 118
The Beauty of the Holy Spirit — 120
Freedom in God's Will — 122

> *"Assuredly I say to you, unless you are converted and become as little children, you will by no means enter the Kingdom of Heaven."*
>
> Matthew 18:3

You were once a little child much like what the Bible describes. Regardless of your surroundings or how you grew up, you had no concept of responsibility, worry, or doubt. Fear wasn't in your tiny vocabulary. You were totally dependent upon someone to take care of you. Do you remember when? Take a few moments and think about what it might have been like when you were so young.

- You might have fallen and hurt yourself, and someone made it feel better.
- You cried because you were hungry, and someone gave you a nutritious snack.
- You needed your shoes tied, and someone bent down to help you.

Even as an adult, I can see similarities in my life now that remind me of childhood. There are times when I make mistakes and fall, and the pain is more than I want to bear. Yet the Lord is there to pick me up, dress my wounds, and make me feel much better about myself. I remember when I felt empty inside and yearned to have the void filled. The Holy Spirit quickened the perfect scripture to my spirit that was food for my soul. It is impossible to recall all of my needs that Jesus met as He bent down with loving compassion to help me. Perhaps you relate in much the same way.

In *Living in His Presence*, we talked about the carefree attitude of a little child. Children are generally happy and content as long as someone is looking after them. They don't know how the next meal will come; they only know that it will. There isn't time to doubt and worry because children are busy having too much fun to think about burdensome cares. There is innocent dependency upon someone bigger, more capable to ensure their safety and well-being.

Here in the Kingdom of God, it is much the same. There is Someone much bigger than we are who welcomes innocent dependency upon Himself.

We were never instructed to "grow up" and make the world tick on our own. God didn't cut the apron strings and send us merrily on our way to succeed in life without Him. In fact, the scripture in Matthew that you just read tells us that we won't be able to enter God's kingdom unless we do it in a childlike fashion. And if we can't enter, then we won't get to live there either.

We have to allow ourselves the luxury of returning to a childlike state of being with God if we are going to learn to live with Him moment by moment in His kingdom.

Pause a Moment

Give yourself the wonderful opportunity to live like a child of God in His presence today.

I want to tell you a brief story about my daughter when she was just four years old. Amber enjoyed playing with her favorite doll and had a pink buggy to wheel her around the house. The buggy was fairly heavy and almost bigger than Amber. One day, I ran to the upper level of our house for only a few minutes while Amber and Ryan were just two floors beneath me, playing in the basement. Suddenly I heard giggling down the hall in Amber's room and ran to see what was going on there. I discovered Amber playing with her doll and buggy in her bedroom, but her little brother was still in the basement. I asked Amber how she got her heavy buggy up two flights of stairs to her room all by herself. She told me that she wanted to play upstairs but needed help getting her buggy all the way up to her bedroom. In a matter of fact sort of way, Amber said that she asked Jesus to watch over Ryan and help her carry her buggy up the stairs, and He did! She had a genuine, child-like expectation of her Savior, and she knew He would take care of her need…period. I was a bit anxious that her little brother was alone in the basement, but I was extremely proud of her for trusting in the Lord for a need that was bigger than she was. Ryan was fine and together the three of us thanked the Lord for taking care of Amber's need.

Picture this!

Your good friend has the dad of all dads. He is strong, courageous, and supportive of his daughter no matter what. He has an established business in town where he is well known. Her dad is the king of clout because of his creative accomplishments and invaluable service to the people of the community. She loves it that others know she is his daughter because being related to him keeps her close and makes her feel a lot like him. Your friend's dad takes care of everything she needs; all she has to do is ask, and he responds in her best interest.

One day your friend tells you that her dad has more wealth than you could ever imagine. He provides for her and takes care of all of her needs. He tells her that as long as he is alive, she never has to worry about anything. There is nothing too good for his little girl. When your friend goes out into the darkness of night, her dad sends a few guards to secure her safety without her knowing they are there. She always returns with a heart of gratitude toward her perfect father because of his provision and protection. She knows that without him, she would have nothing and be nothing. Yet sometimes she ventures off on her own, but her dad always watches with eyes like an eagle. He allows her to make mistakes knowing she will come back and realize just how much she needs his loving direction. When she gets sick, her daddy nurses her back to health.

Then one day you ask your friend if she ever considered cutting the apron strings and moving away to accomplish great things on her own. She tells you that she can't imagine ever doing that! She loves living with her father and being his little girl; she is glad to be totally dependent upon him. Your friend tells you that she knows the world isn't perfect, but that the unconditional love and guidance of her father is enough to put wind in her sails and guide her anywhere she needs to go in life. Suddenly you understand your friend's great fortune and realize how much you would like to have a father like that too.

I have a father like that, and so do you! But sometimes we don't see our Heavenly Father in that light. We get caught up in the world we live in and forget that God the Father is the ultimate dad of all dads. God is everything and more than the dad we have just pictured above. We simply need to change our way of thinking. How can we do that when our culture dictates and demands independence from our Heavenly Father?

Our society primes us for independence from God at an age when we are too young to understand what is happening. At a very young age we learn to say words like: no, never, me, and mine. When we grow up, we take charge, push full speed ahead, and knock over anyone who stands in our way.

We take pride in all we know, choose what we want, and we reason according to our own agendas. We attain financial stability, we keep up with and even surpass the neighbors, we treasure what we've acquired, and we feel pretty good about what we've done. It doesn't matter whether we do these things on a large or small scale. We still make it all happen, and we do it all in the course of a normal lifetime. "We" can do it all.

That might sound like an over exaggeration, but I assure you that everyone can relate to some of what **we** do. It's difficult to admit to any of what I just mentioned. It sounds selfish and inconsiderate, doesn't it? Yet those selfish tendencies affect our relationship with our Father everyday, and they are inconsiderate of His perfect will.

Your Father never created you to work independently of His presence. He didn't give you a mind to devise your life plan without considering Him.

God gave you brilliance so that you could bring Him glory, reason according to His will, and make choices to obey His Word. You don't become absent minded the day you give your life to Jesus Christ. Your mind is re-newed as you develop the mind of Christ, thriving in the Kingdom of God where it comes into peaceful submission to the will of the Father.

Have you ever compared yourself to Jesus Christ? When I think of His life and compare mine to His, I am humbled. Jesus was perfect and continues to be the role model for all those who are willing to follow Him. Yet Jesus said that He could do nothing without consulting with the Father.

> *"Most assuredly, I say to you, the Son can do nothing of Himself but what He sees the Father do; for whatever He does, the Son also does in like manner."* (John 5:19)

Doesn't that scripture remind you of a little boy imitating his dad? Picture that little guy. He walks in his dad's footsteps, repeats his dad's words, and tries to be just like him. He does it all because his dad is a giant in his little world. His dad can do nothing wrong. Jesus lived like that little boy we just pictured. God the Father was Jesus' spiritual giant in the fallen world that He came to live in. Jesus walked in His Father's footsteps, repeated His words, and was a perfect representation of His Father.

When I compare myself to Jesus, I realize that I am nothing more than a pitiful sinner aside from His saving grace and daily leadership in my life. Wouldn't you agree when you compare your life to His? So where did we get the idea that free will means we can think and thrive in this world without God's leading moment to moment?

Why do we wander off expecting to make a significant mark on the pavement of life outside of God's plan? To the Father, we **are** little children whether we dress up and pretend to be big or not! Since Jesus could do nothing of Himself, then we can't either.

**If we want to identify with Jesus,
then we must recognize our need for the Father as well.**

You might be thinking that you do a good job of navigating around town in the presence of the Father. You love God with all your heart. You pray about where to work and live. You ask God to protect and provide for yourself and for your loved ones. You go to church and do nice things for others. Doesn't that count for living as a child in the Kingdom of God? Perhaps it does, but you will learn to reach higher if you are willing!

Time to Reflect

▸ What has been your perception of God the Father? How is He like a real dad to you?

▸ Is Jesus **really** your role model, or is someone else? Who is that person?

▸ Do you live like a child in the kingdom, or do you play dress-up most everyday?

▸ When are you more willing to be child-like, and when is it most difficult?

_____
_____
_____
_____

Living Application: Pray and ask God the Father to help you desire and learn to be more child-like in your relationship with Him. Ask God to help you to recognize your need for Him on a moment to moment basis. Then envision God as a dad, much like the one we just pictured together. If you have trouble seeing God as your true Father, then pray for a clear revelation of His fatherhood to you. Even though it is hard to do, take some time to compare yourself with Jesus. Do this so that you will have a better understanding of why you need to be totally dependent upon the Father. Begin to desire the same child-like attitude that Jesus had toward His Father.

Trusting God

How does one get to the place of trusting in the Lord as a little child would do? Can we automatically turn over control and obey **at will**? Many have tremendous will power and discipline, but I don't think that sheer will or discipline take you over the trusting threshold of life with Christ. Remember that we really can't do anything without God, not even something as simple as deciding to trust Him. We can only cross the threshold by the power of God through our relationship with the Holy Spirit.

If you don't know God, then you can't trust Him completely. Many think they are trusting God when oftentimes they have only offered a quick prayer and then proceeded down the path without His true leading.

In order to trust God the same way a small child would trust, you must recognize His sovereignty, understand your helplessness, and learn to get to know Him on a personal basis. That is why we discussed the first two ingredients before getting to the trusting component of learning to live with God.

You must work at keeping God on **the** throne at all times. You can't afford to make Him less of a priority in your life, even for a short time. The Father has to have the place of distinctive honor in your heart moment by moment.

Your prayer life with God needs to be two ways. You can't do all the talking; the Holy Spirit needs to hold the microphone too. Practice listening for His voice in the daily circumstances of life. The more you get to know the Father through the Holy Spirit, you will sense how trustworthy He really is. You will love God more, your faith will grow, and you will want Christ to be more and more at home in your heart.

"...that Christ may dwell in your hearts through faith; that you, being rooted and grounded in love, may be able to comprehend with all the saints what is the width and length and depth and height- to know the love of Christ which passes knowledge; that you may be filled with all the fullness of God" (Ephesians 3: 17-19).

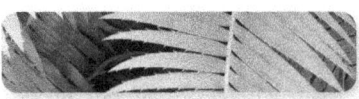

Prayer Poem Ministry
"CHILDLIKE DEPENDENCE"

The excitement in your faith is contagious; your child-like dependence upon God brings joy to His heart. God can fulfill each desire in your heart, every need, heal every wound, and make a sunny day for you... if you desire Him to. As you come to the place where He wants you to be, don't question why or when...only submit and surrender your whys and whens to the Father. It is not necessary to know these things at once...it's only necessary to know that everything is in the care of your Heavenly Father. Who knows God's timing? Not even the Son. Jesus walked in His Father's will, leaving the timing to Him. He was concerned only with the will of the Father who sent Him. Your covering is supernatural, from God Himself. He is your all and everything. With God you will accomplish much, and you will also receive much.

Let your genuine faith excite all those around you. When the world is exposed to your child-like dependence upon God and your faith, it will take notice. God's heart is dripping with joy every time you trust Him and testify to His faithfulness. May the Lord fulfill every desire that He places within your heart. May every need and every wound be dressed personally by God. Desire God and may your days be sunny, bright with His presence, and filled with His faithfulness. Give your whys and whens to God, and watch as you submit to His authority and authenticity. Watch your Father's care for you with attentive eyes, eyes that see Him for who He really is.

Viewing Your Dependence

Trials and hurdles in the world were never meant to be overcome alone. Jesus said, *"These things I have spoken to you, trust in Me that you may have peace. In the world you will have tribulation; but be of good cheer, I have overcome the world"* (John 16:33).

Remember that the Kingdom of God is all around you and that even though you live within the boundaries of this world, you are not **of** the world. You live by the principles of the kingdom and have access to Christ through His Spirit.

When tribulation comes and takes your life-giving breath away, call upon the Holy Spirit. He delivers rescue breathing that resuscitates you and puts the wind back in your sails.

We tend to view dependency as a negative thing in our culture. We learn of those who become dependent upon drugs, alcohol, tobacco, and other addictive substances. We criticize others who won't support themselves but depend upon the government or allow relatives and friends to carry their weight. How about those who constantly burden others for advice and stability; they wear you out, don't they? The elderly will tell you how much they dislike it when they must depend on others for their daily needs.

Keeping these kinds of examples in our subconscious, we strive for independence in every way possible. It is understandable that we don't want to fall into any negative category. I hope that you can begin to see why dependence upon our Heavenly Father could have a negative connotation to so many. We condition ourselves to be independent in every way, and that can harm our ability to lean upon God for everything.

Let's look again at the narrow and wide gates that I mentioned in *Living in His Presence*. They both open up onto a pathway, but it is surprising how the terrain changes as you get further down the road. Many don't stop and evaluate what the terrain could be like down the road. They are off and running before they realize it, oblivious to the possibilities or the consequences of a hasty decision.

Perhaps you might decide to try both paths to see where they lead.

You find yourself squeezing through the narrow gate, and you feel like your feet will barely fit on the little path just inside of it. You set out on your journey and wonder if you will be able to stay balanced on that confining pathway. But when you push the wide gate open, you notice that you can move about in any direction you choose on that pathway. You dart down the road and marvel at all you can do on that spacious path.

Yet something strange happens to both paths. After traveling on the narrow path for a while, it suddenly widens. You sense the freedom to live, move, and have your being in fresh air that brings life to every step you take. While living it up on the wide path, you suddenly lose your footing. Oddly enough the wide path narrows, causing you to stumble and fall to the ground. The air is heavy, you can't catch your breath, and you feel as if your life is being snuffed out.

What happened? The wide gate looked so inviting; there was room for several choices on that path. Yet the narrow gate was totally unattractive; there wasn't even enough room for one thought of your own.

Here's what happened. The wide gate opened out onto the road of independence from God. At first it felt quite freeing. You could pick and choose according to your good pleasure. But after leaving the picking and choosing to your own will, your sin nature kicked in. Suddenly freedom fled, there were consequences to face, and your life's path was very confining.

On the other hand, the narrow gate opened out onto the road of complete dependence upon God. At first it seemed quite controlling. You had to pick and choose according to God's good pleasure. But leaving the picking and choosing to God's will turned out to be a positive experience. Suddenly you were peaceful beyond your own understanding. You were walking with God's approval, and your life's path broadened within the will of God.

There are only two paths, and everyone must choose one.

Sometimes we start out on one and then switch to the other. Through various seasons of life, we find ourselves switching back and forth. But every time we change the path, we lose ground. You can't make strides on the path of dependence upon God if you are tip toeing on the path of independence from God as well.

We can always claim to love God no matter what path we take. But if we want to learn to live in the presence of God moment by moment, then we must make up our minds to choose the right path. The moment to moment component is the key here. It is why we are spending time together. You want life in His presence, and you want to experience it every moment.

Does trusting God and thriving on His path seem difficult? All you need to do is make the choice and then leave it up to the Holy Spirit to help you. God is aware of the temptations we face daily. He knows how difficult it is to walk **any** path without His leading. That is why He sent the Holy Spirit after Jesus lived on the earth. You must choose the wise path and then cooperate with The Holy Spirit's leading from there. You always have a choice. God doesn't take your free will away. Thankfully, when you are in close relationship with God, it isn't that hard to make wise choices.

"He who trusts in his own heart is a fool, But whoever walks wisely will be delivered" (Proverbs 28:26). Walk wisely with God. Be aware of His presence each moment, and you won't struggle as much with the foolishness of your own heart. *"...he who trusts in the Lord, mercy shall surround him"* (Psalm 32:10).

How do you want to live? Do you want strife and judgment to encompass your life, or do you want to be surrounded by God's mercy? When I meditate upon who God really is, I always realize how much I want to be engulfed in His great mercy rather than the alternative.

Time to Reflect

- Is your nature more submissive or dominant? Do you have trouble trusting others?
- How dependent are you upon God? Do you give Him control moment by moment?
- When are you more likely to trust God, and when are you more hesitant?
- At which gate and path do you spend more time? Why are you there most often?

_____
_____
_____
_____
_____

Living Application: Think and pray about your tendency to trust others. Determine how that tendency might affect your ability to trust God. Sometimes we are unaware of what is going on inside our minds and hearts, so ask the Holy Spirit to reveal areas in your life where trusting God is a struggle. Now pray about your areas and ask the Holy Spirit to help you deal with them one at a time. Be patient; it takes time to develop trust. Keep in mind that everyone struggles with the trust factor, so don't be overly critical of yourself.

Roadside Perks

The Bible is filled with promises about the benefits of trusting God.

Here are a few that really encourage me and speak to my heart:

> *"As for God, His way is perfect; the word of the Lord is proven;*
> *He is a shield to all who trust in Him."*
> 2 Samuel 22:31

> *"Oh, taste and see that the Lord is good;*
> *blessed is the man who trusts in Him!"*
> Psalm 34:8

"Commit your way to the Lord, trust also in Him, and He shall bring it to pass. He shall bring forth your righteousness as the light and your justice as the noonday."
Psalm 37: 5, 6

"He who heeds the word wisely will find good, and whoever trusts in the Lord, happy is he."
Proverbs 16:20

"But he who puts his trust in Me shall possess the land, and shall inherit My holy mountain." Isaiah 57:13

These scriptures go against the grain of our culture, don't they? When the world tells you to make your own way, build your own empire, and trust no one but yourself… you have the rebuttal. You have timeless wisdom from the Bible that is tried and true, and that promises great and lasting benefits when you put your trust in God instead of yourself.

Who doesn't want the King's protection as a shield about them, or His blessings? Who wouldn't welcome the backing of the King and enjoy watching His plans come to fruition? Who isn't seeking good and happiness on a daily basis? And who would turn down the favor of the King and His inheritance?

Oddly enough, many still turn away from these incredible promises and more because it means having God lead the symphony when they would rather have their own arms in the air directing the music. It is a matter of pride, and we will discuss that later on.

My favorite perk is that He promises peace to anyone who trusts in Him. In Isaiah 26:3 it says, *"You will keep him in perfect peace, whose mind is stayed on You, because he trusts in You."* I pray this scripture for myself and for my family almost every day. Having peace is like having life to me! It doesn't matter what is going on around me, if I am at peace… I am just fine.

The physical, spiritual, and emotional side effects of peace are immeasurable.

When I am trusting God, my mind stays focused on Him, and I am living in His presence at that moment. That is why trust is one of the ingredients that we must have in our lives if we are going to live with God moment by moment.

We all have our favorite "comfort foods." These are special foods we enjoy that invite comforting memories; they are delicious, pleasing to the palate and to the emotions. They make us happy. Oftentimes when we go through difficult situations, others might bring our favorites to eat, in hopes that we will be comforted. That's how it is with God's peace.

When I am at peace, I feel the comfort of the Holy Spirit all through me as if I were eating one of my favorite dishes. There is no substitute for the peace of Christ. But as the scripture in Isaiah says, peace is a delightful by-product of trust in God.

We must get to that place of entrusting everything and everyone to God, knowing He is in control.

In the world we live in, stress is a well-known, underlying cause for death. Recently, my husband did a short study on stress and worry, and I would like to share a snippet of it with you.

Mike said that stress is epidemic in the western world. Over two-thirds of office visits to physicians are for stress related illness. Stress is a major contributing factor either directly or indirectly to the six leading causes of death in the United States. Stress aggravates many other physical conditions as well as mental illness. There can also be family discord and violence because of stress.

The stress epidemic is extremely costly to the health industry, the business world, and to families. Mike also taught that stress is both additive and cumulative. It adds up over time until a crisis is reached and symptoms appear. I am sure you could also add what you know to the atrocities of stress.

Mike agrees that stress will always exist in the world we live in. Yet he did attest to one very viable remedy to curb the stress epidemic for those who follow Jesus Christ. Learn to trust God daily, moment by moment in every circumstance of life. Stress and worry go raging out the back door when we are at peace with God and our circumstances. Just think how differently you might react to a stressful situation when you hear the Holy Spirit speak peaceful words into your heart and you trust God for the outcome. You know your problem is in more capable hands than yours, and you have restful sleep, free from fret.

It sounds very simple, but that kind of peace won't come on a regular basis without time on the practice field working on your relationship with God. You won't trust the still, small voice inside time and again if you can't recognize it. So, I encourage you to incorporate the first two ingredients into your life. Your heart of gratitude toward God and your ability to communicate with Him will help you trust Him in every circumstance.

Learn to focus upon God, and need Him in the good times. I assure you that He is waiting for you even when you think you are sailing along just fine and don't need God's moment to moment touch. If you follow Jesus even when times are good, you will have an easier time recognizing Him in times of need and pain. And then the peace that surpasses all understanding will guard your heart and mind.

I must warn you that there is an endless list of counterfeits out there that provide only a momentary fix when worry and stress knock on your front door. There is nothing wrong with some of them, but they won't cause you to trust God for His lasting peace. They mostly treat your symptoms and wear off within a short period of time.

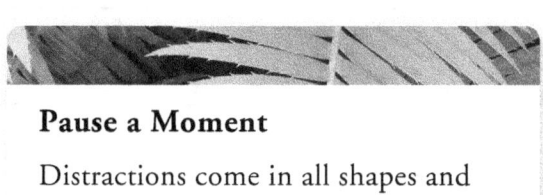

Pause a Moment

Distractions come in all shapes and sizes. Don't let them hinder your pursuit of God.

Any distraction or diversion will treat symptoms of stress. Vacations, money, or material goods will certainly help temporarily. Of course we are all aware that substance abuse and addictions are not only counterfeits to peace, but they are incredibly dangerous in every way. The only way to obtain the peaceful blessings that the Bible describes is by learning to trust God through your relationship with Him.

"Come to Me, all you who labor and are heavy laden, and I will give you rest. Take My yoke upon you and learn from Me, for I am gentle and lowly in heart, and you will find rest for your souls. For My yoke is easy and My burden is light" (Matthew 11:28-30).

Perhaps you are familiar with these famous words of Jesus. This passage of Scripture has been quoted frequently in church and Bible studies. While I am not going into a full teaching on it, I do want to reference these comforting words to point out another benefit of trusting God. We all suffer with the load of responsibility just as the Jews did when Jesus offered these words to help them. Sometimes our burdens become heavier than we can bear. They stress us out, make us weary, and wear us down. Our productivity in life and for the Kingdom of God is severely affected by our wearisome burdens. Yet we don't always unload them onto the shoulders of our Savior; we choose to carry them instead.

Why do we carry our own burdens? Maybe we take ownership of them because they belong to us, and we don't think to get help. There can also be an issue of trust. When we navigate our lives with an independent spirit instead of one of total dependency upon God, we tend to carry our burdens and allow them to drag us down on the path of righteousness. But when we have complete trust in God for **everything**, there is a natural tendency to off-load the heaviness of life onto the sturdy shoulders of Jesus Christ. Only then can we experience true rest from the heavy weights we struggle to bear.

Jesus offers relief from your burdens, but you have to trust Him for that. Don't be afraid that Jesus won't be there for you when you unload. Remember to practice working on your relationship with Him so that in times of need you will be able to release your cares in good faith.

Time to Reflect

- What other benefits can you add to our list of roadside perks for trusting God?
- What possible changes do you see as a result of total dependency upon your Father?
- What stress do you have now that might leave if you were more dependent upon God?
- Do you have counterfeits today that mask God's peace for tomorrow? What are they?

_____
_____
_____
_____
_____

Living Application: Look up more scripture references from the Bible about trusting God, and begin to memorize and meditate upon them. Pray and ask the Holy Spirit to bring those verses to life in your mind and heart and help you to become more trusting of God. Spend time reading about Jesus, your role model, and His dependency upon the Father for everything. Start to picture your life totally dependent upon the Father, and watch things change. Spend time on the practice field living with an attitude of praise and thanksgiving toward God, and work on your two-way prayer life through the Holy Spirit. Identify the stresses and burdens in your life, and practice trusting God for them…one at a time. Pray for the peace that surpasses all your understanding.

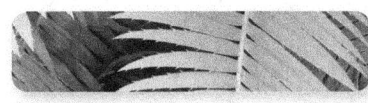

Prayer Poem Ministry
"TAKE CONTROL"

The Lord is all about trust, dear child of God. A life that trusts in God is solely dependent upon Him. A life that trusts in God is a peaceful life. A life that trusts in God knows that He is trustworthy…knows of His trustworthiness because that life has experienced it. To trust in God is to give in, let go, and let loose of the desires of the flesh and the mind. Those who trust in God lack nothing, for they thrive on His very existence. They expect to see His provision in every area of life. Oh that the world would let go and let God take control. Dear child of God, you must trust in Him, in His never failing love and character. You will indeed see yourself live the life that you were created for.

The Father calls you His dear child. He looks upon you with great love and pride because He created you to be in His family. God is drawing you close, near to Himself so that you will know His amazing love and plan for your life. When you learn to trust in God, you will realize just how dependent upon Him you really are. Bask in Him and in His ability to navigate your life. Be excited to let go of what you want in exchange for your Father's best for you. Remember your Father's clout, and cling to Him so that you will lack no good thing. Thrive upon your Father's existence and expect Him to provide for you in every area of your life. May you come to know Him as a loving father and then relinquish control. But remember that you are in His family already; may you trust in His never failing love and character. And may the Lord open your eyes to see yourself and the life that you were created to live.

Drawing Close

How is it going on your practice field? Are you learning to draw close to your Father through your relationship with the Holy Spirit?

You might have a tendency to step off the field and take a breather from time to time, but that isn't ever a healthy thing to do when you are pursuing God. You have to remain committed at all costs just as you would do when you chase something worthwhile in life.

When you take a break from your pursuit of God, you always lose ground. It might not seem that way because we take vacations or breaks in most everything we do in life. But don't compare your relationship with God to anything else in life. There is absolutely no comparison to make…period. The Holy Spirit never stops drawing you close, and God doesn't take breaks away from you. In fact, after the resurrection one of the last things that Jesus said before he ascended into Heaven was, *"…and lo, I am with you always, even to the end of the age"* (John 28:20).

The Holy Spirit lives within you, always at work. Tune in and cooperate with Him!

The more you cooperate and allow God to draw you in, the more you will trust Him for everything. God won't take control of your will; He is simply waiting for you to give it to Him. You might be wondering how to draw close to God on your own. Always remember to let those first two ingredients lead the way for you. I know that when your heart is rightly living in an attitude of gratitude before the Lord and when you pray and hear the voice of the Holy Spirit, you will automatically draw in. It is difficult to turn your back on the loving words that you'll receive from God on a regular basis. Your heart will naturally turn to God and His will for you. Soon you won't know how **not** to trust God for everything.

Establish God's fatherhood in your life, and it will be easier to draw close to Him.

When you see God as your dad and provider, the one in control of everything, and the one worthy of control, you will be more apt to relinquish your will and draw near. Think of the benefits again and again so that you can see how much better off you will be when you draw close and trust God.

> I want to introduce you to a couple who are very good friends to our family. Their names are Doug and Becky. They have really learned to draw close to God and trust Him as their Father through their relationship with the Holy Spirit. We have noticed that whenever there is a decision to be made, they almost always tell us that they will pray about it and ask the Lord what He thinks. They are very serious and deliberate about that! They don't just say they will pray about it…they really do it. We have even watched as they depend upon God for direction for the smallest of decisions. Because they have learned to draw close to God and have practiced listening for His voice, they are able to trust Him as His children should. Yet their child-like attitude before their Father has caused them to mature spiritually. The more they pursue God and depend upon Him, the stronger they become in the spirit. Doug always says that it is God's job to take care of this or that because he knows God to be his dad, his provider, and protector. He finds it easier to hear God's voice when he is in a place of trust and dependence. Then he can rest assured knowing it is God's job and not his. When Doug and Becky went through difficult times, they had great faith to endure and trust God.

They had already learned to draw close to God and had seen His faithfulness time and again, so when the tough times came, they were more prepared to trust Him. They would say that it was also during those more difficult times that they learned to draw close and trust God more. Various issues still come their way, but Doug and Becky try to remain close to their Father and continue to learn to trust Him as little children. Once you draw near and establish God's fatherhood in **your** life, it is easier to practice trusting Him. Begin trusting God for small things while you work on your relationship with Him. When you exercise your faith in those smaller things, it will grow strong enough to trust God for issues of greater magnitude. You will see the faithfulness of God when you take a step of faith and trust Him as your dad, provider, and protector. When you go through difficult times, you will have already drawn close and will have the faith to endure and trust God just as Doug and Becky did.

Are you burdened by your circumstances? Does worry over your spouse, children, or other family members zap the life out of you? Have you allowed stress to consume you enough that you have had to go back later on and pick up the pieces of your life? You will catch yourself nodding yes if you aren't connected to the true Source in total dependence.

Distractions and circumstances cause you to forget about the moment to moment connection with your Savior. It feels like you've been locked out of the kingdom without a house key. What can you do?

Your key is within easy reach. It is in your heart, where trusting God goes hand in hand with drawing close and exercising your faith. As we discussed before, you can't trust someone you don't know. I encourage you to get to know God more. Know Him as your Father, your Creator, your King, and your everything. He **is yours**! Keep God sovereign in your heart. Spend a great deal of time with the Holy Spirit, and build your relationship with God the Father so that you will learn to live in His presence moment by moment.

Remember that your relationship with God is an on-going process, a real journey. Be persistent and press into your journey every day, and get excited about your progress. But don't become prideful or allow your heart to boast of your relationship with God because you will be in danger of a serious setback. Always be mindful that you are His child and that God is the Father. When you understand your position before the Lord, you will travel well with Him.

Identify with Your Foundation

What kind of foundation is your life built upon? Do you build on the wavering theories of the world you live in, or on the timeless principles in the Bible? Is your identity in what you do for a living and all you acquire, or is it in the will of God as a servant in His kingdom?

Of course we all want to be spiritually correct in answering those questions, but we have to be honest if we are going to move forward on this journey. In *Living in His Presence* I copied a quote from an email that our son, Ryan, sent to us when he was a freshman in college. Again, here is what Ryan wrote about the apostle Paul. "Paul's character was founded so deeply in the will of God that not even the fear of torture and death could persuade him to act out of selfish ambition."

If anyone could have boasted about his character or identity, Paul could. He was considered to be quite the Jew because of his background and accomplishments. Yet when he encountered God and established a right relationship with Him, Paul's character changed. Suddenly his identity was in the will of God as a servant in His kingdom. Paul learned to identify with his firm foundation, Jesus Christ.

Jesus is your foundation and He is mine, and when you and I identify with Him we recognize our need for the Father. The more we imitate His example for our lives, the more we realize that we can do nothing without God. Jesus never intended for us to live aside from His examples and revelations. He meant for us to walk in His footsteps and climb mountains with His strength and character. His power within us allows us to take the steps and climb the highest peaks. If His power and identity are not firmly established in each of us, we will only backslide spiritually.

We can make progress on the journey when we learn to live in Him and in the will of the Father. That is why we need the Holy Spirit desperately. It is only by the power of the Spirit that we can operate as Jesus did, totally dependent upon the Father for everything.

You might be thinking that you already identify with Christ and depend upon God. But I challenge you to examine your life. It is my hunch that when you are totally honest with yourself and with the Lord that you might realize how much independence you still exercise in your life on a daily basis. When I reflect upon my own ways, I always find hidden spots of independence that I have to give over to the Lord.

Always be mindful that living with God moment to moment requires more than an occasional exercise of trust.

It takes true humility and a heartfelt commitment to learn to live with God and have genuine intimacy with Him. You have to set your mind and heart upon the will of the Father. But how **do** you set your mind and heart upon God's will in today's demanding world, and how can you identity with Christ? We could dedicate an entire conversation to cover this, but for now lets just look at a few practical steps that could help.

Begin prayerfully, and ask the Holy Spirit to help slow you down so that you can become more mindful of His will. We operate at such a fast pace that oftentimes we don't even think to ask God what He has to say about life. This doesn't mean that you have to change what you are doing in your life unless God reveals that to you. It means that you need to be more aware of your thoughts and actions moment by moment.

Slow down enough so that you can actually hear what you are saying and watch what you are doing at all times. Envision yourself as a helpless child, totally dependent upon your Heavenly Father for all of your needs. Then expect to see your Father actively providing for you. Embrace His thoughts and ways as you faithfully meditate upon the scriptures in your Bible.

Study the gospels with increasing intensity so that you can start to identify with Jesus. As you identify with Christ, your identity will be in Him as well.

When you practice those steps on your training ground, you will make better progress. I must tell you that it isn't always easy to slow down and be cognizant of our thoughts at all times. I am a perfect example of one who struggles with that. Sometimes I feel like my thoughts travel faster than the speed of light. I can be quick to make a choice and then forget what I was just thinking about because I am already onto another thought or decision. I frustrate myself when I allow that to happen. The more I practice what I just mentioned, the more I identify with Christ and depend upon the will of God for my life.

Think of what it's like to identify with someone other than Jesus. Most look for similarities and compare themselves to others. Many try to find ways to identify with those who are well known or have financial wealth. We do our best to get as close as possible to those of influence because it makes us feel good to be associated with them.

While none of that is sinful, it is spiritually beneficial to use our time and energy to identify with Christ and become more intimately associated with **Him**. Anyone who spends time with Jesus will naturally learn to identify with Him and His dependence upon the Father. Jesus becomes the one you relate to, the one you identify with, and the one you associate with each moment. That's when you will feel the best about yourself! It happens moment to moment when you are pursuing the Father, consciously aware of your need to identify with His Son.

Time to Reflect

▸ What foundation have you built your moment to moment life upon? Describe it.

▸ In what areas is your character deeply founded in the will of God?

▸ As you identify more with Christ, what changes do you expect to see in your life?

▸ When is it easier for you to slow down and be mindful of God's will?

_____
_____
_____
_____
_____

Living Application: Once you know what your moment to moment foundation really looks like, decide what changes need to be made for it to look more like Jesus Christ. Spend more time meditating on the life of Jesus so that your need for God will be firmly established moment to moment. Then pray and ask the Holy Spirit to change your heart, rebuild your foundation, and help your character to be founded more upon the will of the Father. Practice slowing down, giving one thought or decision to God at a time. Don't be afraid to be child-like before your Heavenly Father!

More or Less

Have you ever used the phrase "more or less" in your conversations? I know I've used it, and I hear others use the phrase as well. It doesn't really express anything definite; it refers to some of this and a little bit of that, which is a bit like lukewarm instead of hot or cold.

If we are not deliberate about following Jesus Christ, we risk becoming "more or less" Christians. Our relationship with God can become watered down, casual, or even occasional. Here are the words of Jesus found in the book of Revelation:

"These things says the Amen, the Faithful and True Witness, the Beginning of the creation of God: I know your works, that you are neither cold nor hot. I could wish you were cold or hot. So then because you are lukewarm, and neither cold nor hot, I will vomit you out of My mouth" (Revelation 3:14-16).

The reference note in my Bible says that the Lord rejects the half-hearted efforts of self-satisfied Christians; they are lukewarm. That is a pretty somber statement, for sure not one that I enjoyed reading! Yet when we can't trust God and depend upon His will for everything, we really can become self-satisfied Christians.

If what we do in God's kingdom is out of selfish ambition, or even out of God's will, then our efforts are half-hearted because they don't reflect the full heart of God. The note in my Bible also talks about how hot and cold water had purpose. There was no specific use for lukewarm water then. It is the same for those who are serious followers of Jesus.

Those who have their identity in Christ and seek the will of God in every way, have real purpose in God's kingdom.

Some are hot and some are cold according to their specific purpose in the will of God. Those who operate independent of God's plan can easily slip into the lukewarm category.

Pause a Moment

Your identity is in Jesus Christ. Seek the will of God and have lasting purpose in His kingdom.

You and I need to be "more **and** less" Christians…more of God and less of ourselves. Unfortunately, in our culture there is too much of a focus on having more. We want more for ourselves… more wealth, more material possessions, more free time, more opportunities, more travels, more advancement, more attention, and much more. Not only do we want more, but we want it now.

If we are not careful, any one of us can fall into the "more pit" easily because human nature is selfish. Human nature demands more for self and merely sends the leftovers to God. It offers the Kingdom of God a mere morsel of its wealth, possessions, free time, opportunities, advancement, or attention.

> **When we are led by the Holy Spirit,
> we become generous givers of self
> and hand our personal agendas off to the Father.**

God stays in control, and human nature won't dictate. When you have eyes to see what the Father is doing, you will avoid the snares of selfishness that trap and send you down into the "more pit" of life. Being led by the Spirit doesn't mean that you fade into nothingness, or that you don't matter anymore. The opposite happens when you submit to the will of God. If your attitude reflects more of God and less of yourself, God will take very good care of you and your needs.

"Humble yourselves in the sight of the Lord, and He will lift you up" (James 4:10). Just as He raised Jesus, God will raise you above your circumstances when you humble yourself before Him.

What does it mean to be humble? Many equate humility with a down cast spirit. I used to think that humble Christians walked around with their heads scraping the pavement. They were the ones with low self esteem and became the world's doormats. That is not the case at all!

Healthy Christians have their identity in Christ and walk with their heads up toward the Son. They approach the world with a healthy outlook, and their countenance is bright. Christians who enjoy good, spiritual health are focused on Christ Jesus, and they know that every good thing within them comes from Him. They gladly take their position under the greatness of God and respectfully submit to their awesome Lord.

That is why genuine humility is a grand thing. When you are humble, you are dependent upon God. Your spirit is up, cast where it is light and airy. You walk holding your head high because you are a child of the Most High God, leaning upon Him for everything. Your identity is in Christ, so your sense of self esteem couldn't be higher.

The Father knows you are His, and no one in the kingdom should ever take advantage of you. So be humble and desire more of God's will and less of your own. Eat humble pie before the Lord, and enjoy every bite of it. In that sweet state of complete dependency upon God, you'll find true and lasting freedom in His kingdom.

Three Hidden Benefits

First Benefit...Less Sin

The Bible says *"Whoever abides in Him does not sin"* (1John 3:6). It's my desire to never sin, but the sin nature that I was born with has only been curbed, not removed. It will never be totally gone until I come face to face with Jesus in Heaven. Yet as I learn to live in Christ and choose to be led by the Holy Spirit, I will become more resistant to sin.

You will resist sin too because you are seeking the Kingdom of God just as I am. We are on the same journey. Together we will notice how much more of God there is in our lives and how much less of our sinful ways we still have when we are more dependent upon God. The Bible also says *"Therefore submit to God. Resist the devil and he will flee from you"* (James 4:7).

When you are living in a posture of praise before God and you are listening for His voice, trusting and depending upon Him... you are more likely to resist the temptation to sin. The more you practice this on your training ground, the less you will fall into sinful traps. Remember that as you spend more time with God, you will naturally become more like His Son. There isn't anything you can do to overcome sin; it is simply the work of the Holy Spirit in you as you live with God moment to moment. That takes you out of the equation and puts God into it. Once again it is more of God and less of you.

Beware of the tendency to strive to overcome sinful ways. You could find yourself wrapped up in your own methodology where it is impossible to abide in Christ. You didn't earn your citizenship in Heaven, and you won't work your way through sin.

You must simply abide and live in His presence. Listen for God's voice through His Spirit, and go with what He says. Don't be too quick to act upon temptation. Slow down enough to check in with God; that alone will change how you handle temptation. Get into the habit of reflecting upon your day. When you reflect and recall the times when you fell short, don't be too hard on yourself. Those are the perfect times to pray, repent, and then go for a fresh start.

Always be mindful of your journey. You will make steady progress, and that always pleases the Lord.

Second Benefit...More Direction

Have you ever wandered aimlessly, hoping you will find your way? Those that know me well, understand that I am direction challenged. I don't have a natural sense of direction, and I'm not good at reading complicated maps. Without written directions I tend to wander aimlessly. I even have a difficult time reversing directions when it is time to leave. You might be laughing at this, or perhaps you can relate. There is probably nothing I can do to change my natural inability to navigate my way. I have to rely on directions for safe, timely arrivals.

That is how it is with the Lord too. The more I pursue God and get to know Him, the more I realize my inability to steer my way through life. Then I remember that I was never created to run on my own course because when I navigate it myself, it becomes more of me and less of God. Thankfully, God loves us very much and desires to give us as much time as we need in order to help us navigate through life according to His plans and purpose.

He knows we will arrive safely and on time when we depend upon Him for direction.

I can't tell you how many times I have prayed and asked God for direction in specific areas of my life. Without His lead, I know that I will wander aimlessly, needlessly, and unsuccessfully… and still not arrive safely or on time. In *Living in His Presence* I likened my journey of trusting and depending upon God to a long road trip in the car. Now I will embellish that word picture a bit and invite you to come along for a ride with my father and me.

> **Picture this!**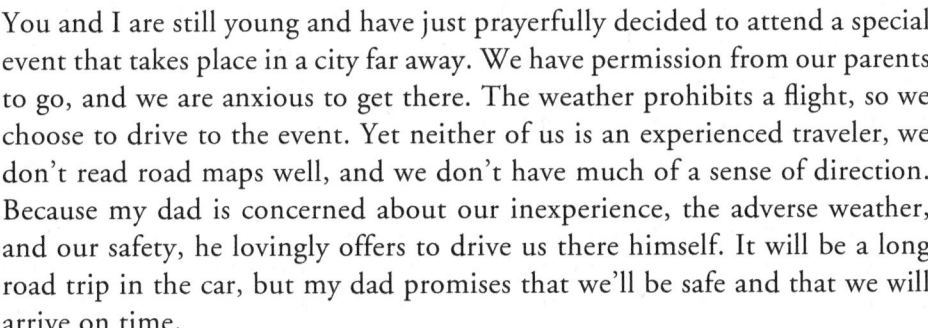
>
> You and I are still young and have just prayerfully decided to attend a special event that takes place in a city far away. We have permission from our parents to go, and we are anxious to get there. The weather prohibits a flight, so we choose to drive to the event. Yet neither of us is an experienced traveler, we don't read road maps well, and we don't have much of a sense of direction. Because my dad is concerned about our inexperience, the adverse weather, and our safety, he lovingly offers to drive us there himself. It will be a long road trip in the car, but my dad promises that we'll be safe and that we will arrive on time.
>
> It's time to leave, and my dad suggests that we both sit in the back seat; he wants to chauffeur us. Then he can have the map spread out in the front, and we will be more comfortable. My dad tells us that he has the entire trip planned out, confident of where and when we will stop to refuel, eat, and rest. In the car, my dad talks about how much experience he has on road trips; he does this often. He'll make all the right turns to maneuver around heavy traffic jams. He knows how to avoid dangerous accidents, road blocks, and unnecessary side streets that lead to frustrating dead-ends. That kind of experience is hard to come by; we feel privileged to have my father lead the way.
>
> The weather is indeed adverse, and it seems like we're going to slide off the slippery road, but we don't. My father's hands are steady upon the wheel, his eyes are peeled on the road, and he is in control. When the car does slide, my dad is steadfast. He never wavers a bit, and keeps us on the road with little effort. Even though my dad is in perfect control, we still panic. But he is so patient and kind; he puts us both at ease and suggests we focus on our destination and the fun we will have there.

Before long the weather subsides, and my dad decides to alter the course to take a scenic drive for a while. He says we have plenty of time, so why take short cuts? It'll be nice to enjoy the journey and take in special sights when we can. But impatience knocks on our door, and suddenly we want the trip to be over. We whine and complain about some of the pot holes along the way and about how long it is taking. Again my father's patience is so evident. He lovingly reminds his little "back seat drivers" not to rush the final destination **too** much for we will surely miss the best parts of the journey. He calms our anxieties and helps us sit back, relax, and experience the rest of the trip.

I am reminded of how very faithful and trustworthy my father is; he always comes through for me. Why should I worry when he is always in control? We arrive at our final destination in perfect timing. We are glad to be there, but we are also thankful for safe travels and the experience of the road trip. What if we had flown or insisted on short cuts along the way? What if we hadn't trusted my dad for a safe, timely trip? Perhaps neither of us would have any fingernails left! It would have grieved my father and hindered my relationship with him if we hadn't placed our confidence in him. Finally, you and I agree that without my dad's leadership we might not have even arrived at our final destination. We take the time to thank my dad for all he did for us, and we trust him to be our chauffeur every time.

By now you are seeing the correlation between my father in the car and my Heavenly Father. Life is a series of journeys, much like the road trip we just experienced together. We all like to think that we "know the way." We set out to tackle the world, but we forget about who created the world and who is the best navigator.

No one likes to be without direction and purpose. Yet many wander aimlessly day after day, clueless as to what to do with their lives. Many don't know how to begin once they determine a purpose. Still, the natural tendency isn't to check in with God for advice and direction. Most tend to rely upon themselves, which really means they operate through trial and error. You don't have to be anything like that!

You have a relationship with the Most High God! Your beginning, middle, and end lay in the hands of the Almighty. So why not trust Him to direct your path and save you from the heartache of trial and error time and again?

Practice resting in God's ability to navigate your life.

Third Benefit...Less Stress

We talked briefly about stress and how it can be an obstacle for peace. In *Living in His Presence* we talked about good and bad stress. Both are sneaky attention getters, and they come between you and God. When you are stressed, life is more about you and less about God. Whatever consumes you, will be your focus. Even though we tend to pray about the stress, we still focus on it. Stress stands up, demands attention, and wreaks havoc in the lives of almost everyone. It sure has ruled supreme in my life from time to time.

There was a time when I was dealt a wild hand in life. It was the most stressful period of time that I have ever experienced; the intensity of it didn't let up for a few years. Maybe someday I'll share the details of that time with you. But for now, I want you to know that even though my intention was to stay close to God during those rough years, stress consumed every aspect of my life, and I took many matters into my own hands. My relationship with God was fairly new, and I had just begun my journey to pursue Him intimately. Because I didn't know what I know now, I allowed the magnitude of that stressful time to control me instead of depending on God.

I didn't stop to ask God how to deal with the trauma; I just took off on my own. My intentions were good, but I flew solo many times and couldn't see through the clouds. I spent all of my emotional reserves tending to the trauma, and it was quite costly in every way. I ran the marathons of motherhood, but almost drowned in my efforts to keep my marriage afloat. In an attempt to remedy the situation, sometimes I caused more pain. I did my best to tackle the demands of normal life, but I could never really get my arms around everything. Instead I grew weary and became frail in every way. My life was filtered through a trauma lens, and I worked harder and harder, to no avail. The magnitude of the stress was more than I could bear, but I took it on for however long it would last. Fortunately it only lasted for a few years. But unfortunately, when it ended many repairs were needed to rebuild my happy life that was severely damaged.

What are you supposed to do when dealt a difficult hand in life?

You can go through the motions like I did when my turn came. You can pretend to be super human and put on a poker face so that no one sees your pain; I did that too. You can push in all your chips and bet on a good outcome. I recall that quite well. You can plan based on what you see on the table, hoping to beat the odds. I became very good at that! You can also fold your hand and walk away from the table, but I couldn't do that. All of these options require more of self and less of God, and none of them will alleviate stress.

Looking back, I know there was nothing I could have done to eliminate that particular season; that's just part of life. But I would have handled it differently. I still would have spent countless hours in prayer, but I would have also spent more time listening for God's direction. I would not have piled everything upon my own shoulders. Instead, I would have relied on God, placing those day to day cares into the hands of my Savior. Then I would have been more resilient to the burdensome stress, and I would have experienced more of God's peace. Even though it seemed dark and I felt no joy, I would have made a sincere sacrifice of praise to God. Surely He would have lifted my spirits! Even though my little children demanded my attention, I would have given my faithful husband more of my time as well.

The nature of our circumstances kept me outward focused, and for that I am grateful. I didn't have time to feel sorry for myself; I was compelled to maintain as much normalcy as possible. I do think that kept me from slipping into a darkened state of depression.

Most of all, I would have placed all of my trust in the Lord, more dependent upon Him instead of my good intentions. Then perhaps I would have eliminated much of the stress, my relationship with God would have come first, and my precious little family wouldn't have suffered as much.

Time to Reflect

▸ In what areas of your life do you most need more of God and less of yourself?

▸ In what ways can you see sinful ways diminish as you learn to submit more to God?

▸ Who sits in the driver's seat in your life? How will you allow God to steer more often?

▸ Where have you felt the most stress? What did you learn from my personal example?

_____
_____
_____
_____
_____

Living Application: Examine your heart and think about the times when you have felt like a "more or less" Christian. Now continue to examine yourself and note where you tend to have more of God and less of yourself in your life. Stay aware of your tendencies. Then slow down your life video and watch yourself to see if you are behaving more like Jesus or more like your old self. Sometimes, once you are aware of your shortcomings it is easier to deal with them. Ask the Holy Spirit to help you move into a lifestyle that is leaning more toward God and less toward yourself. List other, hidden benefits that will come from total dependency upon God. Continue to contemplate the life of Jesus and His total dependency upon the Father. Post scriptures so that you can meditate upon the Word of God and become dependent upon your Heavenly Father for everything.

Prayer Poem Ministry
"STAY OF REST"

Go, little child, and enter into God's rest… for your soul has been worrisome and your faith is always being tested. You must cling to Jesus for your entrance into God's rest. He will bring great peace and rest to your soul. Your faith will be renewed in all that He is and in all that He will do. You desire provision for blessing and abundance, and you shall receive it all. Be mindful, dear child of God, to watch for the blessings…for they come wrapped in packages of many colors. But your name is upon each one. Be patient as you wait for the fullness of God's blessings, for they are surely on their way and you will have them. Such joy, such peace, and such contentment will be upon you and yours. The Lord loves you, dear child! Now begin your stay of rest in His arms and know that He will do great things in your life.

May you enter into God's rest and be refreshed. May you learn to trust God and depend upon His never-ending provision; then your worries and doubts will disappear. For God never intended you to carry your burdens alone; Jesus gladly bears each one with you, so that you will flourish in His will. Now flourish, and may your faith be renewed in Christ Jesus. He will provide the blessing, the abundance that you desire. Stay close to the Lord and watch for your colorful packages of blessings. May the Holy Spirit grant you patience as you wait for the fullness of what God has for you. Trust in Him for your joy, peace, and contentment. Bask in the Love of God, cherish His love, and find your stay of rest in the arms of Jesus. He will do great things for those who place their trust in Him and in His will.

> **Picture this!**
>
> You are staying in a lovely cottage built just for you. It is designed specifically for you with all your favorite amenities. The colors are inviting, and the warmth of the fire melts the frost of the outside world around you. You have no responsibilities in your haven of rest. Everything is provided for you because you are of royal descent. Your comfort and well being is of the utmost value to the King, and He is thrilled to provide this refuge from the harmful elements of the outside world.
>
> You are basking in the loveliness of the cottage when suddenly you have a visit from the King. His Majesty enters, and the room is filled with an irresistible aroma. You attempt to rise and meet your King, but you can't move. The King comes to you and wraps His loving arms around you and calls you His child, His very own. Time stands still while you are enveloped in the love of God; you can't think of anything else but Him. The King steps back, looks upon you with incomparable love and acceptance, and whispers your name. You understand that you belong to Him, and nothing else matters. You know that no one can separate you from the love of the King and you rest, you simply rest.
>
> Who wouldn't desire this cottage of refuge and rest? Yet it is available to each of us anytime we want to visit. Place your trust in God, and allow Him to take you places created just for you. You live in His presence; you belong to Him, so welcome any encounter with your Lord.

Watch Out!

"Trust in the Lord with all your heart and lean not on your own understanding; in all your ways acknowledge Him, and He shall direct your paths." (Proverbs 3:5, 6)

Why is it so hard to lean **not** on our own understanding? The Bible is crystal clear, yet everyone still struggles with this.

One reason we struggle is because the power of the will is so strong. It can be a benefit, but it can also be quite a hindrance. You've known the positive side affects that come when your will is strong and you accomplish goals. Perhaps you have even watched someone beat the odds and survive a serious surgery partly because they had a strong will to endure and live. You and I could list many beneficial effects of a strong, positive will.

Yet we have also seen how a strong will can grow to be a determent. If the will does not come into quiet submission when necessary, it can become destructive. A strong will that is left to fend for itself hurts others and strays from the principles of the Bible and God's best. Eventually, determination that goes unchecked cannot thrive in the presence of God. The Father must be in charge, but the stubborn will fights for the lead, and our relationship with Him dwindles.

It's also difficult not to lean on our own understanding because the more knowledge we acquire the less likely we are to accept what others have to say, even God. We learn a great deal about a subject, become an expert in that field, and think we know it all. I remember when I graduated from college and felt that way. My mind housed a great wealth of knowledge, but my inflated ego opened the window for arrogance to pay a little visit. Thankfully, it didn't take long to settle down because the day to day challenges of my career brought me back to earth. How easy it is to puff up, stand out in a crowd, and have others notice just how great we are!

Leaders must check their attitudes and motives continually. Leadership comes with great responsibility. A Christ-like leader is not only responsible for others, but also needs to be responsible for himself and the condition of his heart.

> **When a leader doesn't remain humble before the Lord
> or allows human nature to lead the way,
> he could stumble onto a dark, prideful alley.**

It doesn't take long before he is feeling good about himself, proud to be in a position of authority. The focus shifts more toward self-accomplishment and selfish ambition than on others. This makes it difficult to trust God and grow in relationship with Him.

It's tough not to lean upon what we already know because human nature says that we need to be top dog and compete for that.

We strive to be smarter, faster, stronger, better, more successful, and even more spiritual than the average person. We like to think more highly of ourselves than we should, and before long we become our own source. Suddenly we're not only knowledgeable in one field, but we become experts on life. We expect others to cater to us and agree with our ways because we need to be right. We like to associate with people of influence, affluence, and fame. Power becomes essential, and weakness is unthinkable. A strong tendency to control develops, and eventually we need no one… not even God.

Watch out, because what I have just exposed is pride at its worst. You might be thinking that this does not apply to you. You aren't the pride monster that I just described. But I caution you because every one of us struggles with pride, whether we recognize it or not.

An arrogant heart and stubborn will are a turn off to God! The Bible says that *"God resists the proud, but gives grace to the humble"* (James 4:7). You have to decide what you want most in life, your way or His way. Your way will not bring you closer to God. You will only gravitate to God when you are seeking **His** way.

Humility before God destroys the pride monster within you and makes you less vulnerable to your own human nature. When you become dependent upon the will of God, you won't have to work overtime to achieve your own independence. Remember to walk through the narrow gate that leads to the wide path, not the wide gate whose path closes in on you after you enter.

Perhaps this is hitting home with you. But it still seems too difficult to trust God completely. Are you wondering why? We've become complicated beings even though God didn't create us to be that way. Before the fall of Adam and Eve, mankind was sinless, and life was simple. Adam and Eve's disobedience complicated their lives in every way because sin entered the picture. It also altered the course of history and dictated how the rest of mankind would live.

Even though our sins are forgiven and we have the gift of eternal salvation through Jesus Christ, our sin nature remains, and that makes us complicated human beings.

Each day, we face decisions and make choices with our sinful nature hovering over us. The Bible says, *"For all have sinned and fall short of the glory of God"* (Romans 3:23). Without the moment to moment **leading** of the Holy Spirit, our sin nature will always get the best of us. We will filter life through our own eyes, look at it our way, and choose not to trust God for everything.

We must give God what rightfully belongs to Him…our willingness for Him to lead and direct our paths. We'll be able to filter everything through His wide angle lens instead of an old, narrow lens that's fogged with our sin nature. Then the strong will submits to God's perfect will. Selfish ambition won't play the leading role in life. Arrogance won't be able to bulldoze those we care about the most. Knowledge will be for the glory of God instead of our own credit. Self appointed power loses its appeal because God turns our weakness into something powerful for His purpose.

Jesus said, *"My grace is sufficient for you, for My strength is made perfect in weakness."* (2 Corinthians 12:9)

We are reminded of how much we need the power of God in our lives every moment, and we remain humble.

Time to Reflect

▸ When is it most difficult to submit your will to God? When is it easiest?

▸ In what areas do you have to tame your pride and curb arrogant tendencies?

▸ When do you catch yourself running the show instead of allowing God?

▸ Describe the lens that you use to filter your life. Are you content with the one you use?

_____
_____
_____
_____

Living Application: You've identified the areas in your life when you struggle to submit your will to God and deal with prideful tendencies. Now pray and ask Jesus to help you give them to Him one by one. Be sure to only give one at a time so you can welcome the Holy Spirit's input and listen for His voice. Then watch for your spiritual life to improve before your eyes! When you find yourself taking charge and not trusting God, be willing to stop mid-stream and pray. Remember that all the Holy Spirit needs is your willingness.

Faith or Fear?

When you decide to trust God for direction in your life, what is going to happen, and how will it occur? Will God impose radical changes that are gut wrenching and painful? Does He automatically send you to a far away land to fulfill your time of service unto Him? Are you going to have to give up your gift of free will and become God's puppet? **Or** is it all going to be well with your soul?

You might get a chuckle out of those questions, but I assure you that others have asked some, or all of them; I know I have! When I was first learning to trust God, those kinds of questions came up often. I always thought I trusted God because I loved Him. But soon I realized that my love for God was partially based on my own theology, not on Biblical principles, and I trusted Him on my own terms. I was afraid that everything would be ripped out from under my control. I also feared that God would force me to do certain things for my own good that I was uncomfortable with.

This is a good time to discuss the fear factor. Fear is the opposite of faith. It cripples, stifles, and snuffs the life right out of anyone who is trapped by it. It stops many from becoming all they were meant to be in Christ. Fear certainly limits how much we can live in the presence of God moment to moment. You and I could go on and on to list all the damaging possibilities of fear. For now, let's discuss how fear prohibits us from trusting God.

Many will tell you that they hesitate to depend on God and place their trust in Him because they are **afraid** of what they will lose, particularly their freedom of choice. They will tell you that God gave everyone free will and that having to trust God and depend upon Him takes free will away. Does that sound familiar? Your free will doesn't go away; you always have the choice to do it God's way or not.

You can expect to lose a few things when you choose dependency upon your Higher Source. You will lose selfish ambition, a controlling spirit, an arrogant attitude, and all your heavy baggage and burdens that you have been lugging around for so long.

You might be surprised at some of what you will gain. You will find yourself basking in the peace of Christ. You will have clarity of mind and heart, confidence, and the joy of the Lord. These are good trade offs, don't you agree? The world's system tries to belittle these genuine gains and replace them with enticing losers of great deception.

A selfish world system hurls an insatiable love for power, money, and success at all of us. And it does it so subtly that many embrace it without knowing. Yet God uses these things everyday for the good of His kingdom. But when they replace total dependency upon the Father, they corrode and corrupt every tender heart where the Holy Spirit dwells. So remember that depending upon God is not a losing proposition; you have all the best to gain. Trust Him and see if all is not gained from the hand of the Father Himself. *"But seek first the kingdom of God and His righteousness, and all these things shall be added to you"* (Matthew 6: 33). You will find peace when you trust God.

What about faith?
"Now faith is the substance of things hoped for, the evidence of things not seen."
(Hebrews 11; 1)

Faith is a sweet confidence in the hope that we have as followers of Jesus Christ. How do you get it? Do you drum it up by sheer will and determination? Does God choose certain ones to carry His precious commodity?

The Bible says *"So then faith comes by hearing, and hearing by the word of God"* (Romans 10: 17). We must listen to the message that comes concerning the Word of God and the Good News about Jesus Christ.

If we pursue God in praise with a thankful heart, through intimate prayer, and offer ourselves to Him in quiet submission, faith will surely find us. You can't make faith deposit automatically by sheer will or by convincing yourself that you believe enough. Then faith comes from you and not from God.

Pause a Moment

God will give you a great measure of faith according to your need and desire. Trust Him for that.

Always remember that everything good comes from God. God has no favorites, and faith is available to all who believe. Some beat themselves up because they can't muster up enough faith to move the mountain that is in the way. Sadly, Christian self-worth is sometimes based on levels of faith. In Romans 12: 3, the Bible tells us that *"God has dealt to each one a measure of faith."* So, we even need to trust God for faith.

We need a dependent mindset; then it isn't as hard to trust God for faith. Don't be afraid to ask Him for greater measures of faith. Do all you know to do in order to pursue Him the best you can, and leave the rest to Him. Really, it is all about relationship. If you want to muster something up; then it should be your desire to pursue God with all the gusto you have. That is all He is asking; He'll handle it from there.

Time to Reflect

- How does fear affect how much you trust God for your finances, job, and family issues?
- What else do you stand to "lose and gain" when you choose to trust the Lord?
- Do you have your own terms for dependency upon God? What are they?
- How does your relationship with God need to change in order to trust Him for faith?

_____
_____
_____
_____
_____

Living Application: Imagine that your personal world has just shattered all around you. Perhaps its a loss of job or immediate family member, or even a financial catastrophe. Then pray and ask the Holy Spirit to show you hidden areas in your life where you could still be afraid to trust Him. Journal what you feel like God is saying about that. Ask God to make any adjustments in your heart that are necessary in order for you to operate more out of faith instead of fear. Spend some time in your Bible reflecting on the life of Jesus and his dependency upon the Father, even at a most fearful time...His crucifixion and death.

Stumbling Blocks

Weakness

No one likes to admit weakness. Indirectly, it implies failure or a "no can do" mentality. What will others think if they know my areas of weakness? Will I lose my good name or reputation within my community and circle of friends? The fear of man's opinions and the repercussions prohibits us from admitting areas of weakness. We don't even want to mention our weaknesses, let alone discuss them with anyone.

Yet the Lord said to Paul, the apostle, *"My grace is sufficient for you, for My strength is made perfect in weakness"* (2Corinthians 12: 9). Paul writes about his desire to boast about his flaws so that the power of Jesus Christ would come and help him move from his own weakness to God's lasting strength. Paul said, *"For when I am weak, then I am strong"* (2Corinthians 12: 10).

Sometimes it's uncomfortable to discuss our imperfections and struggles with others. But we can learn from the words of Paul and his dependence upon God and then find strength in His words of power. Paul knew that if he would identify and admit his weak points, then he'd be one step closer to having them turned into great strength. When he let go and allowed the Holy Spirit to take control, he found tremendous strength in what God did in spite of his own tainted efforts, and his relationship with God grew to enormous heights.

We like to think of Paul as a spiritual hero who could do nothing wrong. But aside from the power and strength of the Holy Spirit, Paul was just like you and me, a helpless sinner in need of God's grace and strength.

You might be wondering how you can be strong when really, you feel very weak. It sounds like somewhat of a dichotomy, doesn't it? Yet it is simply the recognition of your need for God in every area of life.

- Do you struggle with telling the truth?
- Is it tempting to tell a "little white lie" instead of speaking what you know is right?
- Do you worry about offending others with what is true?

Don't feel badly if you have to admit to these struggles. You are in good company because many feel weak in these areas as well. But when you identify your weakness and plead for the intervention of the Holy Spirit, suddenly it is not your problem. It becomes God's issue, and He gives you the ability to overcome the temptation. You realize that you just moved from temptation and weakness to victory and strength in Christ.

Your weak obstacles will diminish when you place your trust in Jesus and the power that comes from the Holy Spirit.

Performance Expectations

If you spend much of your life striving to meet your own expectations and those others place upon you, performance tendencies will affect how your story reads. You are pursuing God with artificial light glaring in your face, and all you can do is filter it with the standards of our world system. Go ahead…work harder, get tougher, be a pillar, move that mountain, and do it all on your own! That is what the world conditions us with.

Our society admires a "self-made" man or woman. No wonder we are out there beating ourselves up, working harder everyday, and burning out. It is all about what we can achieve on our own.

If you adopt this philosophy for your life's journey, you embrace a counterfeit plan. You stumble into the land of self pride and selfish ambition. You plow through life all on your own and leave God out of your efforts.

When you spend your time seeking the will of your Heavenly Father and place your expectations upon His ability to guide you through the night, you journey with brilliant Son light glowing on your face. Your eyes are fixed on Jesus Christ. You don't need a filter to walk in His light because you are operating within the standards of the Kingdom of Heaven. Now go ahead… trust God and work smarter, be soft and pliable so that He can mold you, admit your weakness and watch Him make you strong, move your mountain with the strength of the Holy Spirit, and do it totally dependent upon God.

In God's kingdom you're encouraged to be a "God-made" man or woman.

You don't have to be doomed to stress out, burn out, or wear out on your journey. The expectations should be upon your Heavenly Father instead of on yourself so that the load is light. Jesus said, *"Come to Me, all you who labor and are heavy laden, and I will give you rest"* (Matthew 11: 28). Why wear yourself out meeting every expectation when you can unload it all on Jesus Christ? Rest in His ability to do immeasurably more through you than you can do on your own.

Defense Mechanisms

Because of the staggering numbers of broken relationships and personal offenses in our culture, God's precious ones continue to be hurt. Unless hurts mend properly, they fester and leave painful sores beneath the surface of unsightly scabs that are bumped time and again before scar tissue forms. Unfortunately, this unhealthy healing process is quite common all around us, and it even happens in God's kingdom on earth.

Have you ever looked closely at scar tissue? It isn't like the other tissues around it. It's usually well defined with tough looking outer borders that seem to be lacking in rich blood vessel supplies. I know that scar tissue inside the human body can prohibit good blood flow and block necessary bodily functions. In a similar way, scar tissue within the body of Christ prohibits the flow of the Holy Spirit and builds barriers that hinder the bodily functions that Jesus intends for it to have.

How can that happen to a well meaning Christian who loves God? Oddly enough, it happens without an intentional Christian even being aware of it. It can happen to you and to me if we are not careful. Everyday, we face hurts and disappointments that build on all avenues of life. We can't avoid them. We can deal with them with healthful means or in damaging ways; it is always our choice.

Those who go the healthful route choose not to judge or criticize when they experience hurt. They understand human nature and allow enough slack in relationships for room to overlook and forgive. Forgiveness is always the best practice, but it is very much a mindset and a choice. We will discuss this more later on.

Those who allow hurts to fester live in chronic pain and invite the potential for infection and grave damage. Unhealthy mechanisms develop that keep others away from the sore spots, building serious walls of defense that are almost impossible to penetrate. The fear of being hurt again is so great that others are kept at a distance on the other side of the defensive wall, even God. Then isolation chokes out the hope of feeling better, and soon even the power of the Holy Spirit is blocked.

Somewhere in the hurting process and in building the walls of defense, those with chronic pain oftentimes embrace the worst of all lies…that God is to blame and cannot be trusted.

Can you understand why it is so important to focus on the truth about God and embrace what you read about Him in the Bible? You have to practice trusting God in the good times so that when difficulties come your way, you won't develop defense mechanisms that keep God and others away.

I assure you that there will always be those who will disappoint and hurt you. You must choose to overlook much and forgive more times than you thought you could. Allow the Holy Spirit to dress and heal your wounds as only He can do. Always remember that beyond a shadow of any doubt, God remains trustworthy and is never to blame for anything bad. You can always depend upon Him!

Time to Reflect

▸ Is it difficult for you to admit weakness? Try listing weak areas where God can help.

▸ Do you struggle with expectations? How can they hinder your relationship with God?

▸ Are there wounds from the past that keep you from trusting God? What are they?

▸ What other roadblocks do you encounter that alter your dependence upon God?

_____
_____
_____
_____
_____

Living Application: Prayerfully ask the Holy Spirit to reveal the roadblocks that cause you to stumble and fall on your journey of learning to trust and depend upon God. Allow yourself to be open and vulnerable before God so that you can trust Him more and trust others as well. Present your weaknesses to God in prayer, and begin to expect the power of the Holy Spirit to come and turn them into strengths. Ask God to help you take yourself and others off the hook so that you no longer have to swim in a pool of unnecessary expectations. Pray for the warmth and healing power of God to penetrate every defense mechanism that could keep Him and others away. Allow your desire for a life of complete trust and dependency to grow and burn in your heart. Practice listening for the voice of the Holy Spirit, and always live a life of praise to God.

The Look of Trust

What does a trusting relationship with God look like? How does trusting God change the way you live and think? You were not created to live a life of solitude. You might enjoy a quiet day here or there away from everyone and the routines of life, a break for rest and reflection. But no one enjoys it as a steady diet, and loneliness is not a warm or welcome feeling.

We were created with a need for others and for fellowship with God. John, the apostle, wrote "*…that you also may have fellowship with us; and truly our fellowship is with the Father and with His Son Jesus Christ*" (1John 1: 3).

As you learn to live in the presence of God in true and lasting fellowship with Him, you will naturally crave His perfect will for your life.

It isn't difficult to give up your way for His. Instead of fumbling with your will, you find yourself basking in God's way. Each day is a new surprise with God by your side.

You wake to greet God and can't wait to please Him. The Holy Spirit gives you His agenda for the day and soon you are on your way, flowing in His sweet leading. Your heart is full of praise and thanksgiving while you tenderly wait for God to speak into it. God speaks, and you obey. God leads, and you follow. You knock, and God opens the right door. You enter, and He shines light on the path. You take a step, and He enables you to walk. You stumble and cry out, and He lifts you over the rough terrain. You praise, and He smiles. God warms your heart, and you praise Him more. You pray, and God answers. You declare Him faithful and sleep in His peace. You become familiar with the look of trust and wake to do it all again.

Perhaps that sounds a bit like a spiritual utopia, unrealistic, or far fetched. But notice that I didn't present an airtight day in a glass bubble. There were uncertainties and obstacles; I just didn't name each one.

There were probably times of despair, temptation, or trial when God had to lift you over the rugged terrain. You could have been drowning in a wave of confusion when you knocked and God opened the right door. Perhaps you were under tremendous pressure and needed direction, and the Holy Spirit shed light on the trail. You didn't want to, but you still operated with a grateful heart and made a true sacrifice of praise to Jesus. You were rushed and in a hurry, but you took a few moments to pray for someone's need.

When you finally slowed down, you remembered that God was faithful through your busy day, and you could rest in His presence with good sleep. Much of this happened without your conscious effort; you simply lived in His presence and allowed God to be in control.

Whether you live alone or within a family unit, you don't have to fly solo. You might be alone, but not lonely. The decibels in your life might be very high, but there is a quiet place set apart for only you with God. The look of trust is a beautiful thing. Soon you will find that your days are based upon a loving, mutual relationship with your Heavenly Father, grounded in genuine trust.

The Great Artist

"Then God said, 'Let Us make man in Our image, according to Our likeness.'"
(Genesis 1: 26).

Picture This!

You are God's masterpiece. He has already created you in His image and likeness, and He's pleased with you. But let's imagine that God wants to try His hand at a bit more creativity. He desires to paint a picture of your trusting relationship with Him for His art gallery. What's it going to look like?

You get to choose the canvass. Choose one of substantial quality because it's going to have to endure thousands of brush strokes and layers of heavy paint. Your canvass will be like your faith in Jesus Christ. Is it substantial, or is it stretched so thin that it won't hold up to God's brush strokes? Your Christian foundation and pursuit of God with an attitude of gratitude and in fellowship and prayer should provide God with a canvass of exceptional quality to work with. What colors would you like God to use? Is your level of trust most reflected with warm or cool colors?

What kind of picture would you like God to paint? Is your trusting relationship most represented with a landscape painting or one at sea? Landscapes and seascapes can reveal great emotion even without people in them. God will want to depict all the feeling and emotion of your relationship of trust with Him. Will the seascape look stormy, or will the seas be calm? Will the sky be sunny and blue in your landscape, or will there be turbulent skies and tornadoes lurking in the distance? How about the frame?

Will your frame be ornate, showing years of workmanship and carving? Or, will your frame be more contemporary and indicative of recent times? If your frame is contemporary, then rest assured that someday the Great Artist will re-frame your painting when you have had more practice trusting Him. Remember how important it is to have a canvass of great substance because it must sustain years of hard work. There will be times when God will apply more layers of paint to change the emotion of your painting as your trusting relationship with Him develops.

Please know that the great unveiling won't happen a moment too soon. You will get to admire God's art work at the same time He shows you the DVD of your life!

**Already you are learning to trust God.
Take a few moments to reflect upon the picture
of your trusting relationship
with Him.**

Prayer Poem Ministry
"ABUNDANCE OF LIFE"

Surely, dear child of God, when you lift your eyes above to the Father, you will find Him. He is above the rubble, above the destruction, and above all imperfection…there waiting for you, His chosen one…call upon Him! He knows what will fall, what will try to overtake you, and what would cause destruction. Yet, your Father is there for you, above all rubble, destruction, and imperfection, if you choose Him. God's Word brings forth the abundance of life. The death and resurrection of Jesus Christ brought forth the abundance of life. And now the very presence of the Holy Spirit brings forth the abundance of life. How much better to choose the abundance of life over the destruction, rubble, and imperfections of life! Even though they are vastly different, there is still a choice to make. Oh the abundance of life, it is for everyone who chooses it!

Your precious Father sees you and welcomes your love for Him. May He be the lifter of your eyes so that you can see above the troubles in life that come your way. For when the journey is rough, the Lord is there to carry you and take your burdens so you will find strength. May the Word of God resonate within your heart and bring the abundance of life to you. May the death and resurrection of our Lord and Savior, Jesus Christ, bring the abundance of life right to you! And may the presence of God, through His Holy Spirit, reign supreme in your heart. May the abundance of life continue to grow and flourish in your life everyday. May you be strengthened to look higher over every circumstance to choose God's very best for you…the abundance of life!

Precious Patience

While you are learning to trust God, you will develop a precious virtue…patience. If God is in control, then you aren't. Things don't happen at the snap of your fingers or even at will. Everything happens in God's timing and according to His purpose. It puts adventure into each day and leaves the musty smell of selfishness and impatience in the back alley.

I am sure you have had some practice waiting on others for various reasons. Maybe you waited for a return phone call, or an RSVP, or even a ride to the airport. While you wait, you are depending on someone else.

Let's pretend that the person next door offered to plan an outing for your neighborhood. You are anxiously waiting to hear the date and details so that you can plan accordingly. Time goes by, and you haven't heard from your neighbor. You don't know when it will be or what you will have to contribute. You're tempted to call or even take over so that the planning is done properly. Each day makes it more difficult to wait, especially when you know you are qualified to be in charge. You begin to feel helpless, and that leads to utter frustration over what was meant to be such a simple thing. Waiting, dependence, and patience…these are not your three, favorite words! Can you relate?

Oftentimes we hear of the difficulties for the elderly when they must move to an assisted living facility and leave their independence behind. Suddenly, everything is planned for them, and they simply have to abide. They can't pick up and go anymore; they have to wait for their transportation. Resigned to total dependence, some quietly slip into another state of mind and go down hill very quickly. It is tough to give up their independence; it feels a bit like losing dignity. Waiting, dependence, and patience…these **are** three, difficult words! No matter where you are in life, this is a powerful picture of how difficult it is to release control. Perhaps you can relate.

Ryan's Michelle has had a taste of waiting, dependence, and patience. At the same time that her environment at work was changing, she felt like God was doing something different with her career. Michelle ventured out to explore fresh opportunities, yet she didn't sense the Holy Spirit's stamp of approval on any of them. She could feel a new season blowing in the air but waited for God's perfect will. Michelle had to trust her Heavenly Father and depend upon Him for provision. She also developed precious patience while she continued to do her best in her current job and wait upon God to direct her path. In the mean time, a quiet peace came over her as she let God, be God in her life.

In the Kingdom of God, we all need a quiet peace when it comes to trusting God.

We have to lay down our agendas no matter how old we are. But it requires great patience, and unless we have practiced that precious virtue, we will struggle every inch of the way. If we are not willing to be patient and wait on God's plans, we won't thrive in His kingdom, and we won't be able to live in His presence moment by moment.

We all like to get things done. I know I feel quite accomplished when I can check things off my list. We are a fast paced, "got to have it right now" society. We like to be in charge, and we have shortcuts for everything. Even when we delegate, we tend to micromanage others. "I don't have time for this; my time is worth much more than that!" Do you hear impatience beckoning in the background? How about control? Yet we live this way when we don't practice patience.

We simply say "well, patience is just not my virtue." Yet oftentimes what we really mean is that we are too self-centered to be patient. Oddly enough, lack of patience runs in the same circles with selfishness time and again.

When I think about those tragic hours before Jesus was crucified, I am gripped by all sorts of thoughts and emotions. Recently I watched a movie about the life and death of Jesus and marveled at the most flawless display of patience possible. He had every opportunity to lash at his accusers, but instead He received the deadly lashes. He was interrogated beyond all limits and could have hurled vengeance and retaliation at Pontius Pilate and the Sanhedrin. Instead Jesus practiced perfect patience and waited on the Father's purpose for that final hour. It was the most profound example of waiting on God that we will ever see. What an amazing display of peaceful patience!

Patience is not something you "get." You acquire patience over time through practice and prayer. Waiting on God is one of the hardest things to do because we are so eager to serve. We get a glimpse of His will, and we're good to go. Yet sometimes God wants us to simply wait and do nothing until the appointed time.

Jesus waited for the appointed time with loving patience. The Holy Spirit will also give you patience as the visible evidence of His work in you when you yield to God. Whether you need patience immediately, for a difficulty in the near future, or for the long haul, you can count on God when you learn to trust Him for your desired virtue.

Patience is one of the sweet Fruits of the Spirit listed in the Bible in Galatians 5:22. I wish I could tell you that there are shortcuts, but there aren't any. Yet, to the degree that you yield to God, you will receive His precious virtue.

Time to Reflect

▸ What sort of emotions dial up when you think about waiting, dependence, and patience?

▸ When have you had to relinquish control? How did it feel? How patient were you?

▸ How are you feeling about living on "Someone Else's" terms? What are your concerns?

▸ Are you willing to practice patience? What changes need to be made in your life?

_____
_____
_____
_____
_____

Living Application: Begin your quest for patience by being honest with yourself, and list your areas of weakness when it comes to patience. Tackle each weakness one by one, mindful of how you are doing. Evaluate yourself at the end of each day so that you can learn from your mistakes and celebrate your victories. Contemplate those historical hours before Jesus was crucified and how He must have felt. Allow yourself to relate to Jesus because He is your ultimate role model. Pray for the same measure of patience that Jesus had, and expect your life to change. Establish a habit of counting to ten before reacting out of impatience. Use those seconds to quietly call upon the Holy Spirit for help. Watch for the Holy Spirit's work in your mind and heart as you acquire your precious virtue.

God's Faithfulness

When you are first learning to trust God, you might not always have a warm, fuzzy feeling. It is similar to the way Christians learn to love...as an act of the will and unconditional. Oftentimes it is a choice to trust God, even when we don't feel like it. We struggle with that and still tend to grab the reigns, whether we mean to or not.

We don't decide to worry; we simply find ourselves there before we've chosen to bring our concerns to God and allow Him to take over. Sometimes we don't even pause ten seconds to assess the situation before worry grips, impatience brews, and trusting God is out of the picture.

Make your decision to trust God before your issues beckon at the forefront of your mind and bang on the door to your heart. Then when the time comes, you are more likely to depend upon the Lord.

As you get to know God better and experience His faithfulness, you will find that it is much easier to trust Him for everything.

Your life of praise and your attitude of gratitude toward God pave the way. You will naturally want to communicate with the person you are praising, so prayer and loving fellowship with your Heavenly Father become a part of your life. Out of loving fellowship comes a willingness to place all you have into the hands of the Almighty.

I wish I could tell you that it all happens quickly. That is the way we'd all like it to be, but you must establish your relationship with God before you will trust Him for everything. Then you will experience His faithfulness like never before.

Good memories carry me a long way when life is hectic. In the same way, wonderful memories of God's faithfulness help me go the distance when I must trust Him. That is why I continue to work at building them. Yes, you must work at building your memories with God. He will draw you and prove His faithfulness time and again, but you must choose to reach out to Him as well.

I assure you that when you reach out for God to establish trust, you will see His great faithfulness. The more you choose to trust, the more you will see how faithful God is. You will build lasting memories of trust that will serve your mind and emotions well in difficult times.

It is great to journal your memories of trusting God. These memories enrich your testimony. In addition to that, I suggest that you note the memories of sweet by-products that come from trusting Him.

When you relinquished your reigns of control...

- How did you feel?
- Did you sense the weight of the world taken off your shoulders?
- Was there joy and peace in the midst of that time of trust?
- Did the gnawing pain in your stomach go away?
- Were you able to sleep better?
- Was your level of tolerance much higher?
- Could you think more clearly as a result of trusting your Father?

I hope your answers were positive and that you received sweet by-products when you allowed God to be God. I like to call them tokens of His generosity toward me when I let Him be in control.

When you take your eyes off your circumstances and plant them on your Savior, you will build another memory with God. You will see the world and live life through the eyes of Jesus. Oftentimes, the Holy Spirit will show you the bigger picture.

Sometimes you'll get a glimpse of what God is doing with your issues, and sometimes you might only sense a bigger picture yet to be revealed. Either way, your eyes are on the Savior, and you are able to trust your Father just as Jesus did. You shake your head in utter amazement as you watch your world take fine shape around your circumstances.

Time to Reflect

- How are you doing with your attitude of praise and gratitude toward God?
- What is the Holy Spirit speaking to you in your times of prayer and fellowship?
- What are your memories of trusting God like? List some of them.
- What tokens have you received when you practice trusting and depending upon God?

_____
_____
_____
_____
_____

Living Application: Set aside a special, quiet time to praise God for the valuable tokens He gives to you as you learn to trust Him more. Sit in silence for a few minutes, and listen for the voice of the Holy Spirit right after your praise time. Journal and date what you hear from God. Make a practice to sit quietly before God, and just listen. Pray for an excitement and joy in your alone times with God.

The Beauty of the Holy Spirit

As you know, Jesus never promised that our journey with Him would be free of potholes or treacherous terrain. Before Jesus left to go to the Father He promised to send the Holy Spirit to help us make the journey. Jesus said, "... *I tell you the truth. It is to your advantage that I go away; for if I do not go away, the Helper will not come to you; but if I depart, I will send Him to you*" (John 16: 7).

If we didn't need help, Jesus wouldn't have offered to send the Holy Spirit. Jesus already knew that I would need help crossing the rugged terrain. He knew that I'd stumble and fall into the potholes without His assistance. And Jesus knew long before I was born that the Holy Spirit would be very busy helping me make my journey!

When I think about how busy I keep the Holy Spirit, I start to feel a bit selfish, like I am consuming all His time. Then I remember the beauty of the Holy Spirit, that He is God, and can handle all of our needs at once! The key here is that we all have needs. We would do well to recognize that one of our biggest needs is our **need** to trust and depend upon Him.

Thankfully we have mountain top experiences to encourage us, but we still have many low valleys to deal with. We were never meant to walk through these valleys alone. Yet many of us still try to go it alone. We still think it should be our way or no way. Unfortunately, for some who make their choices without God, the consequences are devastating.

If we want to live in God's presence moment by moment, we must do it His way.

▸ Do you really desire to live in the presence of God?

▸ Are you willing to exchange your will for more of God's perfect will?

▸ If you wrote your story, would God be a part of your life, or would you be a part of His?

▸ Are you living life on your terms or on God's terms?

▸ Do you bask in God's presence, or do you struggle with "me, myself, and I" everyday?

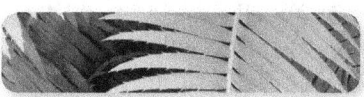

Prayer Poem Ministry
"TRUST IN YOU"

The Lord, the God of the universe, is your strength. He is the only one that is capable of holding you up, of overshadowing you, and surrounding you. Yes, God is sufficient. Oh that you would not run to any other source, only to God! You know that you will find all that you need in Him. Jesus is your stronghold. When troubled times come, He is your hiding place. Your Savior will defend you and your family, and keep your enemies away. Grow closer in love with your King that you may find shelter even from your adversary. Praise to the Lord, your strength, your deliverer, your stronghold! Yes, yes... your great strength! For He will not forsake the one who seeks His face.

Run to the Lord and let Him turn your weakness into strength. Don't be afraid to be overshadowed, for in the shadow of His wings you will rest and build great strength for your journey. When you are looking for more, let God be enough to fill you to capacity. Then you will be ready when difficulties come your way. Run to your Savior and find great and lasting shelter in His presence. He waits for you in the quiet resting place designed just for you. Let the glory of the Lord fill you with everlasting praise and thanksgiving and make you strong in Him.

Freedom in God's Will

Your journey is unique. Enjoy it, and see each step as one more opportunity to know God more. Don't pout about the potholes or rough terrain. See each one as an opportunity to watch God do amazing things in your life while you depend upon Him. Your eyes behold the beauty of the Holy Spirit moment to moment, and you will wait in eager anticipation for more and more of God. Freedom will reign supreme in your heart when you choose to obey God instead of hurrying through the gateway of least resistance.

Freedom in the Lord's will is liberty at its best. Sweet liberty...who doesn't desire to live in a realm of freedom where liberty surrounds them? Walk with God in His freedom; He will dictate your life story, and it will read well.

"Now the Lord is the Spirit; and where the Spirit of the Lord is, there is liberty."
(2 Corinthians 3:17)

Let's pray!

Dear Heavenly Father, I acknowledge your leadership in my life. Thank you for being in supreme control. Please tame my will and bring it into quiet agreement with Your perfect will. I desire to be a vital part of Your life, to please You in every way. Please continue to draw me in and make me the person You want me to be. Help me to stay on the path of righteousness and obey You more and more. When You call, I want to hear. Please help me to fine tune my prayer life and come into sweet fellowship with You moment by moment. I adore You and want my life to be a testimony of praise and worship unto You. As I step out to trust and depend upon You, please meet me on my journey and carry me into Your perfect will and purpose. You are my one and only, I give my life to You once again, and I rejoice in You and in my salvation. Thank you for being my Lord.

Fourth Ingredient

Desire for God...
Heart's Desire	124
You Belong to God	126
Desiring God	128
God is Trustworthy	130
God is Faithful	135
Back to you	139
Knowing versus Doing	141
God's Pleasure	143
God is Compassionate	144
Compassion or Sympathy?	147
Compassion Curbs Judgement	148
God is Merciful	151
Watching God Work Wonders	154
God is Loving	158
Loving God	161
Loving Others	162
What Do They See?	166
No Worries	166
Come to the Buffet	167
Your Desire for God	169

> *"Whom have I in heaven but You?*
> *And there is none upon earth that I desire besides You."*
> Psalm 73: 25

Why does it seem like those who live for Jesus Christ wear a winning smile most of the time? Is that contagious grin for real, or is it a phony front to mask what lies beneath the surface? I used to wonder about that before I became a committed Christian. Quite honestly, I wasn't sure the smile was genuine. Why are they happy all of the time? Perhaps you've had some of the same questions that I had.

- Is life a sweet bed of roses for those who claim to be followers of Jesus Christ?
- Do they ever allow themselves the freedom to be real with themselves and others?
- Is there something that they know or have that I should look into?

Here is what I have come to understand. The Bible says that life is not a sweet bed of roses; it is challenging for all Christians. We live in an imperfect world, and life can be difficult for everyone. You and I have talked about that.

Some Christians put up a front so that others don't know their true feelings. But many followers of Jesus Christ are quite transparent about themselves and have good accountability with others. And yes, the true follower of Jesus Christ has something that everyone should know about that even goes beyond eternal salvation.

There is nothing more important than the assurance of eternal life through Jesus.

Those who are seriously pursuing an intimate relationship with God have even more to smile about. They wear a contagious grin in the most genuine fashion. That grin actually speaks louder than words because it is an outward sign of what is taking place within. I call it the Savior's smile because it reflects the character of God just as Jesus did when He walked on the earth. It says that you choose to live for God, you have cashed in on life, and all that He has belongs to you.

You walk by faith, not by sight, and live a normal life in the presence of God moment by moment. You are on the receiving end of God's goodness. This gives you everything to smile about!

The Savior's smile is unmistakable because it radiates the matchless love of Christ to all those around. Those who carry the smile do it naturally. It isn't a phony front because there is nothing fake about Jesus Christ. It has the keen ability to welcome all who see it, and it receives them with open arms.

The Savior's smile communicates warmth and sends out an invitation for a safe place to be real. It's very attractive because it reflects the sincere attitude of the heart where the Holy Spirit proudly dwells.

Picture this!

You have just accepted Jesus Christ as your personal Lord and Savior and received His free gift of eternal salvation. Your excitement cannot be contained as you anticipate the Holy Spirit's residence. You are bringing God home to your heart of love forever. The right side of your lip starts to turn upward just a bit. You remember that this is a gift and that you didn't have to earn the indwelling of the Spirit. You are also overjoyed because you don't have to prepare anything, clean out the clutter, or dust and vacuum your heart. The Savior's smile is already beginning to take shape. He's there...the Holy Spirit is actually settled and comfortable in your heart. You are so thrilled to have the King residing inside that you cannot be contained.

God's companionship and presence are unmistakable, and you and the Holy Spirit are becoming quite close. Gratitude wells up inside every time you think about it. Your heart is peaceful, and you notice that your struggles are diminishing. You sense the voice of the Holy Spirit directing, guarding, and protecting you. Now the Savior's smile is becoming evident to others. The more time you spend with God, the more His desirable character develops within you. God has become your most prized possession, His desires have become yours, and you desire God more than anything in life. The Savior's joyful smile is starting to feel quite natural to you.

Everyone around you notices the beautiful changes in your disposition. Perfect strangers want to connect and get to know you. Your heart is full, and your joy is complete now that you have decided to follow Jesus all the days of your life. At last, the Savior's smile is there to stay, and your winsome countenance speaks volumes to the ambiance of your heart. You sense the Lord's good pleasure when He gently whispers words of love into your spirit everyday. Is it too good to be true? Is it genuine? It's so good that it **has** to be true, and your genuine, Savior's smile says it all.

Now recall the day when you invited Jesus into your heart. Did your heart sense the Father's excitement to send the Holy Spirit as a permanent roommate and companion? Did you notice that the Holy Spirit didn't make you change or do anything radical before He came to live in your heart? Have you enjoyed the freedom that comes when you are living for God and His attributes become yours?

If you are nodding yes, then I would say that you wear the same winning smile that others wear who follow after Jesus Christ and pursue His presence. You are going to enjoy this chapter and desire more and more of God. If you are unsure, this chapter will bring joy while you learn more about God's attributes and embrace them as your very own.

Time to Reflect

‣ What does your spiritual disposition look like to others?

‣ Do others see the real you, or have you learned to mask hidden, underlying feelings?

‣ Is the Savior's smile a genuine part of your countenance, or is it still a work in progress?

‣ What characteristics of God would you **most** like to see radiate from your heart?

Living Application: Take time to examine your heart. Pray and ask the Holy Spirit to help you to be a reflection of Jesus for all to see. Revisit the word picture that we just looked at, and then paint another one to illustrate your story of bringing Christ home to your heart. Express your emotions and expectations, and be real about your story. Allow your Savior to establish His smile upon your face so that it is genuine and lasting. Remember that you are on a personal journey and that you don't have a track record to meet or beat. Start asking God to deposit His attributes into your character.

You Belong To God

- What does it mean to belong to God?
- What comes to **your** mind?
- How does it make you feel?

Many automatically put up boundaries when they think of belonging to God. They think of the obligations and the time commitments just as in anything else that they belong to. That's the problem...when we contemplate the things of God, we shouldn't compare Him to our worldly values and experiences.

Jesus is the only standard we have when we are trying to understand God the Father. He is the exact representation of the Father. Jesus said, *"Most assuredly, I say to you, the Son can do nothing of Himself, but what He sees the Father do; for whatever He does, the Son also does in like manner"* (John 5: 19).

If you want to see the Father, then look upon the Son. Since you belong to Jesus, then you belong to God.

Oftentimes we get so caught up in selfishness that we miss what it really means to belong to the King. Belonging to God simply means that we are a part of Him and that we are naturally associated with Him. That's good news! It means that you have access to everything that Jesus has because He paid the ultimate price for you. It means that the Father loves you just as much as He loves Jesus and that when He looks at you, He sees His Son. He desires you just as He desires His very own Son.

You are a member of God's household. You are not the housekeeper or cook; you are family. You are a beloved son or daughter. You are His!

If you lived your life with that incredible understanding, others might have to wear sunglasses when they gaze into your heart. There would be so much light in and around you that it could be blinding for others.

I can't tell you how important it is to live with the revelation of God's love and desire for you. Once you bask in His love, you will desire God just as much as He desires you. And when you desire Him, you will also want to be as much like Him as you can.

Everywhere you go, you will want to be as much of a representation of your Father as Jesus was. Don't labor over every move you make as an ambassador for Christ. That will detract from your association with God and put pressure on you to perform. It should never be a struggle for you. Your representation of the Father must be a natural outflow of your connection to Him. How does that happen?

When you practice living with an attitude of praise and thanksgiving to God, your spiritual countenance will reflect a grateful heart. You will watch every thought, action, and feeling agree with your lifestyle of worship for God. Your prayer times become episodes of communion with God, and companionship with the Holy Spirit is your pride and joy. You will crave the will of God more than your favorite foods. Soon the Holy Spirit becomes your personal consultant and most treasured confidant.

You will find that you can barely take a breath without God. Your dependency upon the Holy Spirit will cause you to trust Him instead of yourself for your moment to moment decisions. Soon, your desire for God and His attributes is driving you into the awareness of His presence more and more. Does this sound like an impossible dream?

One day Jesus was talking to His disciples about something that they considered impossible. "*But Jesus looked at them and said to them, 'With men this is impossible, but with God all things are possible'*" (Matthew 19:26). I know that if Jesus looked at me and spoke anything at all, I would believe Him. Jesus would tell us that thriving in His presence, as we just discussed a minute ago, is impossible for a mere sinner. But that as sons and daughters, belonging to Him, looking into His eyes...all things are possible.

We can live the life we were destined for when we remember who we are, who we belong to, and how much we are loved and encouraged by our Beloved.

God draws us unto Himself; we don't strive. We don't take credit for making progress on our journey; we simply abide and enjoy the scenery. When we cooperate with God, we see miraculous changes in our attitude and behavior. You can do this; you have Jesus' Word on it.

I hope you are not thinking that I have mastered this task, because I haven't. At the end of each day when I get ready for bed, I reflect upon my day. Almost always, I find myself apologizing to God for this and that. Oftentimes if it isn't sin that first comes to mind; it is my regret for not practicing each of the ingredients that God specifically told me I need in order to live in His presence moment to moment.

Sometimes, I forget because I start plowing through my day of my own accord instead of abiding in God's amazing love and grace. But when I slow down enough to thank, pray, listen, and trust...I abide in Him and desire God and His ways more than I can express. You will too!

We both need to remember that we are on a journey and that even a little progress pleases our Father immensely.

Desiring God

Nearly every Christian will tell you that they desire God; they would also say that it is a "no-brainer." Every believer desires God! But I'm not convinced that everyone who believes in Jesus Christ really follows Him with a hunger and deep desire for God.

Remember when we talked about how we must become a part of God's world instead of expecting Him to become a part of ours? Your hunger for the ways and characteristics of God is related to the degree in which you are a part of **His** world. When you embrace God's world, you embrace God Himself. And when you embrace God, you will naturally desire Him. But what does that look like?

Desiring God means that first and foremost you desire the person of God... His presence. Your relationship with God and His companionship with you must satisfy your heart more than anything else. Your desire to step into His world has to be established. That means living within His will. You can't desire the things of God until you are passionate about the ways of God. Pray and ask God to settle the issues you might still have regarding your will instead of His.

Plant your feet firmly on The Rock, and echo these powerful words: "...not what I will, but what You will." (Mark 14:36)

Be sure that you are practicing the first three ingredients that we've discussed.

- Live a life of praise and worship to God with an attitude of gratitude.
- Develop your prayer life; include good communication and fellowship with God.
- Learn to trust and depend upon your Father for everything.

Are you ready to ask God to impart His wonderful attributes to you? I could spend the rest of my life expounding on the qualities of God and still not cover them all. But we can look at a few of them together. We will discuss God's trustworthiness, His faithfulness, compassion, mercy, and great love. These are the same attributes of God discussed in *Living in His Presence*.

We both have much to gain when we experience these five attributes of God. Most importantly, they will help us enter into the sweet awareness of His presence on a continual basis, becoming more like our Savior. They are life changing qualities that will improve relationships with everyone we know, including God.

When God's qualities are stirred up and become evident in our lives, our emotional and physical well-being can improve dramatically as we live with less sin, regrets, and offenses.

We will have a powerful impact on the Kingdom of God here on earth when we incorporate them into our lives and they rub off on others.

You are going to enjoy sitting under the Lord's loving leadership when you contemplate His qualities! The Holy Spirit will come along side and reveal hidden truths and secrets to you just as a personal tutor would do. You will be amazed at how easy it is to learn from God when your spirit is open and ready.

Many referred to Jesus as Teacher. He encouraged everyone to come under His teaching and learn from Him. It always brought peace and rest instead of turmoil and burden to those who submitted to His will. Jesus said, *"Come to Me, all you who labor and are heavy laden, and I will give you rest. Take My yoke upon you and learn from Me, for I am gentle and lowly in heart, and you will find rest for your souls"* (Matthew 11: 28,29).

Time to Reflect

- Think about belonging to God. What boundaries hinder your association with Him?
- How does your kinship to God change the way you will live and relate to Him?
- Describe your desire for God. What feeds your appetite for Him?
- Which of God's attributes do you look forward to learning about the most? Why?

_____
_____
_____
_____
_____

Living Application: Pray and ask the Holy Spirit to reveal the Father's heart to you concerning your kinship with Him. Journal your feelings, and document what your expectations are as you desire God more and acquire His characteristics for your own. Practice using the first three ingredients that we have been discussing...Worship God with your life of gratitude toward Him. Establish intimacy with Him through fellowship and prayer, and learn to depend upon God for everything. Focus on Jesus and the flawless manner in which He incorporated the first three ingredients into **His** life. Then watch your desire for God really grow!

God is Trustworthy

We have learned how essential it is to trust God and depend upon Him for everything. Even a small morsel of His trustworthiness is most satisfying. You can't help but want more and more of His delicious presence in your life.

Just yesterday, I was rejoicing in God's trustworthy nature. A friend and I had been praying about doing something together, but we needed others to come alongside and help. We brainstormed trying to make something happen, but realized that our efforts might impose hardship upon others. We weren't willing to do that, yet we still sensed that our little project was God's will. We felt like we should trust Him and not lose hope. It isn't even a long story because within a few hours, the impossible occurred, and all we had to do was be thankful. It was as simple as that! It was one of those little miracles that felt really big. We laughed together because we could go on with our plans. But mostly we rejoiced in God's amazing trustworthiness. We talked about how sweet it is to bask in His trustworthy nature. Later that day, I remembered how much I wanted to be trustworthy like Jesus.

We see how trustworthy God is all the time; it happens every day. When you are on the receiving end of God's trustworthiness time and again, you can't help but desire His nature for yourself. You will want to give to others what you receive from the Lord. As Jesus was sending His disciples out to do ministry, He said, *"Heal the sick, cleanse the lepers, raise the dead, cast out demons. Freely you have received, freely give"* (Matthew 10: 8). How can you give away trustworthiness?

You must become trustworthy before others will trust you. Maybe you think you already are a trustworthy person. I used to think so myself until the Holy Spirit revealed to me some of what goes into His trustworthy nature. Of course, I thought… that is just how Jesus was when He walked on the earth! It's a good idea to go back to the Gospels and notice God's trustworthy character in His Son. Then you can examine your heart and ask the Holy Spirit to help make you more trustworthy.

Jesus had entered the town of Capernaum when a centurion approached Him for help. His servant was lying at home, extremely ill, and in need of a miracle. Jesus told the centurion that He would go to his house and heal the servant. *"The centurion answered and said, 'Lord I am not worthy that You should come under my roof. But only speak a word, and my servant will be healed"* (Matthew 8: 8). This Roman soldier had great faith in what Jesus could do, but there is also something else that he knew about Jesus.

Jesus had a reputation for being dependable and reliable.

The centurion and those all around, knew that Jesus was capable of being depended upon and that they could trust Him with great confidence. Whatever Jesus said He would do, He did. Even those who put Jesus to death marveled at His dependable, reliable character.

How about you?

- Are you dependable and reliable at all times? How easy it is to say one thing, but do something else without even realizing it! It happens more than we like to admit.
- When you tell others that you will return their call within a certain amount of time, do you actually do it?
- Are you consistent? When you agree to do something, do others have a reason to wonder if you will really come through in a timely manner?
- Do you adhere to your priorities?

I know that we are not perfect, but I do think that we struggle with mediocrity and even complacency at times. It is so easy to let others slip through the cracks. Part of being reliable and dependable is having a standard of excellence to live by. It's not that we will ever achieve total excellence, but sometimes we don't even make the attempt. That might sound a bit harsh, and I am certainly not pointing a finger at you. But this is something to consider when you want others to feel like you are trustworthy. They have to know that you will come through, even when you are busy.

It is easy to be timely with others when you aren't busy. The truly reliable person that others can depend upon comes through no matter what the circumstances. That person puts self aside to go above and beyond and place others first. Someone who is reliable doesn't put you on the back burner until a more convenient time.

When you are a priority to someone, they show you that they will follow through no matter what. They walk their talk. That doesn't mean that the truly reliable person is a doormat for others to take advantage of. It simply means that this person does what she says she will do. She learns not to over commit so that she can keep things in proper balance. She isn't super human, but she has integrity. And others know she is trustworthy, reliable to the core.

We all have room for growth in this area, but we must strive for this growth. It isn't going to happen without daily practice. If you fail, then apologize and acknowledge your mistake before God and others. God isn't demanding perfection; He already knows you are incapable of it. But remember that God isn't mediocre or complacent. If you desire His qualities, then you need to commit to Him at a new level.

You have to work at staying close to Him so that you will be sensitive to the leading of the Holy Spirit. You might forget to return a call, but if you are listening to the voice of God, He'll remind you. If your heart is joyful and thankful, you'll find it much easier to abide in the Son of God and live on His terms instead of your own. The more dependent you are upon God, the more of His dependability you will want for yourself.

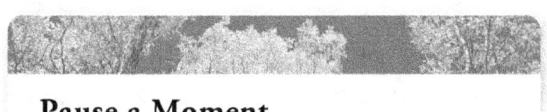

Pause a Moment

Are you feeling challenged? Don't be discouraged, receive God's grace instead. Stay on the path and allow Him to guide you.

It all comes full circle. Spend time with God, and watch His Holy Spirit work wonders in your life to make you trustworthy like Jesus.

"Now when He got into a boat, His disciples followed Him. And suddenly a great tempest arose on the sea, so that the boat was covered with waves. But He was asleep. Then His disciples came to Him and awoke Him, saying, 'Lord, save us! We are perishing!' But He said to them, 'Why are you fearful, O you of little faith?' Then He arose and rebuked the winds and the sea, and there was a great calm. So the men marveled, saying, 'Who can this be, that even the winds and the sea obey Him?'" (Matthew 8:23-27)

I've read that the Sea of Galilee is an unusual body of water because of its size and location with regard to actual sea level. Sudden storms can occur with little warning. It wasn't as if Jesus and the disciples took a risk on a stormy night so that they could go out on the water. The storm was abrupt, and they were actually in grave danger.

Jesus had a reputation for absolute stability.

He was resistant to sudden changes of position and conditions. Not only did He calm the storm, Jesus calmed His best friends. In a helpless state, they frantically woke Jesus up for help. I'm assuming that they didn't have time to think about it...they just reacted. But they automatically knew what to do. The disciples knew from past experiences that Jesus was trustworthy because He'd always been a stabilizing force for them. Jesus didn't waver; He was calm. He had the ability to calm the storm and the disciples.

How about you?

- Are you a known worrier?
- Are you fearful?
- Do others wonder if you are able to endure the storms of life with them in eager anticipation of Jesus' intervention?
- Have they seen you waver or stand firm in your own storms?
- In your quest for God's trustworthy character, are you a stabilizing force for others, or do you topple at the distant sound of bad news.
- Has Jesus been your Rock to hold on to, or have you floundered under the torrential rains with fear and trepidation?

Don't be mistaken, others observe your character all the time. It is not as if they are watching so that they know who is the most trustworthy. People pick up on characteristics just by being with you. When the storms come, they automatically know where to go just like the disciples did.

Jesus proved His trustworthiness over and over in the normal circumstances of life, and so can you. Then you can radiate God's awesome character in stormy or calm waters. Stability isn't something you wake up with one morning. You cultivate stability as you weather your own storms. Unfortunately storms come; it doesn't matter if we are prepared or not. I have had to weather some tragic storms in my life. Looking back, I didn't always do a great job. I buckled, wrinkled, over strained, and almost drowned at times. But through the stormy seasons, I learned how to cling to the only stabilizing force I had, Jesus Christ. Eventually, in the midst of adversity, I automatically went to my Stabilizer. Being on the receiving end of such stability, I desire to be the same way for others.

How can a person cultivate stability in an unstable world? Learning to live in the awareness of God's presence brings unwavering stability. Those times of praise and worship with God clear out fear and worry. Your private times with God will establish peace within your heart and carry you over the turbulent thresholds of life. The voice of the Holy Spirit will resonate deep within your soul and whisper just the right words at the perfect time to calm your anxious heart. Your need for God and His will reminds you that you belong to Him; you are connected. No matter what, you won't topple. You have God's character: you are trustworthy and stable!

Before ascending to the Father, Jesus appeared to His disciples after His resurrection and commissioned them to carry out His ministry. *"And Jesus came and spoke to them, saying, 'All authority has been given to Me in heaven and on earth. Go therefore and make disciples of all the nations, baptizing them in the name of the Father and of the Son and of the Holy Spirit, teaching them to observe all things that I have commanded you; and lo, I am with you always, even to the end of the age'"* (Matthew 28: 18-20).

Jesus had the reputation of being lovingly committed.

He was committed to His disciples and promised to be committed to all believers until the end of time. Jesus lived with His beloved twelve for three years and poured everything He had into each of them. He was committed to the Father's cause and to His precious friends. Jesus had plenty of opportunity to abandon the twelve, with good reason. They weren't perfect, and I am sure they tested His patience from time to time. He had to correct, rebuke, and keep them on track during His time with them. Yet Jesus remained lovingly committed to them and to the will of the Father. His example of commitment revealed even more of His trustworthy nature.

Jesus also revealed His heart of commitment to you and to me. He pledged to be with each of us for our entire lives on earth. He sent the Holy Spirit to live and reign in our hearts. We are never without His presence, guidance, direction, and love...not even for a second. Jesus said He would be with us, **always**. None of us can ever match this kind of commitment because we are not God. But because we receive it from Him, we desire to be as committed to Him and to others as much as we possibly can. This means we must remain devoted to God and to His will.

How about you?

- How committed are you to Jesus Christ and to His cause?
- Do you follow in His footsteps when the visibility is low?
- On rugged terrain, do you turn back, or do you plant your feet on your firm Foundation?
- How do others see you?
- What kind of a witness are you to those around you?
- Are they encouraged to go on because they see loving commitment in you?
- What about your relationships?
- Do you escape when challenge comes, or do you press in with unshakable commitment?

In our world, we are not encouraged to persevere as much as we should be. Oftentimes we are advised to get out when the heat is turned up too high. We are tempted to look out for ourselves, our feelings, and our well-being. "Start over with a clean slate," many would say. The real problem with that shows up later when we are tempted to start over and over, never dealing with the real issues, never understanding true commitment. For those who practice pressing into the presence of God moment to moment, genuine commitment naturally occurs. When your life is an act of worship toward God, your fellowship is on-going, and you are sincerely humble before Him. Trustworthiness will be a beautiful offshoot of this relationship.

We just talked about three aspects of God's trustworthiness: reliability, stability, and commitment. Beware of a common danger that weaves itself throughout all these aspects. That danger is selfishness, and you can become entangled in it. You can't be dependable and reliable if you are caught up in your own conveniences. You won't be able to be a stabilizing force if others can't see that you care. And you will not stay committed when it is uncomfortable if you can't see beyond your own will.

Following in the footsteps of Christ means that you are focused on God, not on yourself. I can assure you that if you truly desire to be trustworthy like Jesus, the Holy Spirit will work in your heart in creative ways so that the character of God will be formed in you. Be assured that God is there for you.

Time to Reflect

- In what ways does your character reflect God's reliability and dependability?
- How have you been a stabilizing force in the lives of others?
- What is the most challenging commitment you have had to make?
- How do you need to change in order to radiate God's trustworthy character?

_____
_____
_____
_____
_____

Living Application: Examine your heart, and allow the Holy Spirit to speak into your life. Ask God to show you where His trustworthy character is lacking in you. Understand that you cannot deposit God's character into your own heart; He must do it as you draw near to Him. Pray and ask the Holy Spirit to give you the same character that Jesus had when He lived here. Be open to character changes that God has for you. Be alert and aware of selfish tendencies, and nip those tendencies so that you won't struggle with them. Spend at least ten minutes in silence before God, and simply listen for His voice.

Thank God for speaking to you, and journal His promptings later. If you didn't hear anything, then continue to pursue God, and ask the Holy Spirit to help you hear His voice.

Prayer Poem Ministry
"SATISFY MY DESIRE"

You are His precious child! The Lord has already given you a taste of what it is like to live with Him. Your hunger for God is enough to cause Him to satisfy you every minute of each day. Taste His sustenance…flavorful, full bodied, and rich in the nutrients for life. You will grow deeper as God's child and desire more and more of His character. Whenever you need more of God and His presence in your life, you will surely have it. For you have already grown in your desire for God. Now take what you have been given, nurture it, hold on to it, treasure what He gives to you, and never take anything for granted that comes from your Dear Father. Your love for God is real, not from a story book or good teaching. Your love for God comes from desire, a desire to know Him intimately and have access to Him whenever you need. But now, dear one of God, you are needing and wanting the Lord more and more. Be the one to tell others what it is like to live in the presence of the Almighty.

Continue to hunger and thirst for God and His character. Don't settle for a mere sample of Him; desire everything He has for you. Allow the sweet taste of God's character to infuse your soul with rich, full bodied nourishment for your life. You have the distinct privilege of growing even deeper into the rich character of Christ so that as you desire more of God, you will have it. God's character feeds the hungers of your heart, so treasure it more than the finest meal on earth. Let your genuine love for God turn into a burning desire for Him and His presence. Access the presence of the Almighty moment by moment, and surely your desire for Him will be contagious to all.

God is Faithful

Have you ever experienced the faithfulness of God? You might agree that it's like a jolt of joy that penetrates your being! Something rises up within, and you feel goodness coming from your Heavenly Father. You log it away in the safest compartment of your memory bank and relish that feeling for a very long time. You even journal the feeling because your words become a faith booster in times of doubt.

> I would like to share a recent story about the faithfulness of God that affected my life and the lives of two others. A few months after *Living in His Presence* was published, I felt like God wanted me to spend more time with you. I went away alone, to pray and fast in hopes of understanding God's will better. I sought wise counsel, and spent time with my friend, Gail, who is a wonderful life coach. It became clear that I was to write *Secrets in His Presence* and that I needed to do it in a timely manner.

Secrets In His Presence ~ 135

The only thing keeping me from really diving into this special project was my job. There wasn't enough time in a week for my job **and** my writing. I can't tell you how difficult that was for me to come to terms with. I really enjoyed my profession and the working environment that I had; I didn't want to give it up. I had been a dental hygienist for almost 29 years; dentistry was a part of me. Yet I knew I had to be obedient and trust that God would take care of all the details; He would be faithful. But first I needed to step out and initiate a meeting with my dentist to express my heart.

The meeting was bittersweet. He understood and was supportive of my newest special project, but really wanted to be sure this was God's will for everyone involved. We prayed that God would be faithful and make it obvious that I was making the right decision. We asked God to hand pick a replacement for my job immediately, even though my time frame was really six weeks. Neither of us was shy about adding in our own two cents about the qualifications of this person! Within about a day, God answered our prayer. There are more details than I have time to share, but I will point out a few so that you can see how God worked a miracle for all involved.

The person for my job was recommended by two, separate sources; neither had knowledge of the other. That usually doesn't happen, especially within a short period of time. We were blessed with an immediate replacement, and her time frame turned out to be exactly the same as mine. The night we prayed for God's faithfulness, our new hygienist was also asking God to provide a job with a specific working environment. It turned out that her specifics mirrored our office exactly! She had also been asking God for an obvious sign that He worked in her life in tangible ways, and her prayer was answered. My dentist prayed for an immediate response. His prayer was answered. I asked God to provide in miraculous ways so that I would know that I was doing the right thing. My prayer was answered as well. We witnessed God's faithfulness in fine form; it was a triple blessing! Then God added an unexpected, fourth blessing. I didn't have to say good-bye to my profession or to those I have grown to love and respect for many years. It worked out that I could remain on staff a few hours a week. I had plenty of time to write, and I didn't have to retire from my profession completely. Can you sense the faithfulness of God in our situation?

"*Jesus Christ is the same yesterday, today, and forever*" (Hebrews 13:8). God never changes and is faithful in every situation. He is faithful on the high peaks of life as well as in the low valleys. It isn't difficult to spot the faithfulness of God during the highs, especially when things turn out like the story I just shared. But how easy is it to identify His faithfulness when life doesn't turn out as we thought? Is God less faithful then?

I have another story to share with you about God's faithfulness. This time things didn't turn out quite like we thought they would, but God was still faithful. When my husband and I first dedicated our lives to Jesus Christ, we couldn't wait to serve Him. Mike wanted to be in "the ministry" and threw his name into the hat with high hopes that God would draw it out soon.

Mike continued to work within his profession in the high tech, corporate world. He had a nice career but never felt fulfilled. We prayed that God would take him out of the business world and put him into a "real ministry" where Mike could serve.

In the mean time, God sent Mike many opportunities to serve while maintaining his full-time job in the business world. Mike was obedient and gladly accepted every assignment that God had for him. For many years, he gave his time and talents to whatever cause God placed before him. God empowered and highly anointed every effort Mike made to be obedient and serve Him. We could see the faithfulness of God every time. We even sensed that God was using Mike's career to prepare him for something down the road. But we still wondered if God would ever call him to serve full-time. Many times we talked and prayed about it, yet we always felt like it had to be God's will, not Mike's. We weren't going to make this happen on our own.

Over the years, Mike let go of his full-time dream and continued to serve God graciously in his "not so spare" time. I remember one day when my husband told me that it was okay that things hadn't turned out the way we had hoped. He would rather be obedient, operate within the will of God, and have His blessing then step out on his own without Him. Yet Mike's vision never perished. I don't think he ever stopped gleaning all he could in case God happened to whisper His name. I marveled at how he stayed the course and responded to God's will. He always encouraged others who were in the full-time ministry. He wanted the kind of fulfillment that they had but wanted God's will more, so he continued to cheer them on and pray for them. As time went on, we remained grateful for Mike's career which always provided for our family. Amber and Ryan would soon enter college.

One day while we were midstream with college and were planning for Amber's wedding, God drew Mike's name out of the hat. Can you believe His timing and sense of humor? It was the most expensive year of our lives, and God was asking Mike to take a significant decrease in pay and go full-time into the ministry. If anyone's circumstances gave him a good reason to say no to God, I think that my husband's did. But once again I marveled at his response to God. Mike sought wise counsel and then went away alone to pray and fast about the opportunity. I stayed at home and did the same. When Mike returned from his prayerful retreat, we both agreed that this was the will of God. My husband would enter his new calling with a grateful heart and not question God's timing.

Even though I was in complete agreement with what Mike was doing, I wish I could say that I had his good attitude. I struggled with the timing and let fear get the better part of me. Yet I remembered…God is faithful. He had always provided for us in the past, and He would continue to take good care of us going forward. But both of our kids were thriving in a private university, we were three months away from Amber's wedding, and I wasn't sure if we would ever be able to put money into the bank again. What was God thinking?

This was not looking the way I thought it would many years ago when Mike first desired a full-time ministry job. Even though I knew it was God's will, it still didn't feel comfortable. Did it have to happen right then?

It **did** have to happen just then. We had the opportunity to look back and see God's faithfulness over the years and exercise our own faith for more of the same going forward. Mike had a full-time ministry all along; it just looked different than we thought. God drew Mike's name out of the hat the same day he threw it in. God was faithful to give him opportunities to serve for many years, and Mike was obedient. God was faithful to use my husband's career of 25 years to train him for what really **was** down the road. God was faithful to encourage us when we wondered if He really could use someone like us in His kingdom. And, God was faithful when there weren't enough hours in the day for Mike to get to everything on his plate and still be a great husband, father, and friend. Because Mike was obedient in doing God's will, God empowered every good work, and somehow he got it all done. What appeared to be the 25 low years of waiting, turned out to be 25 high years of preparation and God's faithfulness to fulfill and use a willing, obedient man. *"being confident of this very thing, that He who has begun a good work in you will complete it until the day of Jesus Christ"* (Philippians 1: 6).

It doesn't matter what your situation is, you can rest in the faithfulness of God every day. God has an excellent track record of taking care of His children in the highs and lows of life. Sometimes God's faithfulness is obvious; it seems instantaneous, and joy permeates your being. Other times you might have to watch for it, trust in it, and be patient as God works all things out for your good and for His glory. I remind myself all the time that God is faithful...period.

Time to Reflect

▸ When has God's faithfulness felt like a real "high" or jolt of joy?

▸ How did you respond to His faithfulness? How did it impact your life?

▸ Name a low season when God's faithfulness looked a little different than you expected.

▸ Did you notice His faithfulness in the journey? What impact did it have on your life?

_____
_____
_____
_____
_____

Living Application: If you had trouble recalling God's faithfulness, then stretch your arms out to Him and ask Him to draw you near. Pray for God to reveal Himself and His faithfulness to you in ways that you will notice. Regardless of where you are on your journey with God, be watching for His faithfulness as it applies to the highs and lows in the moment to moment of your life. Journal God's faithfulness on a regular basis and note your response, attitude, and the impact of His faithfulness on you.

Back to You

"But the fruit of the Spirit is love, joy, peace, patience, kindness, goodness, faithfulness, gentleness, and self-control. Against such things there is no law."
(Galatians 5: 22,23 NIV)

The same faithfulness that Mike experienced from God is also available to you and to me. God is waiting to shower you with the sweet fruits of His Holy Spirit as you walk in the footsteps of Jesus daily. His faithfulness comes right back to you! When we operate in His faithfulness we make a difference as we reveal the character of God to others. How does one be faithful? What does it mean to be faithful?

A faithful person is dutiful and loyal, worthy of trust, and consistent. Actually, faithfulness looks a lot like trustworthiness because it has some of the same traits. When we look into the life of Jesus Christ, we see many, many wonderful character traits of the Father.

Yet when I really think about the faithfulness of Jesus, I realize that He went beyond loyalty and trustworthiness; Jesus took faithfulness all the way to obedience. He epitomized the meaning of obedience when He went to the cross for our sins. Every miracle Jesus performed was an act of obedience in response to the Father's will. Jesus checked in with the Father at all times and left us a flawless example of obedience to follow.

Jesus said, *"If you keep My commandments, you will abide in My love, just as I have kept My Father's commandments and abide in His love."* (John 15: 10)

If we want to live faithfully as Jesus did, we must be obedient children unto the Father.

The word, obey, rubs many people the wrong way. It is similar to dependence in that it puts someone else at the control panel. In a world where self is the focus, anyone who directs or authors your story might be considered the antagonist.

No wonder many will only go so far with Jesus before placing boundaries around their lives. They say they love Him, but few are genuinely serious about obeying the will of the Father, especially if it takes them out of their comfort zone. Obedience to God is simply too confining for most. They can't be in control, so they won't obey God. If it doesn't feel good to us, we ignore God's will and do it our way.

Pause a Moment

The will of the Father was perfect for His Son, and it is perfect for you too! Be encouraged to go the distance with Jesus.

Here is some of what is said when it comes to obeying God:

- Knowing what I need to do is one thing, but doing it is another.
- Disobedience to God is no different than telling a white lie; it doesn't affect my relationship with Him.
- God cares more about how I feel instead of how well I obey Him in this area.
- God gave us a free will, and we have every right to exercise it according to our good pleasure.

Here is what the Bible says about obedience to God:

- *"He who has My commandments and keeps them, it is he who loves Me. And he who loves Me will be loved by My Father, and I will love him and manifest Myself to him."* John 14: 20,21
- *"but those who are self-seeking and do not obey the truth, but obey unrighteousness…indignation and wrath, tribulation and anguish, on every soul of man who does evil."* Romans 2: 8,9
- *"For the time has come for judgment to begin at the house of God; and if it begins with us first, what will be the end of those who do not obey the gospel of God?"* 1Peter 4:17
- *"And we are His witnesses to these things, and so also is the Holy Spirit whom God has given to those who obey Him."* Acts 5:32

Here are a few things to remember about obeying God:

- God takes obedience very seriously. The Bible is filled with stories and examples of those who obeyed and those who didn't.
- If you want to share in the manifest presence of God, then you need to obey Him.
- If we want to live faithfully as Jesus did, we must be obedient children unto the Father.

Prayer Poem Ministry
"PERFECT FAITHFULNESS"

Perfect Faithfulness...a name for your Lord who is faithful through and through. Go to your Savior in honesty and true humility. He will show Himself to you... faithful through and through, inside and out, if you really long to see His perfect faithfulness. But for you who longs for God's faithfulness, there is more than mere performance. You long for God and for who He is, not only for what He does for you. Experience God's perfect faithfulness, and experience God! Desire God, want Him with all your heart, and long for nothing more than Himself. When you are passionate about God, you will pursue Him and stop at nothing. Then you will see His perfect faithfulness shine before you.

Call upon your Lord. Call Him, Perfect Faithfulness, and see His face in all that you do. Humble yourself in complete honesty before your Savior and King, and He will manifest Himself to you. Watch as your King reveals His faithful nature for you to imitate. Then imitate your King, and see the splendor of the Father inhabit your ways and your character. The Lord, your God, will care for you and nurture your life out of relationship with Him. Continue to long for God, desire Him and who He is, and He will lift you higher above your circumstances so that you can share in His faithful nature. Pursue your loving Lord passionately, with humility and honesty. And the faithfulness of God will shine bright before you and through you.

Knowing Versus Doing

Perhaps you have heard some say that the farthest distance to travel is the eighteen inches from your head to your heart. Isn't **that** the truth? I can't tell you how many times I have told God that I understand what He wants me to do but that I can't seem to do it. I want to obey, but can't. Generally, those are the times when my attitude is poor. I'm usually focusing on myself and my undesirable circumstances.

> **When I am dwelling on the hurts and disappointments of the past, I can't see the possibilities of the present, much less the future.**

It never seems like a consequence of disobedience. It feels more like "I can't do it, God!" But really, it is disobedience because those are the times when I am usually not abiding in God or in His love.

Those are the times when I haven't been living in an attitude of praise and thanksgiving. My prayer life was more of a one way system, instead of two ways between God and me. When I can't seem to obey, I am focused on myself, my way, and my timing instead of the perfect will of God. I have a hard time trusting God because my fellowship with the Holy Spirit has been mediocre at best. I have to remind myself that everything good comes out of relationship with God.

How well I abide in the Lord is directly related to how much time I have been spending with Him.

If my relationship with God is slacking, then I am not going to serve Him out of an obedient heart.

How do you travel the distance from head to heart? You have to start by realizing that it is not okay to know better and not obey. When we say that we know better but still can't move forward, it is no different than choosing not to obey God. Disobedience is disobedience when you know better. I don't see various shades of disobedience in God's spectrum. What I do see, is a loving God who knows the condition of each one's heart. He is ready to extend extravagant grace to anyone who is in need.

If you are struggling to overcome in an area, there is plenty of grace and help at your disposal. It all comes through relationship and by the power of the Holy Spirit. Then you won't be tempted to boast about how hard you worked to be obedient to God. If there is any striving to be done, it is in the area of pursuing God through your relationship. That is why the first three ingredients for living in the presence of God are so foundational. If you learn to praise God at all times, deliberately spend time with Him in prayer and fellowship, and commit your heart to Him and to His will... you will realize that your engine is warming up and running. Even if you sit quietly before God for a few minutes to love and thank Him, it is enough to get you going.

While you are walking with the Holy Spirit, you will learn from Him. Where you are weak, He will make you stronger. The Spirit of God will take your strengths and grow them for His use in the kingdom. God will give you insights, understanding, and wisdom so that you can continue to grow. But there will always be times of struggle.

When you struggle with the will of God, pray as Jesus did. "*O My Father, if it is possible, let this cup pass from Me; nevertheless, not as I will, but as You will* (Matthew 26:39). Can't you imagine the heavens opening up to help you accomplish your Father's will when you pray with the same sincerity as Jesus? I can almost hear the glorious sounds of Heaven booming down to earth to help you do it God's way. Then I can hear God say to you, "*Well done, good and faithful servant*" (Matthew 25: 23).

Time to Reflect

▸ Who sits at the control panel of your life? Do you write your own story, or does God?

▸ Do you set boundaries that keep you from obeying God? What are they?

▸ When is the distance from your head to your heart hardest to travel? When is it easiest?

▸ How can your travel plans become more simplistic and enjoyable?

_____
_____
_____
_____
_____

Living Application: Once you have had a prayerful mind-to-heart assessment, ask the Holy Spirit to help you in the areas where you are weak. Pray for a fresh revelation of God's view on obedience. Study the Scriptures, and read about those in the Bible who obeyed God and those who didn't. Allow yourself to relate to some of their circumstances. Even though they lived thousands of years ago, the heart of their issues is no different than yours. Your honesty with yourself and your transparency with God will help turn the engine over so that you can walk with the Holy Spirit to uncover more secrets of His kingdom and live in His presence each moment.

God's Pleasure

"Then Jesus said to them, 'When you lift up the Son of Man, then you will know that I am He, and that I do nothing of Myself, but as My Father taught Me, I speak these things. And He who sent Me is with Me. The Father has not left Me alone, for I always do those things that please Him'" (John 8: 28, 29). What pleases God the Father? We know that Jesus pleased Him immensely. The Scriptures tell of how God was well pleased with His Son. But how can **we** please God?

We give God great pleasure when we operate out of the same obedient attitude that Jesus had. Jesus stuck to the Father like glue; they were two peas in a pod. He lived in the presence of the Father and was obedient even to the cross. Whatever the Father said to do, Jesus did. You won't read about how Jesus reasoned with the Father or bargained with Him so that He wouldn't have to obey; He simply obeyed. You will also give God great pleasure when you obey Him.

You won't be able to feel God's great pleasure when you are disobedient. Disobedience will not cause God to leave you, but it will keep you from the sweet awareness of His pleasure. When we are sinning, we tend to hide from God for a time, just like Adam and Eve did.

Disobedience doesn't change God's love for you, it changes your attitude toward God. Suddenly He is not first, you are. God doesn't move away from us, we move away from Him. Then we tend to re-create the character of God for ourselves.

Have you ever caught yourself justifying your short comings by convincing yourself that God understands and is okay with them? Sometimes I think we forget just who He is! Even though we know that God extends grace and forgiveness, we can't assume that He is okay with disobedience. He is not going to overlook our disobedient hearts just because we say we love Him.

In fact, Jesus said *"If you love Me, keep my commandments"* (John 14:15). It's plain and simple; if we truly love God, we will obey what He commands. And when we obey Him, we please Him!

> **Pause a Moment**
>
> Love, honor, and obey God.
> The Holy Spirit will help you.

Be encouraged that you are living under the New Covenant...thanks to Jesus Christ! If we were forced to keep the law of the Old Testament, we would surely be condemned to the eternal fires, separated from God. None of us has had a perfect track record since becoming Christians. That's why we rejoice in God's wonderful grace that covers our mistakes and allows us to continue to walk with the Holy Spirit without guilt and condemnation. When we blow it, we must repent. That means that we must also change our ways and stay the course with a healthy reverence for God. God's grace was never meant to be taken for granted or misused. It is undeserved mercy that should draw us closer to God and who He really is. And when we draw closer to God, we will live according to His plan and ways.

We all want to hear God's voice. We desire to feel close to Him because God created us to love and know Him.

Everyone has an inner void that needs to be filled. Some fill it with the presence of the One True God and others attempt to fill it in other ways. For those of us who journey together in holy pursuit of God, there is the reward of His presence moment to moment.

The more we learn to live in the presence of God, the more obedient we are. And the more obedient we become, the more God will use us in His kingdom on earth. We will find ourselves bearing God's faithful character and earnestly desiring more of Him. And the pleasure of God will rest within our hearts forever.

God is Compassionate

Living with God gives us incredible opportunities to experience more of His character everyday. It isn't difficult to spot the heart of God in the midst of a normal day of events. His character marks everything that is good.

Look for God, and ask Him to shower you with more of His magnificent nature. Have you noticed that the more you walk with the Holy Spirit, the more of God's compassionate nature He reveals to you?

Once I imagined God to be like a fine governess, perhaps a Mary Poppins type. God is busy directing my steps, but He also helps me walk and live out His plan. His love governs me with a spoon full of sugar! God actually feels my joy, grief, pleasure, and pain. His compassionate nature pours over me all through the day. Even though the Lord is serious about His will for me...He's not stoic, without feeling, or distant. God is right there on the path of righteousness with me, feeling every emotion I have. He is always there to dress my wounds, wipe my tears, and re-tie my shoes.

I know that I am never alone; I sense His presence and compassion moment to moment. Oftentimes, the Holy Spirit and I sit right on the path together and have fun. That's when I sense that God is feeling my joy and imparting **His** joy back to me. Oh the beauty of living in the presence of God! His compassionate nature hovers over us and softens even the hardest heart.

Journey with me!

Let's take a short walk together through some of the Gospels and follow behind Jesus. I'm sure we will see some of His compassionate nature for people.

Matthew 14:14…*"And when Jesus went out He saw a great multitude; and He was moved with compassion for them, and healed their sick."*

Matthew 15:32…*"Now Jesus called His disciples to Himself and said, 'I have compassion on the multitude, because they have now continued with Me three days and have nothing to eat. And I do not want to send them away hungry, lest they faint on the way.'"*

Matthew 20:30, 32, 33…*"And behold, two blind men sitting by the road, when they heard that Jesus was passing by, cried out, saying, 'Have mercy on us, O Lord, Son of David!' So Jesus stood still and called them, and said, 'What do you want Me to do for you?' They said to Him, 'Lord, that our eyes may be opened.' So Jesus had compassion and touched their eyes. And immediately their eyes received sight, and they followed Him."*

Mark 1: 40, 41…*"Now a leper came to Him, imploring Him, kneeling down to Him and saying to Him, 'If you are willing, You can make me clean.' Then Jesus, moved with compassion, stretched out His hand and touched him, and said to him, 'I am willing; be cleansed.'"*

Mark 6: 34…*"And Jesus, when He came out, saw a great multitude and was moved with compassion for them, because they were like sheep not having a shepherd. So He began to teach them many things."*

Luke 7: 12-15…*"And when He came near the gate of the city, behold, a dead man was being carried out, the only son of his mother; and she was a widow. And a large crowd from the city was with her. When the Lord saw her, He had compassion on her and said to her, 'Do not weep.' Then He came and touched the open coffin, and those who carried him stood still. And He said, 'Young man, I say to you, arise' So he who was dead sat up and began to speak. And He presented him to his mother."*

Doesn't it almost feel like you were there? Can you imagine the emotion welling up inside of Jesus? Wasn't His compassion compelling? Right now, I am overwhelmed by the compassion of our Lord in those precious circumstances!

Now I'd like to share some of my own thoughts and emotions about each of those scriptures with you. Then maybe you can do the same thing as you remember experiencing the compassion of Jesus Christ in your own life.

Matthew 14:14...I remember the time when Amber and Ryan were very young and both woke up sick. We had something special to attend early that morning. Jesus must have seen my tears and was moved with compassion because they got better within a few minutes, and we were able to get ready and go.

Matthew 15:32...I can remember pursuing God about a certain issue. I fasted and prayed, pressed in very hard, and stayed the course with Him. I was hungry for the heart of God in the matter. God must have been moved with compassion because the Holy Spirit spoke directly into my spirit and I was finally satisfied as with the richest of foods.

Matthew 20:30, 32, 33...I remember crying out to God to open the eyes of my heart to let me see as He sees. Jesus must have been moved with compassion because suddenly the eyes of my heart were enlightened, I could see through the circumstances into the light, and was able to follow the will of God.

Mark 1: 40, 41...I remember milling over my selfish feelings and stumbling so badly about something that I actually felt unclean and totally unacceptable to God. I asked God to forgive me and make me feel cleansed and acceptable to Him once again. Surely He was moved with compassion because it was as if He reached His arms of forgiveness to me and cleansed me of my unrighteousness right there on the spot.

Mark 6: 34...I remember telling God that without His leading on the path, I would feel lost and all alone. The Good Shepherd was moved with compassion to lead and guide me through that dark hour into the light of day.

Luke 7: 12-15...The Lord heard my many desperate prayers of protection for my children and kept them from perilous times and dangers too grave to fathom. Indeed He was moved with compassion by a mother's prayers and the humble tears of total dependency upon Him for their safety and well being!

Time to Reflect

▸ How do you view God? Do you see Him as a God of emotion or more of indifference?

▸ How often do you notice the compassion of God in the ordinary circumstances of life?

▸ When do you sense His compassion the most?

▸ When was the last time you sat with God and felt His laughter and joy over you?

_____
_____
_____
_____

Living Application: Journey back through the six scriptures we just experienced together. Pray and ask the Holy Spirit to help you recall times when He was moved with compassion to help you continue on your path of righteousness. Write them down and save them for times when you need a faith booster. Then spend some time praising God with a full and thankful heart for His great compassion toward you.

Compassion or Sympathy?

For the longest time I interchanged these two words. They meant the same thing to me, so I used them synonymously. But a few years ago, I heard a teaching about the compassion of God and how Jesus reacted to people in New Testament times. I realized that sympathy is more of a feeling or state of mind, and compassion refers to an action.

When I am sympathetic, I'm more understanding of someone or their circumstances. Oftentimes feelings of sorrow accompany my sympathy. While it is nice to be understanding of what others are dealing with, it is only an awareness. Sometimes my understanding is expressed through kind words, and other times there are no words. I don't actually share in their distress; I simply feel sorry for them. Don't misunderstand and think that there is no use for sympathy. It is simply the initial step toward true compassion. You can stop at understanding and feeling sorrow, or you can go on.

On the other hand, compassion is powerful. We just looked at how the compassion of Jesus Christ ministered to the multitudes and changed the lives of others. We also journaled the ways in which God's compassionate heart has influenced our own lives. Compassion goes beyond the initial feelings of sorrow or pity, and it takes understanding to a new level. It goes from an inclination to an action because something unique happens to you.

Compassion says, "I feel what you are feeling."

It causes you to move on behalf of the other person's unfortunate circumstance. The reason you move on their behalf is because you **are moved**. Something inside compels you to do something about the adversity that is staring you in the face and breaking your heart.

Moving with compassion was a vital part of the ministry of Jesus Christ. Jesus didn't just feel sorry for those He came in contact with. He healed, touched, wept, fed, and did much more. That's because He felt what they felt. He experienced the emotion and the various degrees of pain and suffering of the people. The humanity of Jesus felt the burdens of people so that He could minister to them. His Deity enabled Him to minister to them in a flawless manner.

Pause a Moment

Desire the heart of God. Then you will be moved with compassion just as Jesus was.

Let's look at what compassion did for our eternal salvation.

"Surely He has borne our griefs and carried our sorrows; Yet we esteemed him stricken, smitten by God, and afflicted. But He was wounded for our transgressions, He was bruised for our iniquities; the chastisement for our peace was upon Him, and by His stripes we are healed. All we like sheep have gone astray; we have turned, every one, to his own way; and the Lord has laid on Him the iniquity of us all. He was oppressed and he was afflicted; yet He opened not His mouth; He was led as a lamb to the slaughter, and as a sheep before its shearers is silent, so He opened not His mouth." (Isaiah 53: 4-7)

- What do you hear in that powerful passage of Scripture?
- Can you feel the compassion of Christ for you?

When He carried our sorrows and grief, Jesus felt every single one. Jesus felt the consequences of our sins, and He was wounded for them. He took on the burden of our moral wickedness and the punishment for our lives of sin. And through it all... Jesus was moved with compassion, right to the cross for you and for me. There is no greater example of love and compassion for us. It looks a lot different than plain sympathy, doesn't it?

Compassion Curbs Judgement

One of the hardest things to overcome is the tendency to be judgmental. Sometimes we don't even realize that we are judging others; it just happens. Judgment also comes with a corrupt partner, criticism. Hand in hand, they destroy to the core.

Most of the time, judgment and criticism do their work silently. They capture your thoughts and affect your actions. When we destroy others silently, it is subtle. We don't notice that we are judging or criticizing. It's when we verbalize it that we catch ourselves in the act. Either way, it is just as dangerous because we hurt ourselves, others, and we damage our relationship with God. We know we are hurting others, but it is easy to overlook the affect it has upon our own lives.

Oftentimes if I am operating with judgment and criticism, I find that adversity tends to come my way. It feels like I step out from under the protection of the Holy Spirit when I get into a judgmental frenzy. I always notice that not much good happens when I lock myself into that frame of mind and heart. A few years ago, I was really sulking about something that was a real injustice to me. The more I thought about it, the more I sulked and carried a bad attitude. I found myself criticizing and judging every time I thought about my situation. It felt like a downward spiral, yet I'm embarrassed to say that it also felt good to justify my bad attitude. At least I thought it felt good. A few awful things plagued me during the weeks of that bad attitude season. Perhaps it was all a coincidence, but maybe it wasn't.

Later, I felt like the Holy Spirit showed me that judgment and criticism had created distance between the Father and me. I wasn't living in the awareness of His presence. I was behaving selfishly, was caught up in a judgmental attitude, and I had been badgering others in my heart. It even affected the way I was treating them. It was far from God's ways and attitude, and it was out of character for me to behave that way for so long. The Holy Spirit helped me to understand my need for repentance.

During that time of remorse, I learned something valuable about compassion that I'd like to share with you.

If I had stopped and listened to the voice of the Holy Spirit, I probably wouldn't have had to undergo that dizzy spiral. God would have given me eyes to see the situation as He saw it. I would have been moved with compassion instead of selfishness.

When I think of the hours I wasted judging and criticizing when I could have been moved with compassion for my adversaries, I am filled with sorrow.

God would have shown me their logic and hurts, and I could have been more like Jesus to them. When I realized that, I was moved with compassion, and I loved and served them with an unselfish heart. It felt good, and that's how you know you are operating with a right spirit. I pray this scripture on a regular basis for myself because I know how easy it is to slip into judgment instead of being moved with compassion.

"Create in me a clean heart, O God, and renew a steadfast spirit within me. Do not cast me away from Your presence, and do not take Your Holy Spirit from me. Restore to me the joy of Your salvation, and uphold me by Your generous Spirit" (Psalm 51: 10-12).

Let's look at some ways that compassion can triumph over judgment.

There is someone you know who bothers you and everyone else whenever she is around. You tend to avoid that person because she really is unpleasant. You can judge, or you can ask the Holy Spirit to reveal why this person behaves this way. Oftentimes, God will reveal a strong insecurity and show you how miserable that person really is. Then you are moved with compassion and want to reach out like Jesus would, instead of judging and criticizing.

Your friend never returns your phone calls and doesn't ever initiate communication with you. You always have to do the calling or emailing. It is so frustrating that you are tempted not to do it anymore. You can judge, or you can ask God to show you what is hidden behind the scenes. Perhaps the Holy Spirit will show you that your friend is overwhelmed with daily life and has trouble keeping up with relationships. Your friend wants to be different, but fails miserably every time. Then you are moved with compassion and don't mind being the initiator. You might even be moved enough to offer to help.

For over a year, you've been meeting with a group once a week for Bible study and fellowship. A new member joins the group, but talks constantly. Everyone in the group is annoyed, and gossip begins. You can go to God and ask Him how to handle it, or you can join in with judgment and criticism. The Holy Spirit might tell you that this person is quite nervous and insecure about being the only, new one in the group and is overcompensating in order to fit in. You imagine yourself in the same position. Moved with compassion, you understand and become more accepting just as Jesus would.

You will find that God always knows something you don't know, even when it involves others.

Generally I find that I am more of the problem than they are! Most of the time, we are too busy thinking about ourselves to incorporate the second ingredient for living in the presence of God. We forget to communicate with God, so we find ourselves judging and criticizing instead of moving with His compassion. Compassion will keep you out of trouble with yourself, others, and with God.

The Bible tells us not to be judgmental.

Jesus said, "*Do not judge others, and you will not be judged. For you will be treated as you treat others. The standard you use in judging is the standard by which you will be judged.*" (Matthew 7: 1,2 NLT) That sounds very serious. But we don't have to be concerned if we are in tune with the Holy Spirit and move with God's great compassion.

Remember that compassion is not just an understanding or sympathy; it moves you to action.

It is a very desirable character trait that we can glean from the Holy Spirit as we desire to live and move as Jesus did. We will have peace and find ourselves flourishing in the presence of God more often.

Time to Reflect

▸ How do you view compassion and sympathy? How will you change your thinking?

▸ Have you ever been truly moved by compassion? What happened?

▸ When you struggle with judgment, how can it affect your kinship with God?

▸ With whom is it difficult to avoid judgment and criticism? How can you change that?

_____
_____
_____
_____
_____

Living Application: Pray and ask the Holy Spirit to reveal your biggest obstacles that prevent you from moving with compassion toward others. Ask God to remove those obstacles and deposit the compassionate character of Jesus Christ into your heart. Practice incorporating the second ingredient for living in the presence of God by sitting quietly before Him, listening for His voice. Ask God lots of questions about how you can be a blessing and move with compassion instead of judgment. Sincerely desire a compassionate heart over a judgmental one!

God is Merciful

Mercy is a comforting word, and it emits a fresh aroma wherever it goes. It's what you and I welcome everyday because we have so many imperfections. Human nature tells us that we're going to blow it from time to time. We all need a few merciful handouts before each day comes to a close. I've never known anyone to oppose a generous helping of mercy when needed; it is always gladly received.

Our heavenly Father is lavish in His mercy, more than we can even fathom. Maybe He works hard while we sleep to prepare His merciful handouts for the next day so that they will be ready to go! However it happens, the fresh aroma of God's mercy is available for all who love and respect Him. Yes, it is God's own mercy that is extended to His children in need. God gives it straight from His character in its purest form, to ours.

When Mary was carrying Jesus in her womb, she praised God exclaiming..."*For He who is mighty has done great things for me, and holy is His name. And His mercy is on those who fear Him from generation to generation*" (Luke 1: 49, 50). Many generations later, here you are. You have accepted Jesus Christ as your Lord and Savior, and you love and respect God... so His mercy is upon you. God's **own** mercy is given to you for you to rejoice in.

What does mercy look like? Mercy is a lot like Christian grace because it is undeserved. It comes straight from the heart of God to those who love Him through Jesus Christ. When we stumble and fall on the journey, mercy is there to help us up as we look to Christ.

It doesn't matter what causes us to sin, mercy is always available as we change our ways and turn to the Savior.
Oftentimes, mercy says, "I forgive you" and extends kindness and compassion to our enemies and those who offend us.

You've seen the loving manifestation of mercy throughout the gospels when Jesus extended mercy and grace to everyone in need. Your devotion to your Savior drives a deeper desire for more of what He freely gave away, the merciful heart of the Father.

Yes, mercy is another one of God's radiant characteristics within your reach so that you can experience life in His presence more abundantly.

Mercy travels with a faithful companion, forgiveness. In fact, forgiveness likes to go arm in arm with mercy. It has a sharp affinity for mercy's personality. Likewise, mercy enjoys the company of forgiveness because the two of them accomplish great things together in the Kingdom of God. That is why it is also important for you to understand forgiveness if you are going to live with God moment to moment.

"And when they had come to the place called Calvary, there they crucified Him, and the criminals, one on the right hand and the other on the left. Then Jesus said, 'Father, forgive them, for they do not know what they do'" (Luke 23: 3,34).

Let's gaze at the most powerful display of forgiveness in history. The entire foundation for our assurance of eternal life rests upon the power of the cross of Jesus Christ over two thousand years ago. If Jesus didn't choose to go to the cross and bear our sins once and for all, we wouldn't even be thinking about living with God. We might not even exist today!

Because Jesus chose to accept the Father's divine mission, we are forgiven of our sins, and Heaven is our eternal home. It was all about living, dying, and rising from the dead, but forgiveness was certainly at the core. I can't express in words the beauty or the power of God's forgiveness toward us. I only know that without it, we are doomed.

The Bible tells us that we must forgive.
In fact, if we refuse to forgive, we are in grave danger!

Jesus said, *"For if you forgive men their trespasses, your heavenly Father will also forgive you. But if you do not forgive men their trespasses, neither will your Father forgive your trespasses"* (Matthew 6: 14, 15).

Even though these words of Jesus seem more like a cause and effect, I interpret them to be a definite mandate. I know I need to be forgiven, so I have to forgive...period! I also know that I **have been** forgiven, so I must forgive. That's easy to say, but it's not so easy to do! Don't you agree?

That's because free will and the desires of the flesh rage against our good intentions to forgive. They are so loud and obnoxious that it's almost impossible to ignore them and turn away. They hurl insults, threats, and even phony enticements in an effort to stifle the promptings of the Holy Spirit in you. They activate your pride to defy forgiveness and keep you from entering into a powerful encounter with it.

A serious battle takes place between good and evil to combat the power of the cross and the beauty of forgiveness. But because of the power of the Holy Spirit within, you have the ability to forgive, just as Jesus did.

You might be wondering what the Holy Spirit does inside of you that brings victory over your fleshly desires. *"...for it is God who works in you both to will and to do, for His good pleasure"* (Philippians 2:13). This scripture reminds us of when we gave our lives to Jesus Christ, and God gave us the supernatural desire and ability to overcome obstacles.

You will triumph over your hurdles when you submit to God, depend upon Him, and desire His will over your own. That's why we've already spent time talking about trusting God and depending upon His will for your life. Before you will ever have a sincere desire for God and His characteristics, He must be in charge.

When you focus on God's kingship, fellowship with Him, and practice trusting God, you will notice His unmistakable characteristics oozing from your spiritual pores. Mercy and the ability to forgive are precious companions as you travel on your journey to live with God moment to moment.

I'm sure you have noticed that your journey isn't always smooth sailing. Obstacles and road hazards are plentiful on the path of righteousness. One of the most dangerous stumbling blocks on the path is unforgiveness. It's like a black hole in your heart.

Unforgiveness feeds pride and invites bitterness and rejection to the feast. There is a whole guest list of negative consequences that are scheming for an invitation to the supper table where unforgiveness is the host. Nothing good ever results from feeding your selfish pride.

Why is unforgiveness so dangerous? The central message of Jesus Christ is one of love and forgiveness. When we refuse to forgive, a dagger penetrates our relationship with God and hardens our hearts toward Him and others. We turn away from the power of His cross and the beauty of God's forgiveness for our sins.

Refusing to forgive is direct disobedience to God and hinders us from going forward in our relationship with Him.

It makes it impossible to flourish in the presence of God because we can't help but pull away from Him and who He is. Unforgiveness welcomes a dark cloud that hovers over our thoughts and attitudes, eventually dictating our actions toward others. We veer away from our goal to be like Jesus and find ourselves on a dark alley, far from obtaining His merciful character.

The good news is that you can choose to forgive! Forgiveness puts love into motion, protecting your heart and relationship with God.

It is the key to moving forward when offenses threaten to shove you into reverse. Forgiveness frees you to experience the Holy Spirit.

It's not as if you have to muster up your own kind and loving feelings when you choose to forgive. Most aren't in a loving frame of mind when there has been an offense. In fact, it's quite the opposite. There's a good chance that you have a bad attitude when you've been hurt or offended, at least for a while. That's because you have feelings, and oftentimes they dictate your response to what comes your way.

It doesn't matter how deeply you feel, once you acknowledge your feelings you must react properly. You have to activate your choice to forgive. If you do it before your attitude gets out of control, then you will prevent the harmful consequences we talked about earlier.

Many think that forgiveness is a long process, but it is only a simple choice followed by a sweet prayer. Here's what you can do when an offense comes your way.

Make a decision that you are going to forgive the person who offended you. Then pray something like the following prayer:

Dear Lord, I have been offended, and I acknowledge my feelings to you right now. (You can even be specific about how you feel if it is helpful to you.) I don't want to harbor anything negative about this situation, so I am asking for your help. I forgive (name the person) because you have forgiven me, and I refuse to allow this offense to harm my relationship with You and hinder all you have for me on my journey. Holy Spirit, please protect my mind and heart and help me to walk in genuine forgiveness now and always. Thank you that You are doing a good work in me and that you help me keep my eyes on Jesus and not on the offense. (Then you can say "amen" to that!)

Time to Reflect

- Do you spend time rejoicing in God's mercy, or tend to take it for granted?
- Are you merciful, or are you stingy about extending mercy and grace?
- When were God's mercy and forgiveness unmistakable in your life. What was it like?
- How quick are you to forgive? What hinders your ability to forgive?

_____
_____
_____
_____

Living Application: Try to be more mindful of your opportunities to thank God for the undeserved mercy and grace that is freely extended to you. Don't focus on your faults; focus on God's merciful heart, and begin to desire this characteristic of God. Pray fervently about forgiveness and its impact upon your life and relationship with God. Ask the Holy Spirit to bring great revelation to your heart and mind so that you will choose to live a life of forgiveness instead of holding others captive in your heart. Listen for the voice of God as He whispers words of love, not condemnation, about His forgiveness for your sins. Practice trusting God by placing Him in control of your life's adventures so that you can learn to walk more freely in forgiveness and in His presence.

Watching God Work Wonders

Is forgiveness **really** a simple three step plan? As far as your part in forgiveness goes, it **is** that simple. Forgive, pray, and let go of the situation. The rest of the work is up to God, but you must cooperate.

The Holy Spirit will help you to not dwell on your situation. By forgiving, you hand the person over to God to deal with so that you don't have to. You will be tempted to do more or take matters into your own hands.

You will also be tempted to override your prayer and your decision to forgive. That is why all the other ingredients that we have discussed are so vital.

Make a point to stay connected to the Holy Spirit in your praise and gratitude toward God with prayer and fellowship. Trust God, and depend on Him to deal with your situation; it's His responsibility now. Always remember that God will take very, good care of you.

> **When you do the right thing, you have victory and become more than a conqueror.**
> *"Yet in all these things we are more than conquerors through Him who loved us."*
> (Romans 8: 37)

Jesus loves you so much that His Spirit is willing to act on your behalf to bring more good out of the situation than you can imagine. Just remember to remain in God's presence and let Him work things out His way and in His timing.

Forgiving, praying, and handing a situation over to God is a spiritual matter; you've done your part. After some time has gone by, how do you know the Holy Spirit is still working and that you haven't subconsciously taken matters into your own hands? Has forgiveness **really** taken place?

The beauty of the Holy Spirit's intervention is in His ability to see the whole picture. God knows the situation better than you do. Remember that the Holy Spirit lives in your heart, so He has a much better view of it than you do. He also knows the other person completely. He's taking care of the whole situation. Maybe you will see a change in the other person, and perhaps you won't. For sure, you will notice a difference in yourself.

The first thing you will notice is a sense of peace about your situation. Right after you pray, you will feel peaceful. That peace will linger to remind you that God is in control.

You might not have warm, fuzzy feelings about your offensive situation or the person involved. Depending on the circumstances, you might not even see that person again. But you can always count on the Holy Spirit to change your heart and attitude toward those who hurt you because we serve a God of restoration. You work at hearing God's voice for times like this. The Holy Spirit might prompt you to take a friendly initiative. That's easy because when you are prompted by God, He has already prepared your heart and the other person's heart as well.

The Holy Spirit does amazing things behind the scenes, and it is always for the better. The list of examples is endless because God goes to great lengths in order to help His children rebuild. You'll recognize sincere forgiveness when the Holy Spirit produces this kind of fruit in your your situation: love, joy, peace, patience, kindness, goodness, faithfulness, gentleness, and self-control.

I've watched the Holy Spirit deposit those sweet fruits in the life of a dear friend who chose to forgive instead of holding a grudge. My friend and her husband enjoyed working for an organization where they felt like their talents would be used to support and promote business. They shared a car, so being employed in the same place was a tremendous blessing. Although they were not working in the same department, they enjoyed having lunch together everyday; it felt like home!

A few days before the couple was scheduled to take vacation, my friend's husband was told that his employment was being terminated immediately. He was completely taken by surprise; actually they were both shocked. It is an involved story with much emotion on both sides. I only want to discuss what it was like for my friend. She felt her husband's termination of employment was unjustified. Many shook their heads in disbelief because they appreciated the job her husband had done and enjoyed working with him. This couple had been through serious financial difficulties and felt very blessed to be employed and have the opportunity to get back on their feet again. Unfortunately, this would be a serious set back for them. She was devastated by what felt like an attack on their livelihood; job opportunities in her husband's profession were hard to find. She was also concerned about returning to work the next day. She might have to interface with her husband's manager and others who were involved. It is one thing to be severely hurt, but another to interact with your offenders on a daily basis. What was she to do? A rebellious resignation was out of the question. It wasn't the right thing to do because the motivation behind it would not have been led by the goodness of the Holy Spirit. It would have been driven by selfish pride. They also needed the income from her job, so she had to return to work.

The Bible tells us that we are not to take vengeance on anyone; it is God's job to avenges us." *You shall not take vengeance, nor bear any grudge against the children of your people, but you shall love your neighbor as yourself: I am the Lord*" (Leviticus 19:18). In Deuteronomy 32: 35, God says, "*Vengeance is Mine.*" My friend was about to come face to face with learning to forgive.

I know I've said that the forgiveness process begins simply, but it isn't always easy to initiate. Disappointments and hurts get in the way, and sometimes anger affects a person's ability to move toward forgiveness. Over the next couple of weeks, the Holy Spirit helped my friend to come to terms with the situation and prepared her for the process of forgiveness. She understood that in order for her relationship with God to grow, she had to forgive. She told me that she and her husband prayed many times to release the situation into God's hands, choosing to forgive.

It still wasn't easy for her to return to work, but the Holy Spirit enabled her to go back and be gracious to everyone. She chose not to gossip or criticize, and that made a difference. My friend told me that each week got better for her as she placed her trust in God. **When she gave God control, He gave her self-control.** She felt peace beyond her own understanding and was able to be faithful to her commitments there.

The Holy Spirit helped her to be patient and kind. She has been able to extend goodness with the gentle nature of Christ. Her joy in life and in her Savior was never robbed from her. Recently, my incredible friend told me that the Holy Spirit has actually given her a new love for those who hurt her and her husband so deeply.

Regardless of who was right or wrong, my friend was dealt a perilous hand and chose not to hold anyone captive in her heart. She has never expected anything from those who caused the hurts. When she placed the matter in God's hands, she trusted in His ability to take care of it...period. I'm sure she prayed a prayer similar to the one you just read. Perhaps she had to pray it more than one time when she was tempted to respond to her challenge in ungodly ways. But the Holy Spirit gave her courage and strength to endure the grave hardship. She chose to forgive, and you just saw the evidence of the sweet fruits of the Spirit in her situation.

Can you imagine being in her shoes? Wouldn't you like to respond the way my friend did? I know that her behavior has been an inspiration to me. I hope that hearing her story helps you make better choices about forgiving.

We must be willing to do the right thing, forgive, and submit to God. Our willingness to forgive can alleviate distress and bring relief to hurtful situations. The Holy Spirit will bring peace and comfort instead of turmoil. Unforgiveness will have no power over you or me if we choose wisely in those challenging times. And the best part is that our relationship with God will continue to grow so that we can flourish with God moment to moment in His presence.

Prayer Poem Ministry
"INNOCENT LOVE"

Dear child of God, just as there is no substitute for God's presence, there is also no substitute for your presence and love for Him. Many will do what they may to gain God's acceptance, His approval, and even His favor. But the one who simply loves God with all innocence and sensitivity to His Spirit will receive His approval and even His favor. Dear child, here is a truth for you to grasp...Innocent love is everything! Out of innocent love comes obedience and perseverance. Patience is acquired from innocent love, and all that is required for life is found in love. That is why love is the greatest gift. Love is the beginning and the end. A devoted heart of love will enter into God's presence, and He will cherish it dearly!

God desires you! Run into His arms because they reach out to you now. God desires your love and presence just as you desire His; no one else will do. You are uniquely created to love and spend time with your Heavenly Father, so run into His arms of love. Don't be concerned with gaining great things from God, only gain His presence. Allow your child-like innocence to hear from God with incredible sensitivity. Listen to His approval for you and receive His favor in that sweet, innocent place.

When you radiate obedience, perseverance, and patience...praise your Heavenly Father for lavishly filling you with His own character traits. Cherish God's attributes, but live in His greatest gift to all mankind...love. God will cherish your heart of love for Him and others as you thrive in His presence forever.

God is Loving

"*As the Father loved Me, I also have loved you; abide in My love. This is My commandment, that you love one another as I have loved you.*" (John 15:9,12)

What is love? "*Love is patient and kind. Love is not jealous or boastful or proud or rude. It does not demand its own way. It is not irritable, and it keeps no recored of being wronged. It does not rejoice about injustice but rejoices whenever the truth wins out. Love never gives up, never loses faith, is always hopeful, and endures through every circumstance*" (1Corinthians 13:4-7 NLT).

While we discuss God's loving character, I'll be referring to this passage from the chapter on love in 1Corinthians. God's loving character cannot be duplicated because we couldn't possibly love as perfectly as He does. But God loves us so much that He is willing to give out as much of His loving character as we truly desire.

The key is in truly desiring God's love; it is different than ours.

When I read this passage on love, I can't help but share my thoughts with you.

"*Love is patient and kind.*" Have you ever been impatient enough that you come across as uncaring or indifferent? I know that impatience is sometimes associated with anger or other undesirable actions. But patience is always accompanied by kindness. Think about times when you have been very patient with others. They might not have even noticed your patience; but they tuned in to your kindness toward them. That is why I believe the scripture puts patience and kindness in the same sentence; it is almost like they are one.

"*Love is not jealous or boastful or proud or rude.*" These four words are what love is not. They work together to produce an unhealthy attitude. When we are envious, which comes from insecurity, we attempt to mask it with pride and arrogance. We try to appear better than we really think we are so that others don't notice where we are lacking. A bad attitude always produces rude behavior whether inward or outward.

"*It does not demand its own way.*" Love doesn't have a tantrum, nor does it force its way through life. If love demanded its own way, it would be very lonely. No one stays in the room very long with a spoiled brat who has fit after fit in order to win. Even when the fit is internalized, others pick up on a sour attitude and shy away.

"*It is not irritable, and it keeps no recored of being wronged.*" Many times, irritability comes from keeping track of transgressions. You've been wronged time and again, so mentally you log it all away. Before long your disposition changes and others are affected by your irritable mood swings. You never learned to forgive, so now unsightly consequences surface and affect others.

"It does not rejoice about injustice but rejoices whenever the truth wins out." You don't have to worry about how you might react to injustice. Stay connected to the Holy Spirit, and listen for His voice. Most often God will speak enough truth into your heart to turn on the light and affect your reaction to adversity. Then you will have a winning response to life's unfairness.

"Love never gives up, never loses faith, is always hopeful, and endures through every circumstance." It's as if I can see some of love's companions riding together with the wind of the Holy Spirit at their heels. I see the ruddy complexion of persistence, the depth in the eyes of faith and hope, and stamina pursed on the lips of endurance. There is strength in numbers, and these companions will make a real difference wherever and whenever they ride. They will finish strong!

These verses from Scripture inspire you to love as God wants you to love so that your journey is a reflection of Him. Perhaps the journey is to begin with kindness and a patient demeanor that puts everyone at ease when they are around you.

Your patience and kind heart will win the hearts of others, and you receive them with loving arms.

Soon you radiate the joy of the Lord for others when they succeed or achieve what you haven't yet. Your joy is so heartfelt that you actually experience their joy as if it happened to you. Bad attitude days become few and far between when the love of the Lord becomes yours.

There is no need to worry about yourself because you are living life on God's terms. You won't control anything, nor feel the need to put yourself first because you yield to the Holy Spirit's will in your life. God is putting you first. Eventually you go beyond knowing you have been forgiven, to understanding it, feeling it, and extending it to others. You will be surprised that your first inclination is to give the benefit of the doubt instead of judging and focusing on what is wrong.

Soon, truth becomes like a lamp stand where **you** will stand and shine God's light into every circumstance of life. Your courage to shine for righteousness and justice comes with a compassionate heart. In your courage, you will persevere in life with the kind of faith that moves mountains because hope tells you that you can expect the best from God.

Alas, God's love will amaze you when you find yourself running the race before you with great endurance, sure to finish well.

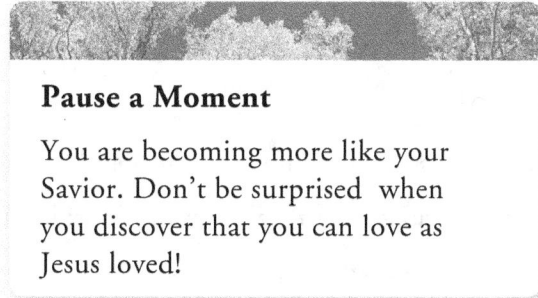

Pause a Moment

You are becoming more like your Savior. Don't be surprised when you discover that you can love as Jesus loved!

> **Picture this!**
>
> Now let's pull the verses of the scripture in 1Corinthians together to paint a picture of love. I am going to start in the center of the painting and sketch some kindness. It has a soft pastel look to it, but I am using a very thick, oil based paint that cannot be penetrated. The kindness looks so thick that you can almost see God's thumb print in it. There's enough kindness there for the whole world! Now I will smear the kindness a bit and feather it out across the canvass to leave a patient hew everywhere.
>
> Whatever else we do to the painting, you will always see the underlying effects of patience. There are some strokes of subdued color near the kindness. Although they don't boastfully stand out, they bring strength to the painting and won't reflect contrasting colors. They will naturally overshadow shades of jealousy, pride, and rudeness to add goodness to the painting.
>
> Next, I will put an inviting color on the canvass, a beautiful goldish red. The other colors of my palate can hardly wait to mingle on the canvass with my warm red. This inviting shade of red is compatible with everything else and brings out the best in the other colors in the painting. Now I add a very forgiving color to this love masterpiece. Its strokes will be plentiful and will look nicely with the patient undertones throughout. This color has the potential to wipe a dark slate clean with peaceful tones of forgiveness.
>
> In an effort to paint an effect of light all over the canvass, I will need just the right color and brush stroke. The color has to be bright, yet with enough transparency to not overwhelm the beauty of this masterpiece. Brush strokes of light and truth will emit from everywhere on the canvass, burning away injustice and unrighteousness.
>
> Lastly, I will blend a special formula together as a durable coat of resilience for the canvass. It won't matter who handles the painting or where it is hung. There is enough persistence, faith, hope, and endurance in the matrix of this formula to last an eternity! This original masterpiece simply cannot be duplicated. Though you might not be able to picture or fully understand the ways in which it was painted, you know it's a beauty and that there is no price to be placed on it.

There is also no price to be placed on love and no greater gift to receive. That is why we rejoice in the love of God that was put in our hearts through Jesus Christ. Even though we will never achieve perfect love, God is willing to share some of His loving character with each one of His children.

Time to Reflect

▸ When are you most patient and kind? With whom are you the most patient and kind?

▸ In what areas do you most struggle with jealousy? With pride? Are you ever rude?

▸ How do you respond to adversity and unfairness?

▸ When are you tempted to give up or lose hope? When is your faith most tested?

Living Application: Make a conscious effort to practice patience and kindness toward those you struggle with the most. Be mindful of your challenges, and pray for help in your areas of need. Ask the Holy Spirit to give you supernatural joy so that you can rejoice with others and experience their joy as if it was happening to you. Work at your response to adversity and unfairness by praying for eyes to see what God sees in your situations. Pray and ask the Holy Spirit to establish God's supremacy within your heart so that life won't be about you, but about Him and His will. When you are tested, shout to God with a loud cry for help. Then expect the Holy Spirit to renew your faith, hope, and endurance for your journey.

Loving God

We read about God's loving character throughout the Bible, and we walk in the loving footsteps of Jesus in the Gospels. The Holy Spirit reveals the love of the Father, and we experience His love first hand. Although we will never fully understand God's love and ways, we do embrace it and bask in it daily. But what does it mean to love God?

It is so easy to say that you love God; every Christian says that. What **do** they mean? Is it gratitude and joy about your Creator? Many will say that they "just know "they love God like they "just know" they love others; it is a feeling, and it's very private.

Perhaps part of loving God is a feeling, but true love for God goes deeper.

We are to love God just as He loves us, and His love for us goes far beyond a simple feeling. Jesus said, "*This is my commandment, that you love one another as I have loved you. Greater love has no one than this, than to lay down one's life for his friends. You are My friends if you do whatever I command you. No longer do I call you servants, for a servant does not know what his master is doing; but I have called you friends, for all things that I heard from My Father I have made known to you*" (John 15: 12-15).

This might sound like an impossible mission, but really it isn't. In the same way that the Holy Spirit helps you with everything else, He also helps you to love. God never intended for you to fend for yourself, and He won't leave you to journey alone. Yet God isn't going to do everything for you. Your Christian walk is a partnership with Him, and you have to do your part too. That is why you have been working to incorporate the necessary ingredients into your spiritual life.

By now I hope you are putting the pieces together concerning your journey and that you've used them sequentially. Remember that your part starts with living in an attitude of gratitude toward God, praising Him for everything. Your prayer life should be starting to look more like an intimate relationship with your Savior. By now you are developing a trusting friendship with the Lord, giving Him full control of your life. You desire God and His characteristics enough to ask the Holy Spirit to deposit them into your life so that you will be a true reflection of Christ. Continue to do your part by cooperating with the Holy Spirit. You have come really far on your journey, and I am very excited for you!

Let's go back to the scripture in John that you just read. Jesus tells His disciples that they are His friends. He calls them friends when they do what He commands and because they have a personal relationship with Him. Out of relationship with God we do what He commands, and we learn to love as He loves. Because we are learning to live with God moment by moment, we can expect His Spirit to help us on our journey. God's very own character traits within each of us enable us to love Him back as He loves us.

Loving God is unconditional and unselfish. It is putting into practice the ingredients that are necessary to thrive in His presence. We've spent time looking at God's character traits; now incorporate them into your life.

Loving God means being trustworthy, faithful, compassionate, merciful, and... just plain loving.

Loving Others

You already know that you are loved by God and that you must also love Him. Out of your love for God, comes a sincere love for others. Let's look at the words of Jesus again.

"Greater love has no one than this, than to lay down one's life for his friends."
(John 12: 13)

You might be thinking that this verse requires more than you are able to give. Only Jesus was supposed to do that! You don't want to die for anyone; nobody does. But do you care about others more than you care about yourself? I think that is what is really required of you. Yet perhaps that is even too much to ask because it suggests that you take from yourself and give to others. What if you don't feel like you have enough love to share? Laying down one's life goes against our human nature.

Loving others as Jesus did shouldn't be a painful procedure. By now you are learning to operate under the influence of the Holy Spirit, and the condition of your heart is improving. God's own Spirit brings revelation and empowers you to step out and love others His way.

Remember that you are looking at life through different eyes now. You are more aware of your time in the presence of God than ever before, and He is pouring His nature into yours. Before getting too nervous about laying down your life for others, spend some time with God and allow Him to teach you what that means. The Holy Spirit jumps for joy in our hearts whenever we seek His help. I can almost hear Him cheering because you need Him! That is exactly why He lives in your heart.

Just as we don't want our children to learn things the hard way, God doesn't want it to be tough on us either. In *Living in His Presence*, I told you my story about getting onto my "high horse" and going off to battle for selfish reasons. If the Holy Spirit hadn't stopped me from launching my attack, there would have been much blood shed. Not only would I have lost the battle, but the casualties would have been more than I could bear. I was planning to fight the battle with blood, sweat, and tears. His plan was for me to win the battle with love. God's love didn't want me to learn a valuable lesson the hard way; His plan was to spare me. Of course He left me with the choice to obey or not. At least the Holy Spirit warned me and gave me viable options. In the end, love won over selfishness; imagine that!

Sometimes it **is** hard to imagine how love can beat out selfishness because selfish pride is so tough. A selfish attitude acts like a bully and works to shove love into a corner. Human nature reminds us of our needs and desires; we don't have to figure that out. We've already got too many reasons why we matter most. We tend to look out for ourselves without blinking an eye. Then we wonder if we have enough for ourselves, so we work overtime to make sure we do. Selfishness fights the battle, but really we lose.

God's kind of love is bigger than selfishness and won't be bullied into the corner.

When love triumphs over selfish pride it looks much different. Love conquers selfishness and locks it up where it can't get out. Love reminds us of the needs and desires of others. It tells us that others matter more than we do because God is already taking good care of us.

Love sees others first and looks out for them.

It doesn't worry about having enough; it uses less effort and makes sure the other person has plenty. Love wins the battle, and there are no losers.

Remember that the love we are talking about isn't the fragile love we see on television or in the movies. God's kind of love is unconditional, and it is tenacious. It endures when fragile love falls apart at the seams. Genuine love that comes from God isn't merely a feeling; it is an act of your will. It is a choice to love someone, especially those who seem unlovable. Loving someone who absolutely frustrates you every time you are together is quite a chore, unless you've made the choice to love God's way.

Let's take a look at loving that frustrating person. You can bite your tongue and clench your teeth in an effort to be loving. You can roll your eyes and murmur to yourself while you fake your feelings. You can even resolve to love that person because you should. Or, you can ask the Holy Spirit to bring revelation about the person.

You've been practicing listening for God's voice, so you are able to hear His perspective. The Holy Spirit might whisper something profound enough to move you to compassion for that person. Suddenly, you have the supernatural ability to love as God does. Does that mean you have loving feelings for that person automatically? Sometimes you will and sometimes you won't. That depends upon each situation.

It is our responsibility to love no matter how we feel.

Anyone who has been married long enough knows that there are times when we feel love for our spouse and days when we don't. It is much harder to lay down your life when you're upset with your spouse. It's also really tough to lay it down when you've misplaced your loving feelings. But Jesus didn't put a conditional clause in His command to lay down your life. You won't find a way out in the fine print. If there is any fine print at all, it might read: greater love has no one than this...Jesus Christ!!

**We have Greater Love living inside of us,
and His love is released when ours gets stuck.**

We don't have to come with anything more than the will to love and the choice to do it God's way. After that, the Holy Spirit does a beautiful job. How do you think people maintain loving, lasting relationships? It is only by sheer will and with the help of the Holy Spirit. Anyone who tells you otherwise doesn't know the true love of Jesus Christ.

"You have heard that it was said, 'You shall love your neighbor and hate your enemy.' But I say to you, love your enemies, bless those who curse you, do good to those who hate you, and pray for those who spitefully use you and persecute you, that you may be sons of your Father in heaven; for He makes His sun rise on the evil and on the good, and sends rain on the just and on the unjust. For if you love those who love you, what reward have you? Do not even the tax collectors do so? Therefore you shall be perfect, just as your Father in heaven is perfect" (Matthew 5: 43-48).

I can almost hear you sigh as you contemplate this difficult passage of scripture. It has never been one of my favorites!

My first feelings about this passage were worrisome. It is difficult enough to pray objectively for my enemies much less love them. I'd have to eat a lot of humble pie before I can do good deeds and bless those who have hurt me or my loved ones. How can I be perfect like my Father when I am a sinner? Perhaps you've had similar questions and can relate.

The Holy Spirit revealed something about this passage to me that I would like to share with you. The only way I can love, bless and do good, or even pray with a right attitude is if I do it through Jesus Christ. And if I do it through Him, then His character traits will emerge. I will trust God and be faithful to act according to His will. I will probably be moved with His compassion to extend mercy and forgiveness beyond my own understanding.

Then the genuine love of God will pour into my circumstances to help me love my enemy. When I pursue Christ, not my sinful ways...I please my Father in Heaven. I hope this helps you like it has helped me!

You've heard others talk about tough love or hard love. This kind of love draws a line, puts up boundaries, and stands firm. None of us likes to be on the giving or the receiving end of this type of love. Even though there are times for tough love, they don't have to be quite as hard as we make it.

Everyone has their own issues and circumstances in life. And every one of those is unique, requiring specific measures. But when we operate with God's love through the Holy Spirit instead of with determination through our own strength, love wins the toughest of battles.

Time to Reflect

▸ How does your life reflect your love for God? What are your strengths and weaknesses?

▸ In times of trial, what does your love for God look like? How about in the good times?

▸ Can a competitive nature affect one's ability to love others? What concerns are there?

▸ How unconditional is your love for those who test your patience...at home, work, etc?

_____
_____
_____
_____
_____

Living Application: Read and meditate upon the following Psalms in your Bible that exalt God's character: Psalm 8, 19, 29, 103, 104, 139, 148, and 150. Spend some quality time praying about God's character and His love. Ask the Holy Spirit to give you insights, revelations, and the ability to love like God loves in order to overcome the stumbling blocks on your journey. Listen intensely for the voice of God, and invite the Holy Spirit to work in your heart as He desires.

A Roadside Perk

Just when we think that God's loving character is all about loving God and others, He sends a roadside perk, a blessing, to make our journey even better. When we love like God loves, we live in peace. I've heard it said that if someone could mix up a batch of peace and bottle it up to sell, they could make a fortune! Yet Jesus said, *"Peace I leave with you, My peace I give to you; not as the world gives do I give to you"* (John 14:27).

There is no price to be placed on the peace of Christ. It comes from Jesus, and it stays with us by the power of the Holy Spirit. It is the unexpected gift that comes from loving others God's way. It is also the gift that keeps on giving. When you receive the peace of Christ, it comes with no regrets!

I really don't like regrets, especially when I can't do anything about them. Regrets affect others and rob me of God's joy. But when I love as Jesus loved, I receive God's peace with no regrets.

I am sure you can name other roadside perks that come from loving God's way; the blessings are plentiful. It's funny how we think we are doing things for God, when oftentimes it turns out to be for our good benefit and pleasure.

What Do They See?

In a culture obsessed with appearance, we are very conscious of how we look to others. Physical appearance is emphasized more than you and I would like to admit. It's effects on our society are astronomical! We could have another whole conversation about that, but for now let's just agree that physical appearance is crucial in today's world.

There is also a tremendous focus on outward appearance that goes beyond how we look physically. Everyone likes to look good to the world and talk about their walk, whether or not they are Christians. How many times have you been introduced to someone and the first question you are asked is: "What do you do?" We like for others to know what we do, what we have, where we've been, and what we've accomplished. We are good at letting them know what we believe and don't believe. We argue our points, and we pick and choose battles. We offer advice and oftentimes have the solution. We like to look good on paper, in the mirror, and to the world.

What do others really see?

- Do others see your God given love?

- Would they sense you are a real follower of Jesus Christ if you hadn't told them?

- I know your love **is** different, but does it **appear** to be different than worldly love?

- Is the love of Christ evident in your life?

It has been said that people are more impressed by what they see and feel, not from what they hear. I challenge you to pay as much attention to your spiritual appearance as you do to your outward appearance. There is nothing wrong with asking others what they do for a living. But sometimes I wish the introductory question was more like: "Why do you think we are all on this earth together?" Depending on the answer, others would have an opportunity to see and feel the love of God firsthand.

No Worries

Let's look briefly at what Jesus said one more time. "*Therefore you shall be perfect, just as your Father in heaven is perfect*" (Matthew 5:48). Does that mean you can't make a mistake? What happens when we make mistakes or feel like we've failed?

We are all a work in progress, and we journey only by the grace of God.

If we were automatically perfect then we wouldn't need a Savior. Does that mean we can ignore God's Word, be oblivious to sin, and live life on our own terms? Paul, the apostle, says no.

"For if we sin willfully after we have received the knowledge of the truth, there no longer remains a sacrifice for sins, but a certain fearful expectation of judgment." (Hebrews 10: 26-27)

Jesus said, *"My grace is sufficient for you, for My strength is made perfect in weakness"* (2Corinthians 12:9). Paul had many struggles; his transparency continues to be an encouragement today. He said, *"Therefore most gladly I will rather boast in my infirmities, that the power of Christ may rest upon me. Therefore I take pleasure in infirmities, in reproaches, in needs, in persecutions, in distresses, for Christ's sake. For when I am weak, then I am strong"* (2Corinthians 12: 9,19).

Jesus knew we would make mistakes when He went to His cross for our sins.

He knows our hearts and intentions. His grace is plentiful; it covers a multitude of sins. Jesus is perfect. Remain in Him, abide in Him, and receive His grace when you need it. No worries, only perfect love through Christ!

1st Corinthians, Love Chapter...check list

- Allow the Holy Spirit to guide you in difficulties, with patience and kindness.
- Rejoice with a sincere heart for others who have what you desire.
- Let go of the strong need for praise and recognition.
- Be a quiet, good listener before speaking truth into hurting situations with others.
- Practice looking out for others more than yourself.
- Respond to others with words and actions that restore instead of destroy.
- Throw away your records of offenses, for future reference.
- Rejoice in truth, and delight in righteousness and justice.
- Keep a loose grip on worldly possessions.
- Invite God to sit at the control panel of your life.
- Let hope win over doubt on your journey.
- Run your race with supernatural endurance, focused on Jesus Christ.

Come to the Buffet

Remember that you have been invited to a buffet feast where you can have all of God that you truly desire. There are no limitations when it comes to how much of God you may have. God desires all of **you**; why not ask for all of Him? *"For to everyone who has, more will be given, and he will have abundance"* (Matthew 25:29).

Go to the Lamb's feast, recline with Jesus, and enjoy everything that He has to offer. Don't be shy or overly polite about your portions; bring your biggest plate for the Holy Spirit to fill. The world we live in has limitations, but God doesn't.

There's more than enough of His delicious character to go around. I can't imagine either of us telling God to stop the huge portions of His trustworthiness, faithfulness, compassion, mercy, or love. God wants us to have an abundance of Him. And we want it all, right? "*Ho! Everyone who thirsts, come to the waters; and you who have no money; come, buy and eat. Yes, come, buy wine and milk without money and without price. Why do you spend money for what is not bread, and your wages for what does not satisfy? Listen carefully to Me, eat what is good, and let your soul delight itself in abundance.*" (Isaiah 55:1, 2)

Let's not waste our time and resources on what has no eternal value. Let's go straight for golden eternity!

The invitation is irresistible, the price is affordable, and the buffet feast is superb! Join me there, and together we will enjoy God's delicious character.

Even when we feast on everything that is of God, there are still plenty of leftovers to give away to others. Many will have their hands out for a helping or two of our Lord without really understanding their hunger. They've been busy spending their money and using their wages for perishable items that will never satisfy them.

When you walk by and God's sweet aroma follows you, the watching world can't help but want some too.

Share what you've been given so that they can be satisfied as well. "*Then Peter said, 'silver and gold I do not have, but what I do have I give you. In the name of Jesus Christ of Nazareth, rise up and walk*'" (Acts 3:6). The eyes of those watching suddenly fix upon the same buffet feast you enjoy. Portions of reliability, dependability, and commitment have never looked so appetizing to them.

They never thought of tasting faithfulness sitting atop plates of loyalty and steadfastness. Helpings of obedience were like icing on the cake! The eagerness to exchange brown bags of judgment and criticism for soup tureens of velvety compassion is quite a sight to see. Then their eyes met mercy and forgiveness for the first time on the buffet line, and they wanted to dish them up in huge portions. But the love of God sitting on crystal, dessert plates was the most appetizing of all. No longer would they be satisfied with the sights and smells at the feast; they want to indulge in the goodness.

The watching world around you wants to rise up and walk, and you can point them to the arms of Jesus of Nazareth. Then they will taste, eat, and be satisfied at the Lord's buffet table just like you. The tastes of God and His characteristics will inspire them on a journey of their own to learn to live with God moment by moment. And it all started with you and the sweet aroma of God that was irresistible to all those around.

Prayer Poem Ministry
"CLOSE TO YOUR HEART"

Your Father bursts forth in love and joy over you. Do you see His buttons of gold? They are so bright that they are almost blinding. Watch, dear child, as the Father's buttons pop and burst to expose His heart of joy over you. Have you ever seen such splendor? Have you seen such a heart of joy? There will never be another one like it.

What you gaze upon is true love, complete and unselfish. It is unconditional love, pure and spotless, accepting of you, and ready to draw you into His arms. Draw near as you step inside, close to your Father's heart. You will be transformed, never to be the same as you draw closer. You won't want to leave your Father's intimate presence. The best part is that you are His little one, and you don't ever have to leave His precious presence.

May the love of God warm your heart so that you burst forth in love and joy over **Him**. Let your joy shine so bright that the world is blinded by the light in your life. God sees your splendor and your heart of joy that reflects His, and He is pleased. Let God's love transform yours into complete and unselfish love. Allow your Father to take you beyond yourself to unconditional love that is pure and spotless. The Holy Spirit is drawing you near, so take a step closer to the heart of God and rest there. Do you sense His intimate presence? Let your Father minister His unconditional love to you and hold you near and dear forever.

Your Desire for God

The more you taste and partake in the character of God, the more your desire for God will grow. You can't ever get enough of your Lord once you sample His ways and presence. The five characteristics of God that we discussed are enough to fill the biggest dinner plate you can find.

Your Heavenly Father waits for you to desire Him as much as He desires you, and He calls you directly to Himself! You practice His presence when you are trustworthy, faithful, compassionate, merciful, and loving.

Don't forget the rest of the rich ingredients that are necessary for you to flourish in God's presence. Spend time sitting with God in praise and worship so that your life will be an act of worship. Be in awe of your Lord and Master when He whispers sweet words of love to you in prayer and fellowship. Never take the voice of God for granted, but treasure every word you hear. Remember that you serve the Almighty and that He must remain in control at all times.

Learn to depend upon God and trust Jesus to live in and through you each moment. The Holy Spirit is much more capable of taking care of the world and your life than you are, so submit to the will of the Father and notice how much more fulfilled you are. Then you can earnestly desire God and all that He is.

Always remember how much you are loved and desired by the Almighty. He is yours to take home to your humble heart and live with each moment. Jesus is Lord, first prize, and your gold medal. Wear His winsome smile for the world to see and rejoice that you belong to Him. Cherish everything about your relationship with God, and allow His Spirit to reign supreme in your heart and keep you happily in love with Him.

Let's pray!

Dear Lord, you could have anything in the world you want, yet you desire me. I am so blessed to be called one of yours and to share in all that you are and all that you have for me. I am overwhelmed by your goodness and generosity. Thank you for infusing your very own character into mine. Holy Spirit, please help me to be the trustworthy one that others know they can depend on. I want to be faithful and operate with the integrity of Christ, so please empower me with your Spirit each moment. Thank you that I am growing sensitive to Your Spirit more each day and that I am moved with the compassion of Jesus by those you place on my path. I receive your mercy and forgiveness and want to freely extend my hand to others so that they will see You in me. Most of all, Dear God, thank you for your love for me; I love you so much! I want to be an ambassador of love in the Kingdom of God; thank you for that great privilege. I pray that others will come to know You as they see Your love in me.

Fifth Ingredient

Abandonment...
Letting Go	172
Lots of Babies	173
Surrender or Abandonment?	175
Terms of Abandonment	177
Your Gift to God	179
Dangerous Road Blocks	181
Kingdom Rights	186
Love and Abandonment	189
Empty Pockets	192
The Peace of Christ	195
It's Well Worth It	197
Don't Settle	199
Time to Get Excited	201
Life Changing Perks	204
Abandonment is Not...	205
Practicing Abandonment	206

> *"I once thought these things were valuable, but now I consider them worthless because of what Christ has done. Yes, everything else is worthless when compared with the infinite value of knowing Christ Jesus my Lord.*
> *For His sake I have discarded everything else, counting it all as garbage, so that I could gain Christ and become one with Him."*
> Philippians 3: 7-9 NLT

We rejoice in Christ Jesus, and we find ourselves undone in His everlasting presence. The privilege of knowing God is what Christians seek on a daily basis because life isn't worth living without Him. All that matters is the joy of knowing God intimately in the moment to moment of life. There's nothing we wouldn't do for Christ!

- Do we have to go to the ends of the earth for Christ?
- Is it alright to place limitations on how far we will go for Him?
- What **would** we do for the sake of knowing Jesus Christ in this life?

Now it's finally time for the last ingredient necessary in order to live in the presence of God moment to moment. Your journey will always be a work in progress, but hopefully you've noticed growth with the addition of each ingredient. Remember that they work together and that they are progressive. That is why we add them in one at a time as you are ready. This last ingredient is just as powerful and vital as the others, and it will take your relationship with God to greater depths. Be sure to add it to your spiritual life so that you can journey with greater strength and confidence.

Your last ingredient will usher you to an ultimate place of intimacy with God on a regular basis.

It will help you conquer your fleshly desires and strong will in the ordinary circumstances of life. Without it you will find yourself tangled in your own efforts to tame the desires of the flesh. Yet **with** this powerful ingredient, you will encounter new dimensions of intimacy with your loving Lord. The final ingredient that we will discuss is called abandonment.

You might recall that in *Living in His Presence* I mentioned how frightened I was at the thought of abandonment. I didn't want to face my new, biggest fear because it was a mysterious unknown. What did God mean when He said that abandonment was crucial to my spiritual growth and relationship with Him?

I wanted to stop my progress with the fourth ingredient and settle for a better relationship with God instead of an excellent one. But the Holy Spirit pursued me; He wouldn't **let** me settle. God knew how much I had grown to depend upon Him and desire Him. A simple settlement would redirect my journey enough to keep me from entering His presence moment to moment. God knew I wouldn't be happy with this in the long term. His Spirit helped me understand abandonment enough to pursue Him on the right path.

In *Living in His Presence,* we talked about the how the Holy Spirit helped me to picture abandonment. A long time ago, before adoption was a choice… young mothers made painful, selfless decisions to let go of their babies when they couldn't care for them. A mother placed her baby on the doorstep of someone who was very qualified to give care, knowing it was the best thing to do. The mother turned her back, walked away, and never reclaimed her child again. She wasn't forced to give up the child; it was her choice to let go. Although it was an agonizing decision to let go of her baby, the young mom knew she did the right thing for her child and herself.

Imagine the internal struggle that took place before she could simply let go. Can't you almost feel the anguish of that struggling mom? Yet through the pain and anguish, a resolve to do the right thing drove the decision. It was a painful decision to live with, but in the end there was great peace and a better life for the mother and child.

Lots of Babies

Unfortunately, we give birth to lots of overwhelming "babies." This can be burdensome and keep us from a better life in the presence of God. For various reasons, we struggle to carry them throughout life. We haul them everywhere we go because we think it's easier than dealing with them. They come in all shapes and sizes, sometimes disguised and undetected.

Without intending to, we fling hurts and disappointments over our shoulders and lug them around year after year. Then after they turn into anger and bitterness, we are dragged down. We bottle up guilt and shame and then store them in secret places where they can only damage the healthy flow of blood supply to the heart. We allow worry and fear to grip our minds and cause dangerous levels of stress.

These are just a few of the "babies" that arrive unplanned and out of nowhere. They require too much time and energy and rob us of valuable rest in the Lord. We know life would be much more fulfilling if we didn't have to tend to them. What should we do with them?

There's only one person who would welcome those kinds of "babies" on a front doorstep. Actually, He prefers that we leave them at the foot of His cross where they really belong. Jesus desires for us to gather up our unwanted "babies," and drop them off for Him to deal with. Just like young mothers long ago, we must leave them and turn our backs. We have to drive away and not return later when we are tempted to get them back.

This is God's perfect plan for us, but I can't say it is always easy to carry out.

**The longer we bear our burdens,
the harder it is to let them go.
Various strongholds seem to tag along.**

Strongholds come in many varieties, and they can be cleverly disguised.

Perhaps you are struggling with sin and don't recognize it because your stronghold is deception. Deception tells you that what you are doing really isn't that bad, so you don't have to deal with it. Deception also hinders your ability to discern the voice of the Holy Spirit and clouds your understanding of God's Word. You can become so deceived that you can't tell right from wrong. You find yourself covering up sinful ways and hauling them everywhere you go just as we talked about before. Deception jeopardizes your relationship with God.

Maybe you have allowed too many hurts and disappointments over the years because your stronghold is stubbornness. Stubbornness keeps you from admitting your feelings and working through your frustrations. Then stubbornness kicks up a notch and spits anger in your face. This stronghold won't let you process your anger and forgive; it just hangs over your shoulders and drags you down into the miry muck. Your relationship with God can hit a stubborn wall and suffer great damage.

If you have guilt or shame bottled up inside, your stronghold might be poor self-esteem. It hurls insults at you and shatters the real you. It always finds fault with you and reminds you that you are less than you really are. Poor self-esteem also affects your relationship with others because it forces you to compare yourself to them. It can break your heart and cut off the healthy flow of blood supply to it. You might not even feel worthy of a vibrant relationship with God.

Suppose worry and fear grip your mind; your stronghold could be false humility. It makes you think you are trusting God, when really you are making your ends meet yourself. False humility smothers faith, and the only thing you breath is self-made oxygen. Soon your supply runs out, faith is crippled, and you can't move forward. You don't understand why you are consumed with your thoughts because you have done everything possible in the name of Jesus to overcome them. You are worn out from the wear and tear of your emotions and levels of stress. Your relationship with God can become paralyzed.

Although I can't begin to name all the strongholds in life, I do hope that I have exposed you to a strong undercurrent that can keep a healthy relationship with God from surfacing.

Life's strongholds dominate and pull us under unless the power of the cross of Jesus Christ obliterates them.

"For the weapons of our warfare are not carnal but mighty in God for pulling down strongholds" (2 Corinthians 10: 3-5). Your true stronghold is Jesus Christ; He is the real fortress and your deliverer. *"The Lord is my rock and my fortress and my deliverer; my God, my strength, in whom I will trust; my shield and the horn of my salvation, my stronghold"* (Psalm 18: 1-3). By His Holy Spirit we can learn to swim without concern for the undercurrents.

You and I will have the opportunity to discuss abandonment more. You will come to understand that abandonment is really a simple letting go. Before long you will have the courage to take your "babies" to the cross, let them go, turn around, and walk away.

Time to Reflect

‣ How are you feeling about adding the final ingredient into your spiritual life now?

‣ What are you most excited about, and what are your concerns?

‣ In what ways do you see abandonment as a powerful tool to live in God's presence?

‣ Name a burden that you'd like to take to the cross of Jesus Christ. Is there a stronghold?

_____
_____
_____
_____
_____

Living Application: Pray about this powerful ingredient, and ask God to give you a glimpse of how it will improve your relationship with Him. Verbalize your concerns to the Lord, and ask Him to relieve any anxious thoughts and feelings so that you can best journey with Him. As we discuss abandonment, if other burdens come to mind, journal about them and ask the Holy Spirit to help you deal with them. Begin to really pray about a desire for an even deeper, more meaningful relationship with God.

Surrender or Abandonment?

In *Living in His Presence*, we discussed the difference between acts of surrender and those that come from true abandonment. I remember that it took me a while to get used to thinking of them separately. Maybe you are still working on that, so let's look at them again.

> Every time I think about surrender, I see a battleground; let's picture it together. It's loud, smoky, and dangerous. There is a profound sense of darkness all around due to the gray haze that lingers from the fire of destructive weapons. Wounded soldiers are being carried off on stretchers into hospital tents that reek with infection. The casualties are too numerous to count. Bodies are everywhere, some with a cloth over their faces while others are yet to be discovered. Military officers are issuing orders right and left, yelling at the top of their lungs over the sounds of gunshots. There's talk of surrender because the battle is too fierce and the casualties are growing. There is a sense of great fear and despair at the thought of surrendering into unknown territory. Everyone knows that some day another battle will erupt when the soldiers are strong enough to fight again. But right now, everyone is either wounded, dead, or worn out; they can't fight anymore. So the surrender flag goes up, and the soldiers are taken captive. There's no peace treaty, only bloodshed. It's not a pretty picture.

A long time ago, in those first years of marriage to my husband, I engaged in numerous acts of surrender. I'll share that story with with you now.

We were young and quite unprepared for marriage. Although we came from similar backgrounds, our family lives were very different. I expected Mike to do the same things around our house that my dad did. When I realized that he wasn't going to be just like my dad, I was furious. Every effort I made to change my husband failed and caused strife between us. Soon after we became Christians and dedicated our lives to Jesus, I learned about surrender. After years of trying to change Mike, I was ready to surrender him to God. As I recall that time, I realize that I had an ulterior motive. In surrendering Mike to God, I was sure to get my way. In my prayer to God, I remember presenting my husband to Him and telling Him that it was now His job to change Mike. When it didn't seem like my prayer was answered, I took matters into my own hands again. All that did was stir up trouble and cause pain in my marriage. Then I surrendered Mike to God again. "I give up, God, **You** make him be like my dad." But Mike didn't start acting like my dad. Guess what I did then? I took back my surrender and went out onto the battleground myself. The injuries became too numerous to sustain, and I knew I was losing the battle. This pitiful state went on for a long time before I realized that I was never going to turn my husband into a younger version of my father. Thankfully, because we were growing Christians, we learned to work through our differences according to the principles of the Bible. If I had an understanding of abandonment then, we might not have had to endure such pain and hardship. My motive wouldn't have been to change Mike. My issue wasn't with him; it was with myself and my selfish will. If I had known better, I would have abandoned my selfishness and asked God to help me understand my husband better. I would have been more open to the working of the Holy Spirit in my heart. Surrender brought much bloodshed. Abandonment would have protected our hearts and brought lasting peace.

When we settle for surrender, we can picture a battleground similar to the one we just looked at and the one I created many years ago. That might seem overly dramatic, but I don't think it is. Because life is what it is…imperfect and volatile, we find ourselves on the battlefield often. We engage in external and internal battles. Sometimes we are at war with others, and then there are times when our struggles are within.

Some of the strongholds that we just discussed lead us into dangerous battles without protection. Our fighting conditions and situations aren't much different than what we just pictured; it can look gruesome. When we can't bear our firearms any longer and have lost hope, we decide to surrender. We tell God that we give in and that we are surrendering it all to Him. Oftentimes what really happens is that we give in for a while, but then life's issues cause us to take back what we surrendered. It becomes a vicious circle of give and take, and it is exhausting, costly, and futile.

There's no peaceful feeling in surrender. Sometimes we end up worse after numerous attempts at surrender than if we hadn't tried at all.

Now let's remember how the Holy Spirit pictured abandonment. Even though it was painful for the mother to leave her baby, she knew it was the right thing to do. She had come to terms with this process. Her child will be better off because she is not able to give proper care. No one is forcing the young mother, she simply chooses to let go of her rights as a parent. There is trauma, but it's not nearly as volatile as the battleground of surrender. When the mother lets go of her child and turns her back to walk away, it is complete and permanent. She will have tearful moments, but eventually there will be great peace. She is trusting that her decision will be good for both of them.

When you choose abandonment over surrender, you've eliminated a brutal battle. You've let go and simply let God! How did you do that? By the time you are ready for abandonment, you have already come to worship and revere the Lord with a grateful heart. Your relationship with Him through prayer and fellowship has deepened considerably. You know you can't do anything without the help of the Holy Spirit. And you desire God and His character traits more than anything. Of course you can let go of your "babies" in life because you are placing them at the foot of the cross of your Savior.

> **It doesn't matter what you're letting go of; it could be struggles, desires, or anything that hinders your relationship with God... simply letting go brings great peace.**

"*and the peace of God, which surpasses all understanding, will guard your hearts and minds through Christ Jesus*" (Philippians 4:7). This amazing scripture tells us that God's peace comes even in the midst of turmoil.

One example of letting go can be seen in the decision my friend made to allow God to work in her spouse's heart and stop flirtatious actions. The desire to confront and control him was great. She was in serious pain and wanted to resolve the issue once and for all. Instead she chose to let go and allow God to work it out. She talks about the peaceful feeling that God gave her. Before letting go, my friend did her best to find peace on her own. But when she placed her issue at the foot of the cross of Christ, peace flowed like a river to wash away stress and strains. What a beautiful choice!

Terms of Abandonment

Before you can let go of anything at all, you have to come to terms with abandonment. You need to understand that it is the right thing to do. Abandonment is a foreign thought to most; all they've known is surrender. Surrender has become a buzz word in accountability groups. We discuss our issues with others, and we surrender this and that. And we do it over and again before we realize it's not working. People usually have to come to the end of their rope before they are ready to let go. Then they aren't sure **how** to let go. That's when it is time to come to terms with abandonment.

You will come to terms with abandonment while you practice using the other four ingredients for living in God's precious presence. As your relationship with God grows to new levels, you will truly **understand** your need for Him. There isn't anything you won't do to live, move, and have your being with God. Then letting go of whatever hinders your relationship isn't that traumatic.

That is why abandonment is the last ingredient that goes into the pot. You can do this because you've already sampled the other four. You don't have to do it the hard way and fail at numerous attempts at surrender before letting go. Instead, you can spend your time growing your relationship with God, already living out the terms of abandonment.

Part of coming to terms with abandonment is facing the fear factor that can act as a road block on your journey. Remember how afraid I was of abandonment? As long as I kept my biggest fear to myself, it grew and gained momentum. Before long, I imagined myself being exiled from my sweet family. I wondered if abandonment meant that I would have to endure grave hardships for the sake of knowing Christ. Would I be diminished to nothing and wonder who I really was? Maybe I would become a doormat and have to turn the other cheek one too many times. It was a downward spiral from there!

One day, I decided to let my fears out and share them with my friend, Terri. Just letting them out was a relief. Terri reminded me that I had already come this far and that the Holy Spirit had been generous with me. She encouraged me to take another step and expect God's goodness to continue. God did meet me in that fearful state, and that is when He gave me the more peaceful picture of abandonment.

If you are dealing with some fear, it is very important that you let it out; don't internalize it. Find someone who will listen, encourage, and pray for you. Then expect God to meet you as well and help you continue in His goodness. Maybe you will be like me, and the first thing you need to abandon is your **fear** of abandonment. God will help you do it just as He helped me. You are not in a race, and you don't have to measure up to anyone. Remember that the Holy Spirit has helped you with the other four ingredients, so He's not going to desert you now.

Coming to terms with abandonment means that God must be in control.

It means that you can't put God in a box and tell Him exactly what He can and can't do with your life. Remember that you are a part of God's life; He is not a mere part of yours. I used to draw lines in the sand and tell the Holy Spirit that He couldn't cross them. My husband calls them show stoppers. They tell God that the show will only go on under certain conditions and that He can only go so far. Surely God would understand my limitations and respect my boundaries, wouldn't He?

What God really understood is that I didn't want to pursue any more growth in my relationship with Him. I was bold to put my show stopper out for God, so He decided to be bold with me.

The Holy Spirit said that either God is God in my life, or He isn't! God reminded me that if a relationship doesn't grow, it will slowly deteriorate. I didn't want that, so there could be no more lines in the sand and no show stoppers for me!

Later, I learned that without the other four ingredients for living with God moment to moment, we will all draw lines in the sand and allow only so much of God's control. We won't be able to let go and come to terms with abandonment if we are only willing to go just so far with God. Don't let that discourage your journey to live in God's presence. We still have a lot more to discuss that I think will be helpful to you.

> **Remember that you have the Holy Spirit to guide you and walk with you every step of the way on your journey.**
> *"For He Himself has said, 'I will never leave you nor forsake you.'"*
> (Hebrews 13: 5)

Time to Reflect

- What have you surrendered and taken back that you need to let go of and abandon?
- How much do you desire God? Are you ready to explore abandonment?
- What fears or anxious thoughts do you have concerning abandonment?
- Do you draw lines in the sand for God? What show stoppers hinder your relationship?

_____
_____
_____
_____

Living Application: Note your experience with surrender and how well it worked for you in specific situations. List your expectations of abandonment and your fears. Journal how you might see your life change and how it will affect your relationship with God. Pray about your limitations with God and of God. Ask the Holy Spirit to help you to come to terms with abandonment and let go of fear and control.

Your Gift to God

Abandonment is like an expensive gift given to God.

You can smell it's costly fragrance through the elegant wrapping. It is presented to God with great humility and reverence. It tells God that He is worth all you have and that there is nothing you won't do for Him. And your gift of abandonment is a true reflection of your deep love for God. There isn't much you can give to God; He already has it all. *"For every beast of the forest is Mine, and the cattle on a thousand hills. I know all the birds of the mountains, and the wild beasts of the field are Mine. If I were hungry, I would not tell you; for the world is Mine, and all its fullness."* (Psalm 50: 10-12).

No one can love God like you can, and everything you have for Him is unique and one of a kind. When you let go in peaceful abandonment to God, He receives your priceless gift with open arms. He sees it as righteousness before Him because you are giving of yourself just as Jesus did. God smiles with great pleasure because He knows that your abandonment is going to bring you closer to Him. He can already see your relationship with Him soaring to new heights. His good plans and purpose for your life are secured in the vault in His heart. They are unlocked and released when your love for God presents yourself in holy abandonment to Him.

You say that there is nothing you won't do for God, but He is telling you that there is nothing He won't do for you! Your gift of abandonment to God returns back to you in the form of His precious presence on your journey to live with Him each moment. You can travel at higher speeds on the interstate when nothing is hindering your relationship with God.

Our son, Ryan, really struggled when it was time for him to buy his first car at the age of seventeen. Ryan pictured a sporty car that he could feel really good about investing all of his savings into. Yet he didn't want to have to work a full-time job in order to have his dream vehicle at such a young age. My husband found a reliable car for Ryan that was within his budget. The only problem was that the color of the car was more appealing to a girl. It was really hard for Ryan because he wanted something reliable, but at seventeen the look and feel of the car was important too. He really prayed about it and decided to let go of his desires and do the right thing. He told God that if his parents thought this was a good car and that if He wanted him to buy it, then he would let go. Here is an excerpt from the email that he sent to his dad who was out of town when Ryan made his decision.

"I have made my decision about the car. I have been praying about it, and this is what I believe God has told me. I think that when buying a used car at the price that I can afford, it is safe to say that I will most likely not find a perfect one. Add my many specifics, and the probability of finding just the right car is low. It could look great, but if it rattles or has too many miles, it could be a bad deal for me. When I look at the car I am driving now, I realize that this newer one looks pretty good! So I am going to give up my idea of the perfect car, and I will do what you guys and God think I should do. For these reasons, I have decided to consider this car as a major possibility and have it checked out to be sure it is okay." Ryan's email really touched our hearts. We were so pleased that he checked in with God and that he was trying his best to honor Him as well as both of us. We knew that his decision was prayerful, thoughtful, yet painful. It was tempting to jump in there and help him financially so he could afford a better car. But God told us not to intervene. Ryan's willingness to let go of his will to honor his parents and his Heavenly Father was like a gift. God must have been very pleased because He gave Ryan a very unexpected gift as well. It is a long story, but I want you to know that the day after our son made his decision, a brand new car suddenly came into the picture. It was sporty, but not fast...thankfully!

The new car was the exact color that Ryan envisioned, and it was less expensive than the used car. It only had twelve miles on it and came with a warranty which would take Ryan through his college years. Can you see the hand of God in this story? Our son will always remember how God reacted to his act of abandonment and gave him his heart's desire.

Ryan never expected a gift or added blessing when he let go of his desires. None of us should let go or abandon anything with an expectation that God is going to give it back or compensate in some way for the loss. That's like playing games with God or asking Him to live on your terms. God can do whatever He desires with your act of abandonment. Never make demands or expect God to perform for you.

Prayer Poem Ministry
"THE INWARD PATH"

Listen, child of God, to the words of love that He brings to you today. Words of encouragement, strength, and peace come your way. For God loves you deep within the inner core of His very being, and the path to His heart has been opened. But it is a path untraveled by most, for it is costly. What price is there to travel such a path? Only that your love for your Father be limitless, open, and subject to His leadership. Only that you would let go and come to Him via the inward path. Then you will find joy, love, peace, and encouragement. For as you seek the inward path unto God's heart, you will find that the secrets, promises, and the truths of His Word will come to life. Seek your Lord this way, and you shall have it all. He opens the access to the inward path today, and you may travel and find God's heart ready and open to you.

God calls you His child, and His words of love are for today and every day. Let His words of love minister to your heart and bring peace and strength as only God can do. Don't hesitate to go deeper with God and allow Him to take you closer to the core of His being every moment. Allow your love to be open to God, and don't limit all He has for you because you aren't willing to travel the inward path. Let go, and abandon all your cares and shortcomings so that you can travel the inward path more easily. Joy, love, peace, and encouragement await you there, so don't delay, only let go and find your place with God. He will uncover the secrets and will fulfill the promises of the Bible before your eyes. You can have it all, but you must seek the Lord in the intimacy of His heart. Let the love of God draw you inward and journey with Him in the safety of the shadow of His wings. He loves you so!

Dangerous Road Blocks

Selfishness

Beware of this serious road block that can appear on any avenue of your journey with God. It is very dangerous because it's almost always at the root of every sin. It is the main obstacle that keeps us from letting go in peaceful abandonment before the Lord.

You might be thinking that you are good at dodging the selfish road blocks on your journey. But I assure you that they come up when you least expect them. You could be rolling along with God at high speeds and have to come to a screeching halt when selfishness blocks the road. Oftentimes you won't even know how it got there because you were doing so well. That's because selfishness is like a hidden tyrant; it dictates without you knowing it. It feeds the flesh, and that feels good to our sin nature. It is a strong desire that must be dealt with each time it appears on your journey.

The best thing you can do in order to bypass selfishness is to be aware that you are not exempt. Everyone deals with selfishness in some form. Selfishness is associated with rebellion, indifference, control, intolerance, egotism, and conceit. It has more companions than I can list, and they stay strong together, to cause you to sin.

It doesn't matter how old you are, you must beware of selfishness. Even little toddlers struggle with a selfish nature. I know we didn't teach our children to say "no;" it just came out one day. We had to teach them not to be so self-centered. Adolescents and teens dabble with rebellion and allow selfish tendencies to dominate and hurt others. What about self-seeking agendas that permeate businesses, institutions, and government?

You would think that adults would have enough maturity to avoid selfish traps, but we don't. Selfishness is rampant and continues to rise to astronomical levels in our society. If you think that you are beyond it, then you are at risk.

Let's look at a few blatant acts of selfishness and see how they lurk in the dark on various avenues of life. You might not stroll down these avenues on a regular basis, but it is important to see what a selfish attitude can do.

- You've extended numerous invitations for dinner to some friends, but they never accept. Now they've invited you and you'd like to go, but you decline because they've never accepted your invitations. That is a rebellious attitude stemming from selfishness.

- Your best friends weren't there for you yesterday when you really needed some help. But they stop by today, and you behave with indifference toward them. You are a bit aloof and short with your comments because they disappointed you. That subtle indifference came from your selfish attitude.

- You are an active member of an important committee. In the last few meetings, you've been overruled every time you try to force your way. You can't control the direction of the committee, so you decide to resign. You need to overrule your own selfishness and be a team player.

- A co-worker is culturally different from you. This person bothers you with their foreign accent, mannerisms, and traditions. You have no tolerance for this, and become rude. You even gossip about this person. That kind of intolerance is selfish because you are focused on your feelings.

- You like to be right, and you strive to be correct at all costs, even when it hurts or offends others. You are feeding your ego and could pay a huge price for your selfishness.

- You turn your nose at those who are unattractive or unlovable. Your tendency is to judge by outer appearance. You've developed your own standard for self-worth, a form of conceit. Selfishness wins.

You might not have guessed that selfishness could be lying underneath each example we just looked at. That is because it is so sly, and it disguises itself. But in each example, self mattered most instead of the other person. That kind of attitude will keep anyone from letting go in genuine abandonment, and any relationship with God will suffer.

Now let's consider a more subtle form of selfishness that is more common. Although it hides in the dark, it can be found almost everywhere.

Oftentimes others are blessed in areas of life where yours might be lacking. You cross paths on a frequent basis, so you have to interact with them.

- Do you have genuine joy for others when life goes their way, or do you struggle with envy?
- Do you wish you had their financial gain or high profile lifestyle?
- How do you feel when their children have privileges or talents that yours don't have?
- If their children grow up to appear more successful in life than yours do, can you handle that?
- Does your heart sink when your friends are more recognized for their work at church than you are?
- Do you ever desire to be like others so that you could have their lifestyle?
- Have you ever secretly wished your spouse was like someone else's or felt like you deserve someone better?

This form of selfishness hits every one of us in the face from time to time. I would be very surprised if you aren't nodding yes to one or more of those questions. It's really hard to be happy for others when they have what we want. We tend to put up a good front and appear happy, but on the inside we struggle to find genuine joy. Yet the Bible gives us a mandate in Romans 12: 15. *"Rejoice with those who rejoice, and weep with those who weep."* You can't muster up sincere joy at will. It is a fruit of the Holy Spirit, the evidence of His influence on your life.

Your deep relationship with the Holy Spirit will enable you to jump selfish hurdles without falling.

Pause a Moment

If you just noticed a few selfish hurdles, don't be too hard on yourself or stop your pursuit of intimacy with God. Cling to Jesus; He's there for you.

Selfish Pride

It's very difficult to let go in genuine abandonment when selfishness blocks the way. Now add pride to the equation, and the sum is astronomical! Selfish pride demands, kicks and screams, and sends you far from the awareness of God's presence. God never leaves you; He is ever present, and it doesn't matter if you are aware of it or not. But when you are all about yourself, you can't be aware of God or become anything like Him. Your desires and your ways will always matter most if you are not walking in the awareness of God. Yet when you are mindful of someone other than yourself, you barge through every barricade meant to keep you from God.

Selfish pride lives life its own way and takes the credit for everything. It would even choose to suffer consequences if it can just be left on its own. It is an arrogant attitude that produces a haughty lifestyle away from God. When needs arise, selfish pride comes first and decides what to do based on self. It won't take the blame because it only sees one side.

Selfish pride squelches the work of God because it won't come under the quiet control of the Holy Spirit. Selfish pride likes the word "me" best, and all other words are antagonistic. It doesn't sound like a very nice person could emerge from selfish pride, does it? Yet you and I will fall prey to its ways and move into the darkness if we don't yield to the promptings of the Holy Spirit.

Selfish pride judges and criticizes at the drop of the hat. It is so wrapped up in itself that others don't quite meet up to its standards. We have to be careful because it also cleverly disguises itself so that it can rule and reign. It won't own up to its own mistakes because it is rooted in sin.

Selfish pride shouts on various avenues of life to say:

- It's my way or the highway!
- Of course they will listen to me…I've invested my time and resources into them!
- Why aren't they catering to me, don't they know who I am?
- After all I've done for them, this is the thanks I get?
- I'll have nothing to do with them; they rubbed me the wrong way.

We might not actually say these things out loud, but oftentimes they are part of our thoughts. Thoughts influence our actions, and actions change our ways to bring about new belief systems. *"…casting down arguments and every high thing that exalts itself against the knowledge of God, bringing every thought into captivity to the obedience of Christ"* (2Corinthians 10:5).

We have to be aware of thoughts that Jesus wouldn't approve of and get rid of them before they cause us to sin. That is easier said than done! If it was that easy, we'd all be breezing along with nothing but pleasing thoughts to God. That is not always the case. I've discovered that when I am doing something mindless, like drying my hair, my mind wanders off to dangerous places. Now that I know that about myself, I am cautious during mindless times.

Sometimes I get going so fast that I don't stop to ponder my thoughts, so I ask God to help me know when my thoughts are headed in a wrong direction. That is why it is important to practice listening for the voice of the Holy Spirit. Oftentimes, He is shouting so that we will hear His warnings. But if we haven't learned to listen in the quiet times, we won't recognize God's voice in the midst of danger. The more we take each prideful thought captive and stop the progression of sin, the less we are tempted with sinful thoughts.

But what can you do when you wrestle with the same thoughts time and again?

Perhaps you struggle because you are working hard to surrender them instead of letting God help you to abandon them. Your struggle will come back if you try to deal with it yourself instead of letting it go and placing it at the cross of Christ. By now you understand that you are not in life's battle alone; you have fellowship with the Holy Spirit. You have the power of God living as close to you as it can get, in your heart. Welcome the work of the Holy Spirit, and you will have victory over selfish, prideful thoughts.

"*Pride goes before destruction, and a haughty spirit before a fall*" (Proverbs 16:18). Here we are warned to deal with prideful tendencies before they destroy us. I am not very good at problem solving. I would rather go the extra mile to prevent something than have to mend fences. It upsets me to hurt others, and I always wonder if permanent damage occurred because of carelessness or selfish pride. If you are like me at all, you will want the Holy Spirit to help you make choices as Jesus would. It is much easier to go with God's route than re-route later to get out of trouble.

We've discussed so many wonderful things about learning to live with God moment by moment. I know I always come away with such a positive feeling, and I am ready to go the next step with the Lord. When we have to talk about sinful attitudes like selfishness and selfish pride, it isn't as invigorating. I don't mean to be pointing the finger at you; I merely share with you hoping to help.

Pause a Moment

When we become painfully aware of our faults, we shouldn't feel unworthy of intimacy with God. We simply stay the course and allow the Holy Spirit to work in our lives.

Whenever I have to come to terms with dangerous road blocks on my journey, I tend to wonder if it's worth the trouble. If you are discouraged and feel like you aren't going to get there, then I encourage you to hang in there and continue on this good journey.

You are an overcomer through your great faith in Christ Jesus, and you have the Holy Spirit leading and guiding you. You have come so far on your journey, and you will learn to let go of everything that hinders your relationship with God. It will be like icing on your cake! *"For whatever is born of God overcomes the world. And this is the victory that has overcome the world—our faith"* (1John 5:4).

Time to Reflect

▸ What selfish tendencies do you have that could hinder your relationship with God?

▸ In what ways do they impact others? How do they affect your journey to live with God?

▸ When do your thoughts roam into unsafe territories? How can you prevent trouble?

▸ In what ways have you been an overcomer on your journey to live in God's presence?

_____
_____
_____
_____
_____

Living Application: Set aside a specific time when you can devote yourself to a period of personal reflection. You might need to get away from your surroundings for a few hours to be alone with God. Pray about your ways, and ask the Holy Spirit to reveal any hidden tendencies toward selfishness or selfish pride. Allow God to be specific and identify those who might have been affected by your tendencies. Then ask the Holy Spirit to uncover hidden unforgiveness toward anyone who might have hurt you through selfishness or selfish pride. Now spend the rest of your time in prayer, forgiving others and asking God to forgive you. Allow God to minister His love and compassion to you. Receive all that the Holy Spirit has for you, and listen for His voice.

Kingdom Rights

Whenever I read the second chapter of Hebrews, I always come away amazed at how Jesus lived even though He was born a king. The author of Hebrews paints a vivid picture of Jesus as a leader. Perhaps that is where we get the term, "servant leadership."

Jesus gave up His kingdom rights so that He could be a perfect leader for us. In order for Him to do that, Jesus had to endure temptation and great suffering. Why is that so important? You would think that as a king, His leadership would be similar to what we see in governments throughout the world. We would expect Jesus to travel with body guards, rule from a distance, or protect Himself behind leaded, glass windows.

Instead, Jesus bent down in the dirt and became dusty and tired. His attire didn't give away His heritage, nor did His choices for companionship. He had no kingly manner to speak of; you would never suspect His royalty. Yet Jesus was the King of all the kings. He simply developed a new style of leadership, servant leadership. He rolled up His sleeves and fulfilled all prophecy as a humble servant.

Jesus walked with the weak, and gave courage to the meek.

He went without sleep, but never stopped tending the sheep.

Jesus fed the hungry crowd, and silenced the selfish proud.

He healed the blind so they could see, and set each and every captive free.

Jesus didn't gloat in glorious fame; instead He took all the blame.

He bore our sins to prevent our loss, and gave life when He embraced His cross.

"Therefore, it was necessary for him to be made in every respect like us, his brothers and sisters, so that he could be our merciful and faithful High Priest before God. Then he could offer a sacrifice that would take away the sins of the people. Since he himself has gone through suffering and testing, he is able to help us when we are being tested" (Hebrews 2:17,18 NLT).

Jesus is a flawless example of servant leadership. He is a true captain of the team, and He is approachable.

He earns the love and respect of His peers by serving them. He leads the way onto the field but then turns to encourage each team member to be their best. When the team is down, Jesus is faithful as a genuine captain should be. He takes a beating on the field with His peers and teaches them never to give up. He feels their disappointments because He is still one of them. And Jesus celebrates victory with His team. He eats with them at the banquet table, and they know they are valued by their beloved captain.

If anyone should have exercised kingly rights, it should have been Jesus. He was born with the right to demand His rights! Yet Jesus gave up His kingly rights and became a servant instead. If Jesus gave up His rights in order to demonstrate true servant leadership, then so should we. Yet everywhere I go, I hear about our rights for this and that. I'm not talking about our political rights; that would have to be a whole, different conversation. I am referring to normal day to day living when we strive to look out for "number one."

Unless we control our thoughts and actions, human nature insists that we demand our way with an attitude of selfish pride. Can you hear the shouts of selfish pride that we discussed earlier? Those shouts come from the need to be "number one" and exercise our rights.

Please understand that as followers of Jesus Christ, we have no earthly rights. The only rights we have are found in the righteousness of Jesus Christ because of what He has done for us.

- We have a right to go to Heaven if Jesus is our Lord and Savior.
- We have the right to be called sons and daughters in Christ.
- We have the right to follow in His footsteps and live our lives for Christ.
- We have the right to proclaim the promises of the Bible as yes and amen.
- We have the right to love God first and then love our neighbor as ourselves.

We also have the right to suffer just as Jesus did.

There was a time when our daughter, Amber, had to let go and abandon her rights. It could have been a harmful situation, but the Holy Spirit worked in her heart to avoid disaster. Amber was a member of a group that was working on a project. One person made the final decisions about the project and would soon decide about Amber's level of involvement. Amber had an expectation of the leader that was based on her own way of treating people. She expected the leader to be fair and do the right thing. Amber also felt like she had certain rights as a member of the group and wanted those rights to be honored. When the leader's decisions didn't meet her expectation, Amber was hurt and disappointed. It wasn't a bad decision, it just didn't line up with her rights as a member of the group. At first, she thought to withdraw and be of no help to the group because she felt embarrassed. But after much prayer, she realized that her attitude could damage her relationship with God. Amber feared that her feelings might lead to anger and frustration. If she wallowed in her sadness, bitterness and unforgiveness would contaminate her tender heart. Her pride told her that she had a right to exercise her rights, but God was telling her to let go. I can't say that it was easy, but Amber chose to do the right thing. She abandoned her rights and let go of her expectations. She decided to trust the Holy Spirit to help her deal with her feelings. Not only did God help her cope, He empowered her to engage in a way that made her a blessing to everyone. She went the extra mile and become a group servant. When Amber abandoned her rights and expectations at the foot of the cross and turned away, Jesus bent down and took them. He changed her hurtful attitude into a servant's attitude. She didn't demand her rights, she became a blessing instead. Amber decided that her relationship with God was more important than her pride.

Are you beginning to understand the idea? It isn't all about you or me. It's about the righteousness of Jesus Christ and His influence in our lives so we will imitate His ways. This was hard for me to understand. I read and heard about it, and I pretty much agreed with it. But it took a real revelation from the Holy Spirit to understand it and be willing to learn to live this way. Leaving your rights and embracing a lifestyle within the righteousness of Jesus Christ is abandonment in fine form.

Love and Abandonment

"A new commandment I give to you, that you love one another; as I have loved you, that you also love one another" (John 13: 34,35). We will learn to obey this command from Jesus when we practice abandonment as part of our lifestyle. It doesn't matter what definition you find for love, if it doesn't talk about giving of yourself, then it is not a valid definition. We've been too conditioned to believe that love is about feeling. Our culture speaks mostly of falling in and out of love. We hear, "I love you, but I am not **in love** with you anymore." It's in the movies, on television, and in real life. And it's so very sad. It's the reason that many marriages end. It was all about feelings from the start. What happened to laying one's life down?

Real love is one of self-sacrifice, putting others first.
"Greater love has no one than this,
than to lay down one's life for his friends." **(John 15:13)**

When we operate with selfish pride, we aren't able to love God or anyone the way the Bible tells us to love. We try, but we fail miserably if we aren't operating out of genuine love. How can anyone lay down their life for someone if self matters the most? It's not like we don't want to help others; its just that we only do it when it is convenient. That's conditional love, not greater love. It hinges upon selfishness and selfish pride which prevents you from loving God. Remember that greater love is one of self denial, and it puts God first.

Perhaps you have seen the movie, *Fiddler on the Roof*. What a delightful depiction of love, commitment, and tradition! There is a scene in the movie where the husband and wife are alone together. The husband asks his wife if she loves him. She answers, "What...do I love you?" He asks her again and she responds in a similar way. Then the wife reminds her husband that she has cooked, cleaned, and washed his clothes for twenty-five years. But the husband asks her again if she loves him. The wife responds again with all that she has done for him in the past twenty-five years and then asks, "If that's not love...what is?" "Then you love me," replies the husband. She tells him that after twenty-five years... she supposes she does. Then the husband tells her that after twenty-five years he supposes that he loves her too! Although there had to be some feeling, they only referred to their actions and commitments.

Love is not just a feeling; it is an action and an act of your will.

You love intentionally, not just spontaneously. Remember our discussion about 1Corinthians chapter 13? Everything the Bible says about love as the greatest gift requires some kind of action. 1Corinthians 13: 4 starts out by saying that love suffers long. I don't think it is talking about a broken heart because of rejection. It is talking about the work and effort we must put forth in order to love like Jesus loves us. It is talking about self-sacrifice and peaceful abandonment. It means putting others before yourself, and that is tough to do on a regular basis.

> Jim, Amber's husband, recently practiced loving abandonment on her behalf when she needed to be on a very restrictive diet for a few months. In order for her health to improve, it was imperative that she strictly adhere to the plan without exception. The list of approved foods was minimal, and the diet was extreme. Convenience foods were taboo, restaurants were almost eliminated, and temptations were everywhere. You can imagine how difficult that must have been for Amber. It would take dedication, great discipline, and lots of prayer. Our families were supportive of Amber, and prayer was plentiful. But Jim went beyond the call of duty as her husband. He decided to put Amber first and do the diet with her for as long as she needed to be on it. You would think that he might be somewhat dedicated around his wife but then maintain his normal diet the rest of the time. That in itself would have been helpful for her. Yet Jim chose to totally abandon his eating habits in order to support, encourage, and benefit Amber. That might not sound like a spiritual matter, but I assure you it was loving abandonment at its best. It was letting go and laying down his desires for her best interest. He placed his cravings at the foot of the cross and turned his back on them. Both would agree that the Holy Spirit gave them the discipline to remain dedicated to the cause. Can you imagine the celebration dinner they had when Amber was released? I picture the Holy Spirit sitting there laughing with them!

None of us can love without giving of ourselves. And giving of ourselves means letting go in peaceful abandonment. How can anyone do that consistently? One thing is for sure; if you work at loving the way Jesus loved, you will fail. It is impossible without the work of the Holy Spirit. I think God designed it that way so that we would need Him. If you could heed the first and greatest commandment on your own, why would you need a Savior?

It becomes a matter of your relationship with God. I hope you can see how this whole journey is coming together to help you. None of us will even trust the Holy Spirit's help without some history with Him. How are you going to let go of your desires if you haven't experienced God's faithfulness? You can't! What are you going to do with your "babies" when you decide they are too much of a burden? If you don't have some solid history with the Lord, you won't know what to do with them. You probably won't even know you **can** unload them. Without relationship and an encounter with God, you will struggle miserably to become a better person and thrive with God each day.

That is why we are spending time together. We've embarked upon this journey, and the ingredients that we've put into practice are going to help us learn to let go of ourselves and take hold of God. Without them we will wrestle with life. I know that without the daily practice of praise and worship, I catch myself murmuring my negative thoughts at mindless times. When I haven't spent time with the Lord and can't hear His voice clearly, I am not happy. I start to think I am out there alone and tend to sit at the control panel too long. Then I forget to trust God and don't desire everything He is and all He has for me. Abandonment is out of the question by then.

Yet when I am living in an attitude of gratefulness, my mind is set on the important things in life. I crave the presence of God so much that I will make time to sit with Him and experience His love. My prayer life goes beyond the mundane to the extraordinary. Then I can't wait to give God the responsibility of making life happen because His will becomes my desire. God's beautiful character traits seem to come out from nowhere to help make a difference in the lives of others. The Holy Spirit shows me things from His perspective, and suddenly I am moved with compassion to let go of myself for someone else. It's a beautiful process that I wish I could practice every moment. But I need to remember that this is a journey and that I won't arrive until I meet Jesus face to face someday. In the mean time, I am happy with steady progress.

Steady progress with the five ingredients is the only way we will ever learn to love as Jesus instructs.

- Live with an attitude of praise and thanksgiving unto the Lord.
- Let your time of prayer include fellowship with the Holy Spirit.
- Trust God, and depend upon Him for everything.
- Desire God and His beautiful traits.
- Let go of everything that keeps you from the awareness of God's presence.

I don't think Jesus would have left the command to love if He didn't think we could do it. The examples from the life of Jesus and the working of the Holy Spirit in our lives are priceless treasures for the journey.

Time to Reflect

▸ What rights have you demanded? How do they associate with selfishness and pride?

▸ How have your rights affected others?

▸ When do you tend to love as Jesus loves you? What makes it most difficult for you?

▸ How has your journey changed your relationship with God? List your hurdles.

_____
_____
_____
_____
_____

Living Application: Read the second chapter of Hebrews. Then picture Jesus as your captain, and draw your own word picture to depict His involvement on your team. Write down a Biblically correct definition of love. Note how it differs from what we perceive in the world. Start with the first ingredient and chart out a desirable course, as I have just done, to show your hopes for steady progress to live in God's presence more and more.

Empty Pockets

In *Living in His Presence* we acknowledged that Jesus gave up everything for us. He laid aside His royal benefits and kingly rights to set an example of servant leadership. We pictured Jesus with the pockets of His robe hanging out to the side, inside out. He had emptied the contents of His pockets out onto the dirt. All of His kingly rights and royal benefits were in the dust. Everything that belonged to Jesus was blowing away in the wind as a sign of His willful, royal abandonment.

When people are convicted of a crime and sentenced to jail, they also have to empty out their pockets. You've probably seen it in the movies. The prisoner puts every last belonging on the counter for the guard to confiscate. That person no longer has any personal items from the past. He has no identity except for the number he is given. He relinquishes all rights in a forced act of abandonment.

You and I have pockets too. Sometimes it seems like mine are over-sized and too numerous to count. For a long time it felt like I carried the weight of the world in my pockets. I had pockets filled with fear, despair, worry, and fatigue. I could hardly tote them around. The contents of my pockets affected my demeanor and my countenance. My pockets were filled with burdens that were too hard to bear. But I didn't know what to do with them, so for years they were always with me.

I remember surrendering my fears in hopes that the fatigue would go away. I thought that if I could just surrender my worries that the despair would leave. I lived through numerous acts of surrender, lost many battles, and grew weary of my burdens. Now I recognize what that was all about and have let them go in peaceful abandonment at the cross of Jesus Christ.

Your pockets might have some of the same burdens in them as mine. Perhaps you have other belongings in yours that I haven't mentioned. Many hold on to their rights, pride, security, stability, and possessions as if they are all that matter in life. Others carry financial problems, family issues, guilt and shame, strife, habitual sin, and bondages. You'd be surprised at all the baggage that we collect along the way and drag through life. All it does is weigh us down and hinder the journey. Burdensome baggage takes all our energy and focus and doesn't leave much for anyone else.

Have you ever been so tired or stressed that you think you've got nothing left to give to your family or to others? Chances are good that you don't have anything left to give to your Father in Heaven either. How can you when you are totally spent because of your burdens?

Pause a Moment

Is there anything that weighs you down so much that you don't have time for God?

Oftentimes our pockets are filled with good things that don't seem to drag us down. We can carry desires, dreams, and plans in our pockets. But if they are not God's best for us, we might have to let them go. Can you let go of what you want in exchange for the will of God? God might ask you to abandon your best desires and dreams so that He can give you **His** best.

> My niece, Katie, chose to empty her pockets and avoid a rugged road of destruction. She was working hard on an academic path with a promising future. She's an excellent student and was at the top of her class in the practical portion of the program. It is a long story, but Katie's college experienced academic mayhem in her third year of school which caused her to be removed from the program. In many ways it seemed so unfair because Katie was brilliant in her skills, and the misfortune brought hurt and devastation. There was nothing anyone could do about the issue; she was a victim of the system. After three years of commitment to a highly specialized field, her academic pathway dead ended. Many would have drowned in self pity and given up, but not Katie. Her pockets were filled with hope, dreams, vision, hard work, dedication, financial investment, purpose, energy, and more. They were heavy, but not burdensome because they carried the future. Chris and Marilyn, her parents, and Andrew, her brother, were by her side. Yet her family was broken over this issue as well because they carried some of the same things in their pockets for Katie. They are a close family, so whatever happened to their beloved happened to them too. One week after Katie's dreams were shattered, something amazing happened. She emptied out her pockets and abandoned everything they represented. She placed the previous three years of effort at the foot of the cross and walked away. Katie didn't give up; she just let go and sought the will of God. Within weeks, the Holy Spirit gave her new direction, precious hope, renewed strength, and He restored her dreams. Now Katie is thriving on a different career path even better suited for her. If she had not abandoned all she had in her pockets, she would have been destroyed on that rugged road. The hurts and disappointments could have forced her down an unforgiving path. She could have added burdens to her pockets that were too heavy to bear. But instead, she harbors no anger or unforgiveness. God rewarded Katie with much more than she let go of. It was hard for Katie's family to watch her endure the trial. My sister could also have been destroyed because she ran along side Katie in that third year. Her dad and brother were there with her too. But instead, we watched as they emptied their pockets and let go of all they carried for Katie. Their abandonment prevented them from anger, retaliation, and unforgiveness as well. This wonderful family now rests in their peaceful abandonment, and God has restored their joy!

You and I can definitely learn from Katie's story. Her pockets were filled with good things, yet God required genuine abandonment. She relinquished control and obeyed God. Jesus has royal benefits and kingly rights in His pockets, not the kinds of burdens that you and I might have. If He could let them go for us in order to obey and please His Father, don't you think we should be willing to let go of our rights, privileges, and burdensome loads? All it takes is a willingness to let go and be like the young mother who left her baby on the doorstep. You **will** be better off!

God doesn't want any of us to be without good things in life unless they interrupt the flow of His presence. There is nothing wrong with being financially stable as long as your real stability is in Christ. Worldly possessions aren't a problem if your grip isn't so tight that you can't let go of them if needed. God gives the best gifts, some tangible and others intangible; He wants us to be blessed. What we do with our blessings is what matters to God. The condition of your heart is what God sees, and He'll let you know what you need to abandon and what to keep. Remember that His Spirit is always there to help you.

When we listen to God, empty our pockets, place the contents at the foot of the cross of Jesus Christ, and walk away...it is always to our benefit.

God knows we've just relinquished our nothingness into His sovereignty, and He is pleased. It is like walking through the narrow gate that widens to freedom after you enter. You can hold your head high once again and breathe in pure Holy Spirit air. You will feel light as a feather because your loads are gone. Joy comes back to share in your laughter and energy. Your mind and heart are in unity once again, and the color comes back into your cheeks. The benefits and positive side effects are immeasurable. Yet all of it came from the simple act of abandonment that you feared would ruin your life.

Prayer Poem Ministry
"COMING FROM LOVE"

Your love for God and His for you will drive away a multitude of evil. Where there is love, there can be no evil. Love the Lord your God with all that is within you, with your whole heart, soul, and mind. God will cause your very being to rise above all the superficial love of the world that you live with. Go deeper with God just as His Son did, to a realm that is deep and filled with selfless, abundant, and graceful love. This realm of love is a wonder to you... a cherished possession, a gentleness like you've never known, peace never imagined, and joy to keep you going in times of trial. No trial will detain you now that you are coming from love. But most of all, your Father draws you closer in love with Him.

What obstacles do you face? What evils lurk around the corner and make you doubt the presence of God and His love for you? No evil can dwell with Perfect Love. Run to your Perfect One, and encounter true and lasting love. Then your entire being will burst with love for God. Yes, your heart, soul, and all that is within you radiate the light and love of Christ. Don't settle for the love in the world; rise above its lust and take the higher ground to a more meaningful love in the presence of God. Just as Jesus traveled to the core of His Father's being, go now and feel the love of a Father for His child. Bask in the selfless, abundant, and graceful love of the Father. Open your eyes to the wonder of peace and joy. Let no challenge derail you, fear no evil, and walk where others can't. Go with your Father to heavenly places created just for you, and love Him as He loves you.

The Peace of Christ

"Peace I leave with you, My peace I give to you; not as the world gives do I give to you. Let not your heart be troubled, neither let it be afraid (John 14: 27).

The world presents peace in a very different light than God does. The kind of peace that comes from the world is temporal and conditional. It has to be earned and hunted down with incredible diligence. Everyone is looking for it because nothing else puts the heart and soul at ease like peace does. People everywhere are looking for peace. The most popular, is peace of mind; it's used all the time to indicate an inner feeling that tells us it's going to be alright. We eat, sleep, and rest better when we have peace of mind. The world's peace doesn't last long, so we're always on the hunt trying to get it any way we can. Since peace of mind is an unusual commodity, we work to manufacture it with depleted resources, and it is a never ending process.

On the other hand, the peace of Christ is a lot like God's love. It lasts forever, and it's unconditional. It is so plentiful that God's reserves are never depleted. We don't have to search for the peace of Christ; all we have to do is ask for it. Oftentimes, it comes without asking. It is one of the most valuable benefits we have as followers of Jesus Christ.

The peace of Christ is priceless, incomprehensible, and extravagant.

We can't purchase God's peace, nor can we understand it because it comes from an extravagant Source. It is often mistaken for peace of mind, but there is no comparison. The peace of Christ doesn't merely give our minds rest. It permeates the body, soul, and spirit to flood them with the presence of God. It doesn't matter what kind of reserves you have or where your factory is, you can't manufacture the peace of Christ.

Letting go and placing your cares at the cross of Jesus Christ brings peaceful abandonment every time; it is not a hit or miss action.

When you abandon yourself to the will of God, He will always take care of you. Every time I engage in sweet abandonment, I am so relieved. That is when I know that it is no longer my issue but God's. It's in perfect hands, and I can watch from a distance to see what God does with it.

Just today, I was praying about a situation that had too many issues and options. It was giving me a headache just thinking about all the possibilities. I was about to bundle it all up and carry the wide load when I thought to let it go in peaceful abandonment. Instead of allowing it to consume my thoughts, I decided to let God take care if it. I've seen His faithfulness enough to know that He is more than able to work on my behalf and do much better than I would. Once I let go, I knew it was in His control. It was great to feel the peace of Christ instead of the heaviness of the load.

I was glad I didn't even carry it for a short time; this time I remembered to do the right thing immediately. The **beauty** of abandonment became so real when I let go before I struggled.

Abandonment ushers in the peace of Christ at times when uncertainties could be playing games with your mind. It isn't often that you will let go of something and know what is going to happen. There will always be uncertainties. The disciples and apostles lived their lives with uncertainties. When Jesus was alive and living among them, life was full of unknowns. We read in the Bible about all the unusual situations that came across their paths when Jesus was with them. He had to calm them down, ease their fears, and preach to them constantly. You know how uncertain life was for the disciples. Then when Jesus went back to Heaven, the apostles were overwhelmed with uncertainty. Thankfully Jesus sent the Holy Spirit to help them stay focused. Those ordinary men operated with the power of the Holy Spirit and turned the uncertain world upside down for Jesus Christ.

We live with as many uncertainties as the disciples did; they are just different. Yet we live and dwell with the Holy Spirit every moment, and His power is available whenever we ask for it. Abandonment brings uncertainty. Yet if there were none, then there would be no need for faith.

Abandonment starts with a need and desire to do the right thing. It operates on your faith, and finishes at the feet of Christ.

You have to walk in faith, knowing that God is at work. Doubts and fears will try to sneak in the back seat, but your faith is strong enough to hit the door locks immediately. When you feel like your faith is not strong enough to hit the locks, ask the Holy Spirit for help. Faith is a gift that keeps coming as you need it. God energizes your faith and convinces you that He is at work. Isn't that comforting? All you have to do is decide to let go, and the Holy Spirit takes it from there. I think the hardest part is the decision to let go.

You might struggle with your decision process. Fear of the uncertainties will try to paralyze you. But faith is the opposite of fear, so remember what we just talked about. God will energize your faith to overcome fear of the unknown. You might be a bit stubborn about losing control. When you reflect on God's faithfulness at the times you have needed Him, you will have the ability to step away from the control panel.

Selfishness will disguise itself as concern to worry you about what you might be giving up in abandonment. Don't be concerned; the Holy Spirit will help you to discern selfishness and remind you that you are doing the right thing.

There can be pain and suffering in abandonment, depending upon what you are letting go of and if there are strongholds attached. The pain is mostly emotional because letting go doesn't appeal to your fleshly desires. Human nature affects the process significantly. Those who are strong willed or have a powerful personality, could have a more difficult time letting go. When control is an issue, then leaving a situation to God could be a struggle. Some drag along unhealthy baggage for so long that it becomes a part of life and resists abandonment. When it's exposed, a real battle might take place before some can let go. Every time sin is involved, the pain and suffering could be grave.

The strongholds associated with sin are tenacious. But that doesn't mean there isn't victory. Remember that the Spirit of the Living God is much greater than any stronghold or powerful personality. God's got you covered!

"For it is God who works in you, both to will and to do for His good pleasure" (Philippians 2:13). God gives you the desire and the ability to let go in peaceful abandonment; it's almost always His idea. It's never easy to abandon the things we've been comfortable with for so long. No one looks forward to discomfort. It's a bit like giving birth to a healthy baby; it's worth the pain. The peace and comfort that come after you let go and allow God to work, are worth it as well. Freedom tastes so good that you'll wonder why you waited so long. Living with God and hearing His voice everyday tastes pretty good too!

Time to Reflect

- What have you carried that weighs you down and hinders your relationship with God?
- Do you clutch your rights and securities for fear of losing them? Name some of them.
- What uncertainties do you have about letting go? Are there still some fears?
- Describe your peaceful feelings. Is it more like peace of mind or the peace of Christ?

_____
_____
_____
_____

Living Application: Take time to sit quietly with the Holy Spirit. Allow Him to rummage through your pockets and help relieve you of your burdens and selfish rights. Don't be afraid to let God see your heart as it really is; allow yourself to be vulnerable with His sweet Spirit. Pray and ask God to help you take your heaviness to the cross of His Son, in whatever form it is exposed. Don't be in a hurry to dump everything at once. Oftentimes, God deals with our issues one at a time as part of the healing process. Journal as much as you can so that you will have a record to review and rejoice in. Start praying and believing for the peace of Christ instead of a mere peace of mind. Remember that you only have to initiate abandonment; God will take it from there.

It's Well Worth It

When I look back at how the early pioneers plowed their way to freedom and success, it makes me tired just to think about it. They worked hard to achieve their dreams and were diligent to the end. You've seen movies and pictures of their lives. Sometimes the simplicity of life then sounds good, but recalling their journey brings us back to our senses.

We don't want to endure their hardships if we can have more with much less effort. We've become a microwavable society. If we can't have it now, we will go for something else.

> I have always had great respect for those who have worked very hard for their success. You read about those who achieved the impossible with sheer determination and a good work ethic. My grandfather worked very hard when he came from Italy to this country. He settled in Southern Colorado where he opened a grocery store in his community. He achieved great success, but more importantly, he earned the love and respect of the community because of his generosity and compassion for all. During the Depression, he fed many out of the surplus in his store. He captivated my attention with his stories; he called them "the good old days" because many cared for others. He always ended by telling me that self-sacrifice is difficult, but well worth it in every way. My grandfather loved Jesus even though his spiritual journey looked very different than mine does today. But he pioneered a journey of generosity and love at a most challenging time in the history of our country. He was compelled to live life the right way, loving God and his family first. A time came when my grandfather was in need. Some suggested that he go back and collect from those he extended credit to during the Depression. But my grandfather wasn't willing to do that. He said it was all worth it and that he was content to live a simple life in his later years.
>
> I wanted to share my grandfather's story because he stayed the course even when his journey was rough. As a young man, he abandoned his rights to a better life in his retirement years. He let go of his surplus during the Depression in order to help others. To go back and reclaim the fortune he let go of was unthinkable. He stayed the course on his journey, and it was well worth the challenges he faced. I am sure he was tempted to go back, but he didn't. My grandfather didn't look back, complain, or blame God for the way life turned out for him. He was simply content to have done the right things in life. In a way, I think he understood abandonment.

It is tempting to "abandon" the whole spiritual journey in an effort to avoid abandonment. Living in the presence of God seems like too much work, and it takes too long. Self-sacrifice isn't on the top ten list of easiest goals to achieve. A life of service to God, weathering the storms, and letting go of self isn't appealing to most. But if you want to thrive in the presence of God, you will have to learn to let go in peaceful abandonment. I can assure you that you will find the journey well worth the effort. You can become a pioneer and help others with their journey. *"Indeed we count them blessed who endure. You have heard of the perseverance of Job and seen the end intended by the Lord—that the Lord is very compassionate and merciful"* (James 5:11).

We've all read quotes from famous athletes who pushed their bodies to the limits in order to attain their goals. Their journeys exemplify self-sacrifice, endless endurance, pain, and discipline.

They didn't slack off much in those challenging years of reaching for their dreams. But everyone of them will tell you that it was well worth the effort and sacrifice. We only see the glamor of today, but they remember the journey.

Physicians dedicate at least ten to fifteen years of their lives to study the human body. Stories reveal their sacrifice of self, family, friends, time, finances, and more during those grueling years of school and internships. While they pressed in without a guarantee of reaching the goal, they will tell you that it is well worth the effort and sacrifice. We see success and a socioeconomic status, but they remember the journey.

Pastors and those who devote their lives to various ministries give of themselves endlessly. They don't usually receive the same financial rewards for their self-sacrifice that others do. Oftentimes missionaries put themselves and the lives of their families at risk to evangelize the lost in remote counties around the world. The preparation, endurance of spiritual warfare, and constant perseverance of those who minister to God's children isn't often evident to most. Just look into the eyes of one who makes continual sacrifice to serve God, and you will sense that is was well worth the effort. We see spiritual respect and authority, but they remember the journey.

The list of those who sacrifice themselves for others and for God is endless. We all know of them because they are ordinary people whose paths cross ours. They quietly let go of themselves in peaceful abandonment on a regular basis and never look back. We read the magnificent stories of those long ago who gave of themselves to accomplish the will of God and His purpose for them. They all said the same thing; it was worth it!

Continue on your spiritual journey, and let the Holy Spirit lead you to that peaceful place of abandonment. Become a pioneer who is willing to help others make their journey. You will have plenty of stories to tell that could encourage the multitudes. They will want what you have and be tempted to hold you in spiritual esteem, but you will remember the journey and give glory to God!

Don't Settle

Notice how different people react to adverse conditions; it can be very revealing. We all do fairly well when the journey is smooth. But when the terrain takes a turn for the worse, we find out how plentiful the sweet fruits of the Spirit really are in our lives. How do you react to adversity?

- When the journey becomes challenging, is there an abundance of love, joy, and peace?
- If the pot holes are too numerous to count, is there enough patience, kindness, and goodness to keep you on track?
- How gentle, faithful, and self controlled are you on the icy roads?
- When you know you need to abandon your dream because it defies the wisdom of the Bible and the will of God, what will you do?
- Will you stay the course and pursue God's presence, or will you settle for a lesser relationship with Him?

The most important thing in your life is your relationship with God. It defines who you are and builds upon your character.

You want an excellent relationship with your King, not a mediocre one. That is why we are spending time together; it is what we both desire. Neither of us would be satisfied if we pulled off the main road and took some other path away from God's best. That would mean settling for less than God's leadership which will keep us from rejoicing in His presence every day.

You probably won't be asked to abandon your dreams unless they are unhealthy or dangerous to your spiritual well being. Remember that by the time abandonment is required, you will recognize the need and follow the lead of the Holy Spirit. Sometimes the Holy Spirit will nudge you along to help you be your best, but He does it with grace and love.

Anytime God initiates something with you, embrace it and allow His Spirit to help you. Even when it is uncomfortable, you can trust God.

Remember that by now, you have learned to depend upon God and trust Him, so an uncomfortable nudge won't put you over the edge. It will cause you to press in with God, developing character and hope. *"...but we also glory in tribulations, knowing that tribulation produces perseverance; and perseverance, character; and character, hope"* (Romans 5:3,4).

Those who choose to abandon the journey always regret it later. They are so close, yet pull away when the cost of following Jesus Christ becomes too high. They become disoriented and abandon the wrong thing in the heat of the day. Oftentimes they come back when they realize that life isn't so grand without the excellence of God's interaction moment to moment. They've dug a pit that is deeper than the normal pot holes and realize they really need God's intervention. That's okay; it is better to find the way back to the main road than to stray onto a dangerous, ungodly path. But it's much harder to get going again than it is to stay the course and pursue God.

The worldly road blocks make it difficult to find your way to good fellowship with God again. Never settle and abort the journey; take the high road to His presence instead.

Pause a Moment

Are you tempted to abandon your journey right now? Stay the course; it is well worth it! And remember...you are not alone.

Time to Reflect

▸ How are you a pioneer? When you only see a journey, what do others see in your life?

▸ How hard are you willing to pursue God? Are there any show stoppers today?

▸ When is it most difficult to stay the course with God? How can the Holy Spirit help?

▸ In times of trial, are you tempted to settle? How can the Holy Spirit help?

_____
_____
_____
_____
_____

Living Application: Pray about how you will share some of the details of your spiritual life so that others can benefit. Even though your journey is life long, you can still make a difference in the lives of those around you as you progress. Be open to transparency, and admit your successes and your shortcomings. Allow yourself to be honest with God about letting go. He already knows your feelings, but acknowledging them will make it easier for you to receive help from the Holy Spirit. Journal your concerns about taking your relationship with God deeper. List all the things you are excited about as well. Openness with God will help you progress instead of settling for an average relationship with Him.

Time to Get Excited

"I can do all things through Christ who strengthens me" (Philippians 4:13). You have access to God through Jesus Christ, and you enjoy fellowship with the Holy Spirit! That should excite you enough to turn your engine over and send you merrily on your way to an extraordinary life with God. Nothing about your relationship with God is ordinary anymore. You have learned to present your life as an offering of praise and worship to God in an attitude of genuine gratitude. Your prayer life is second to none by now because you know how to pray and listen for the voice of the Holy Spirit. Your need for God grows more each day as you realize you can do nothing without Him. How can you live without Him when you desire everything He is and represents? You are probably ready to fall into His arms of love as we speak! That's when you know that you can do anything He asks of you, even letting go of yourself.

Jesus said, *"Nevertheless I tell you the truth. It is to your advantage that I go away; for if I do not go away, the Helper will not come to you; but if I depart, I will send Him to you"* (John 16:7). Doesn't that reassuring scripture give you great comfort? Always remember that you are not alone on your journey. Not only are you not alone, you have the Helper; God Himself is with you every second. And because you are developing an extraordinary relationship with God, you really **can** do anything.

This means that you can come to terms with abandonment and learn to let go whenever you need to! Eventually it will be like a second nature; you will automatically let go because of your trusting times with God. You have seen the faithful hand of God more times in your life than you can count. Now make a point to remember His faithfulness every day, and notice how much easier it becomes to trust God.

We are so busy going for the next thing that we forget about God.

But God doesn't forget about us for a second. I can't imagine the depth of His patience with us as He lovingly waits for us to notice His presence moment by moment. I am not talking about an imaginary friend; I am telling you about the God of the universe who created everything and longs for your heart in lasting fellowship.

Your constant Helper is the Holy Spirit of the Living God! The thought of God's Spirit within you should just make your day everyday. There is nothing you can't do with God's help as long as you are willing to do it His way. You have no reason to fret over abandonment because the Holy Spirit is going to do more work than you are. You are simply going to decide it is the best thing to do and then let God's Spirit take it from there. You'll wonder how you ever lived without God's intervention before.

Have some fun with God, and make abandonment an exciting challenge. Are you wondering how in the world that's going to happen? It can happen because part of the challenge is spending time with God, listening for His voice. You get to be with God! You have the opportunity to ask all your questions about God's will and expect that He will give you answers.

"If you abide in Me, and My words abide in you, you will ask what you desire, and it shall be done for you. By this My Father is glorified, that you bear much fruit; so you will be My disciples" (John 15: 7,8).

If you are like me then you have probably prayed and asked God for lots of things, but felt like He didn't come through. Why are there so many scriptures about asking and receiving if the chances of an answer are slim? When this scripture in John was first written in Greek, to abide meant to stay in a given place or relationship. When I remain close to God and stick to Him like glue, it seems like my prayers are heard and answered more often. If my relationship with Him isn't like it should be, then it feels like my prayers aren't even getting to the right place.

Learning to live in God's presence is so important! Abiding in Christ means remaining in a right relationship with Him. We must keep Him on the throne in every aspect of our lives. Abiding is making a sacrifice of praise to God whether we feel like it or not. Don't just listen for the voice of the Holy Spirit when it is convenient; go out of your comfort zone to meet with Him.

You can't abide in Christ when you are pushing your way to the control panel. If you refuse to forgive and then hold others captive in your heart, you aren't free to love as God loves you. You become imprisoned by your own unforgiveness, and your hardened heart can't desire all of God that is available. How will you ever be able to let go in a peaceful act of abandonment if you are focused on yourself more than others and God? It seems like a vicious circle, but you already know how to avoid it. If you happen to find yourself somewhere on the circle, you can get off. The ingredients for living with God moment to moment will lead you back to the right path again.

There is no precise formula for getting your prayers answered. Yet Jesus tells us that if we stay in relationship with Him, we can expect answers to our prayers. When we are in a right relationship with God, our perspectives change and our prayer life changes too. Remember that your prayer life is two-fold and that the Holy Spirit will be prompting you to pray certain ways. His desires will become your desires, and you will pray accordingly.

When you cry out to God in despair concerning someone, the Holy Spirit will show you how to pray for that person. You have to pray according to God's will until He tells you to stop, and we never know how long that will be. We only know that we can expect God to work and answer your prayer in His timing and according to His will. The Holy Spirit might tell you that it is time to let go and place your prayer request at the foot of the cross of His Son. But He'll help you to leave it there in peaceful abandonment. It all comes out of relationship with God. That is why it is the most important thing in your life.

You have been given the greatest honor imaginable; you are a child of God. You also have the highest privilege on earth, to know God and make Him known to others. You can enjoy fellowship with the Living God every minute of your life, and no one can take that away from you.

It's time to get excited about God instead of worrying about life.

In your excitement for God, you will watch your worries and fears fade into the darkness. And the secret pathway that leads you to abandonment and His presence will shine bright before you.

Prayer Poem Ministry
"FALLEN TRIALS"

Yes, it is true that God allows troubles and sorrows in this fallen world, and they affect you, His child. While God doesn't make it His purpose to send trials your way, He does allow them to mold and shape you. There is enough imperfection in this world for God to use to help shape your character that He doesn't have to create trials just for you. Yet His perfect love casts out all fear, unbelief, sorrow, and even every trial. Walk in God's love and conquer the trials that come your way. His love is deeper and will continue to grow in you each day; it is bottomless! See if this is not true...as you grow deeper in your love relationship with God, you will surely cast aside more and more of the world's imperfections. Beneath your feet is the path of obedience and righteousness. Walk there now, and you shall most certainly find Him there with you.

Don't be afraid of the trials and challenges that meet you on your journey. Your Heavenly Father is there for you, and He will use them to help you in your relationship with Him. Though this imperfect world hurls tragedy and pain at you, don't let it get you down. Embrace the perfect love of your Father. His Spirit will take away your fear and sorrow and leave you with everlasting peace.

When you cannot believe, don't hang your head in shame. Lift it high, and the power of God turns your disbelief into faith. In every trial, the presence of God embraces your weariness and carries you to a place of rest. Let the love of God come, conquer your trials, and take you deeper into His presence where there are no limitations for you.

May your relationship with God be stronger than the problems of this world. May it keep you on the path of obedience and righteousness, and may you embrace the presence of your King every moment.

Life Changing Perks

When I think of how I feared and avoided abandonment for so long, I really get sad. The thought of losing out held me back, and letting go didn't sound like a winning proposition. That was because I didn't understand abandonment. The more I practice this last ingredient, the more I want to use it. The benefits are greater than I expected. The history of my journey tells me that there is something worth looking forward to at the end of the road if I continue to embrace abandonment today.

Everyone has a purpose in life, and many hope to have a good grip on it within a certain time frame. Perhaps it is parenting, a career, or something else on the list of purposes for life. While those are all great and certainly a part of the plan, there could be more to God's purpose. God might be thinking about something beyond the scope of your imagination that requires an excellent relationship with Him.

We've all read about those who did amazing things according to the will of God. And the Bible is filled with ordinary people who made significant contributions to the Kingdom of God. Not only did they do great things, they knew God, and He knew them. You and I can be like those faithful ones who realized all there was to their purpose in life. We can have as much intimacy with God as they had.

Those who go beyond the ordinary to the extraordinary in God's kingdom, practice abandonment on a regular basis.

They accomplish great things for the Kingdom of God, but they also have their visions and dreams fulfilled. Not everyone is meant to travel the world and evangelize those who haven't heard of Jesus Christ. Few people work in a structured, full-time ministry compared to the rest of the world. Yet every follower of Jesus Christ has a purpose within the kingdom that goes beyond the obvious.

When you share intimacy with God, you have access to His will and desires for you. You can go beyond the obvious to the secret place where God waits to whisper in your ear. Life takes on a new meaning because you know God, and He knows you. Out of relationship with Him, you can discover who you are and what your purpose in life really is. Everyone knows the unsettled feeling that comes from lack of direction or purpose. It feels like a void waiting for God to fill. But when you know you are right where you should be, contentment keeps you company. You can weather any storm because the peace of Christ protects your thoughts and emotions.

**Those who practice genuine abandonment are rewarded handsomely.
They can almost hear Jesus say,
*"Well done, good and faithful servant."***
(Matthew 25:23)

Sin becomes less of a struggle because you are listening to the Holy Spirit instead of to your fleshly desires. When you are living in peace with God, all is well. I can't express how comforting that is; you will have to feel it for yourself. If you let go of yourself and allow God to work, stress rolls off like running water. Imagine your life with much less stress; is there anything you won't let go of for that?

Abandonment causes you to grow and mature in your Christianity.

You'll stand strong and not buckle and fold when life is challenging. I am sure you can already think of many more benefits. My best benefit is the assurance that God is in control. When I am reassured of that, then it seems like everything else falls into place. It's easier to submit to God and resist the temptation to sin. I am more content, less stressed, and have lasting peace. Then I grow to new heights with Jesus and thrive in His presence more and more.

Abandonment is Not...

Abandonment is not a forceful act of God to control you. You decide if and when you will engage in abandonment. It's God's best for you if you want to live with Him more intimately, but He won't impose it on you. It is not a game of tug of war that wears you out like surrender can. Abandonment seeks the will of God, but God doesn't control your will. It is not a battleground where the wounded are too numerous to count. Abandonment actually protects you from hurts and fatal shots.

While you practice abandonment, you won't look like a suffering soul. Those around you shouldn't be able to tell the difference in your demeanor. You don't have to keep it a secret, but you don't need to advertise it either. Sometimes it is good to share it with someone who will pray and encourage you along the way. Abandonment can look a bit like Biblical fasting.

Jesus said, *"Moreover, when you fast, do not be like the hypocrites, with a sad countenance. For they disfigure their faces that they may appear to men to be fasting. Assuredly, I say to you, they have their reward. But you, when you fast, anoint your head and wash your face, so that you do not appear to men to be fasting, but to your Father who is in the secret place; and your Father who sees in secret will reward you openly"* (Matthew 6: 16-18).

**As you practice abandonment, you will come to rest in it
much like anything else you do on a regular basis.**

It becomes a natural part of your spiritual well-being. Your spiritual maturity and openness to God carry you over the threshold of abandonment into the arms of Jesus every time.

Time to Reflect

▸ What excites you most about letting go in peaceful abandonment?

▸ How much have you practiced letting go? What has been your experience with it so far?

▸ What is keeping you from practicing abandonment? How can God help?

▸ How is your relationship with God going? Are you abiding in God and His love?

_____
_____
_____
_____
_____

Living Application: Your journey requires the Holy Spirit's intervention. If you have been traveling alone, then it is time to stop and include God's Spirit so you will make good progress. Reflect upon your spiritual journey, and take time to journal some of the details. Ask the Holy Spirit to help you where you feel like you need some assistance. Practice letting go of the easier things in preparation for times when you need to deal with more serious issues. Note how you felt and what you did to let go, for future reference. Practice abiding in God by watching for Him and signs of His love everywhere you go. Make specific choices to do the right thing during your day and journal about it so that you will remember that you did make some good choices. Continue to pray for an awareness of the Holy Spirit in the moment to moment of your life.

Practicing Abandonment

No one is perfect when it comes to the practice of abandonment. Much trial and error takes place before you will feel comfortable. But you have to stick with it because without it, you won't be able to get to that fabulous place with God that you desire.

I wish I could give you a few short cuts, but I haven't discovered any yet. It will seem like you are rolling right along when all of a sudden you hit a road block. You will wonder how it got there because you were doing so well.

Oftentimes the Lord will allow it to reveal a hidden stronghold. It is good to get it out of the way so that you don't have to deal with it down the road. Don't fret about it, just pray and ask God to help move it out of your way. Then wash your hands and continue on.

If you come across a hurdle that you don't think you can get over, don't try to do it alone. It is better to stop and get some Holy Spirit assistance than to ask Him to mend your bruises later. You'll be laid up while you heal, and that could take valuable time away from your journey.

When you make a mistake, just know that you are not the only one. You are always in good company; make sure you have someone to confide in that you trust. Most of all, remember that there is more grace to go around than you can imagine. Go to your Savior with your mistakes, and let Him take care of you. Don't be shy about trying again because you are more than a conqueror!

Adversity comes in all shapes and sizes with the ability to thwart your loving relationship with God. Tribulation and trials are plentiful; they are simply a part of life. What you do with them matters the most. Don't allow them to damage your relationship with God. Instead, remember how powerful this last ingredient is, and simply let go. You will have to trust God, but you have already learned to do that.

When you trust God, He will sustain you as you choose to abandon whatever is keeping you from overcoming your trial. Count on God to carry you across the burdensome threshold into the peaceful arms of your Savior. God will not disappoint you. If it doesn't happen quite the way you thought, spend more time with the Holy Spirit, and He will speak to your heart.

Because this is your journey, you will be tempted to think that it is your responsibility to make things happen. The only responsibility you have is your commitment to Christ. You must love God and pursue Him with all you have. Even when you have so little to pursue Him with, the Holy Spirit inhabits what you do have and gives you the rest. God draws you into relationship and into abandonment if you will just follow His lead. You are ready for this because you have come so far already.

Abandonment is not like your worst nightmare. It is a beautiful encounter with God that helps you fulfill your biggest dream... to live in His presence, moment by moment forever.

Abandonment is the last ingredient because it needs the other four to empower it. As you know, all the ingredients are equally vital to your growth with God. They work together and intermingle to give you what you need to have depth and intimacy with God every moment.

Pause a Moment

Praise and worship God. Pray and have loving fellowship with Him. Trust God for everything and depend upon Him. Desire God and all of His beautiful traits. Then you can let go in loving abandonment to live in His presence.

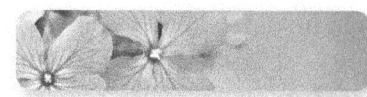

Prayer Poem Ministry

"A FLESHLY FLIGHT FOR LIFE"

You are a child of God, and to die is great gain for that is how Jesus accomplished His mission. And yet, God does not call you to suffer death on a cross as His Son did, but to open your heart to the things that matter the most. If there are obstacles that keep you from what matters most, then die to those very things so that you are no longer hindered. It is your love for God that will bring about death to your fleshly obstacles. As love overwhelms your heart, the ways of the flesh will fade away. Draw near to God and His love will take you wonderfully captive. Your fleshly burdens will die out as you cling to God and to His love. It will not be a wrenching process but a loving one. Abide in Christ, and you will die to the fleshly ways that hinder you. You shall be free, and you will welcome death of the flesh that you may come unto Christ.

You are escaping from all that keeps you from the presence of God. May the power of the Holy Spirit consume you and enable you to let go of all that prevents you from knowing your Father intimately. May you walk in true freedom with your eyes upon your Savior. And may the peace of Christ be your eternal gift and treasure as you live with God moment by moment. *"And those who are Christ's have crucified the flesh with its passions and desires. If we live in the Spirit, let us also walk in the Spirit."* Galatians 5: 24,25

Let's pray!

Dear Lord, I want nothing to keep me from living in the sweet awareness of Your presence. Help me to empty my pockets in complete abandonment unto you. Take my nothingness and turn it into whatever pleases you. Fill my heart with joy as I leave my burdens at the foot of your Son's cross. Help me to turn my back on whatever hinders my relationship with you and embrace all that Jesus has accomplished for me. I want to walk in the fullness of all that you designed for me in this life. I want to make a difference in the Kingdom of God right here on this earth. Thank you for drawing me near in peaceful abandonment. Now may my life reflect your precious presence today and always.

The Blend of Ingredients

Life in His Presence...

The Goal	210
Your Life Song	211
Past or Present?	212
The Fear of God	214
Count Your Blessings	215
Your Heart...His Temple	216
The Miraculous	216
Your Joyful Place	217
He's the Same God	219
Settle the Issues	220
Who Trusts Who?	221
Counting the Cost	222
Less Room for Sin	223
Desire God	224
Love God	224
Obey God	225
Be Compassionate and Forgiving	226
Spiritual Alignment	227
The Refining Process	228
Don't Stress About It	229
Protect Your Relationship	230
"Don't Wrestle; Just Nestle"	231
For You	232

"And He has made from one blood every nation of men to dwell on all the face of the earth, and has determined their preappointed times and the boundaries of their dwellings, so that they should seek the Lord, in the hope that they might grope for Him and find Him, though He is not far from each one of us; for in Him we live and move and have our being, as also some of your own poets have said,
'For we are also His offspring.'"
Acts 17: 26-28

The presence of God is your life line. It really is how you live, move and have your being! Your spirit, soul, and body will flourish in the intimate relationship that you have with God through the Holy Spirit.

Many go into debt looking for peace and contentment on every corner stand of life when all they need is to simply make one stop with God. Everything you need comes from God by His Spirit. He offers no phony bargains, just reality through Jesus Christ.

You were never meant to strive for the things of God; you were created to thrive in His will instead. Sometimes thriving is an encounter with the Living God. Other times you thrive while you stand in faith and meditate upon the promises of the Bible.

It's okay to experience God, so don't let anyone diminish your times with Him. Many in the Bible experienced His presence through tangible manifestations. Their lives were dramatically changed because of God's unmistakable involvement with them.

God gave Abraham a vision. *"After these things the word of the Lord came to Abram in a vision, saying, "Do not be afraid, Abram. I am your shield, your exceedingly great reward"* (Genesis 15:1).

God manifested Himself to Moses through signs and wonders using the burning bush. *"And the Angel of the Lord appeared to him in a flame of fire from the midst of a bush. So he looked, and behold, the bush was burning with fire, but the bush was not consumed"* (Exodus 3: 2).

Peter, James, and John were with Jesus when they had an incredible vision on the mountain. *"Now after six days Jesus took Peter, James, and John his brother, led them up on a high mountain by themselves; and He was transfigured before them. His face shone like the sun, and His clothes became as white as the light. And behold, Moses and Elijah appeared to them, talking with Him"* (Matthew 17: 1-3).

The apostle, Paul, had a radical encounter with Jesus as part of his conversion to Christianity. *"As he journeyed he came near Damascus, and suddenly a light shone around him from heaven. Then he fell to the ground, and heard a voice saying to him, 'Saul, Saul, why are you persecuting Me?' And he said, 'Who are you, Lord?' Then the Lord said, 'I am Jesus, whom you are persecuting.'"*

"So he, trembled and astonished, said, 'Lord, what do You want me to do?' Then the Lord said to him, 'Arise and go into the city, and you will be told what you must do.' And the men who journeyed with him stood speechless, hearing a voice but seeing no one. Then Saul arose from the ground, and when his eyes were opened he saw no one" (Acts 9: 3-8).

The presence of God inspired these Bible heroes to do great things on behalf of the Almighty. The Kingdom of Heaven became their treasure, and they found great spiritual wealth. Their pursuit of God was costly, but their relationship with Him proved to be extravagant and well worth the effort. They received amazing dividends because of God's presence in their lives. Yet none of these spiritual giants set out to make a difference. They didn't decide to go into "the ministry." They simply found treasure in a relationship with the Living God. Then they went out and influenced the world on the Lord's behalf.

Everything comes out of relationship with God.

Once you dig into the ingredients and savor them, you will taste and enjoy lasting freedom from worry of the cares of life. Your freedom takes you into the realm of the Holy Spirit where you can know your Father more intimately. While your freedom to know God comes with no guarantee for a perfect life, you have His Word that your life will have meaning, purpose, and peace. *"Now may the Lord of peace Himself give you peace always in every way* (2 Thessalonians 3: 16).

As you know, each of the five ingredients has its own flavor and purpose. Yet the real beauty of the ingredients is realized when we intermingle them for the purpose of genuine relationship with God. Imagine trusting God so much that you can actually let go and abandon your burdens. Think of what it could be like to hear God's voice clearly in prayer and have faith to act upon His will. How would you feel when you notice that your attitude of praise enables you to love as Jesus loved? The possibilities are grand, and they are countless. The guarantee of an amazing relationship with God will surely boost your faith.

"...and truly our fellowship is with the Father and with His Son Jesus Christ."
1John 1: 3

Your Life Song

If your faith is going to blossom and grow to new dimensions with God, then you must have a willing soul and a thankful heart. Then God will awaken the song of praise that He has placed in you. He will give you the desire and ability to live your life with an attitude of gratitude. You won't have to force yourself to live a life of worship; the Holy Spirit will gently give you a unique life song of praise for God.

Your life song is your expression of praise to God all through the day and night. It reflects your demeanor of praise and the way you revere Him.

It is Holy Spirit driven in a gracious manner so that you can relate to your Father. It is already there; you just need to allow the Holy Spirit to help you nurture it for God's eternal glory.

- What does your life song look like?
- Where does your praise go all through the day?
- Where does your praise go when you sleep?

"...be filled with the Spirit, speaking to one another in psalms and hymns and spiritual songs, singing and making melody in your heart to the Lord, giving thanks always for all things to God the Father in the name of our Lord Jesus Christ, submitting to one another in the fear of God" (Ephesians 5: 19-21).

The Bible says that in all things we are to give thanks. *"In everything give thanks; for this is the will of God in Christ Jesus for you"* (1 Thessalonians 5: 18). Your life song doesn't thank God for your troubles. I've never known anyone who can offer sincere thanks to God for times of turmoil. Your life song praises Him for seeing you through those difficult times. That is when then the peace of God comes and allows you to live in an attitude of praise in the midst of difficulties and challenge. *"Be anxious for nothing, but in everything by prayer and supplication, with thanksgiving, let your requests be made known to God; and the peace of God, which surpasses all understanding, will guard your hearts and minds through Christ Jesus"* (Philippians 4: 6,7).

Sometimes we make it too hard on ourselves. God never meant for us to manufacture feelings of gratitude or peace. But through our relationship with Him and in our pursuit of Him, God takes care of the details and your life song brings Him glory.

Past or Present?

Does your mind stay focused on God's activity in your life now, or do you tend to dwell on the past?

Oftentimes we spend so much time thinking about what did or didn't happen that it affects our ability to fulfill God's purpose for us right now. It doesn't matter if the past is a good memory or a painful one, too much attention on it stifles what you should be doing now and clouds your vision for the future.

The Good Old Days

For some, "the good old days" had very few hurdles, and it was easy to breeze through the cares of life. But when unexpected trials came later, it was a different story; they weren't prepared to handle them. The difficulties were an unwelcome surprise that burst their bubble of joy. It is a pleasure to praise God and love Him when things are easy.

But when the heat turns up and life becomes a serious challenge, many really struggle to give God the praise that came so readily before.

There is a tendency to blame God for allowing trials that darken a bright and cheery outlook. Some question God, and their relationship with Him suffers because they feel betrayed or let down. Praise and thanksgiving take a back seat to resentment and hurt. When this happens many well meaning Christians distance themselves from God and risk falling away from their faith.

Don't become so accustomed to your comfortable life that you can't still flourish in your relationship with God through the tough times. Never allow yourself to be so consumed with those "good old days" that you resent the "here-and-now," no matter how challenging it might be.

Try to remember that God is perfect; He doesn't make mistakes.

If you can keep that in the front of your memory bank, you will continue to live with an attitude of praise toward Him. Acknowledge that your perfectly loving God must know something that you don't. Trust His goodness with a thankful heart, and love Him during the hard times too.

The Not So Good Old Days

For many, the past is so painful that God's purpose for them will never be fulfilled. The hurts and disappointments of yesterday are crippling. All they can do is hobble through the present with doubts about the future.

If you can't release the mayhem of the past, you will struggle to live a life of praise and thanksgiving toward God. A difficult past that has not been dealt with properly will taint your relationship with God and keep you from loving Him unconditionally. How can you live with an attitude of gratitude toward God if you are holding Him accountable for what happened long ago?

The shortcomings of the past can become the crutch that keeps you from moving on in good spiritual health.

Some use the painful past as an excuse for not moving forward in their relationship with their Heavenly Father. They forfeit a bright future because they haven't been able to let go of the past to function normally in the present. They hobble along on their crutches instead of getting on the operating table and allowing the Holy Spirit to do spiritual surgery so they can move on in life.

Don't let that happen to you! If you were dealt a difficult hand yesterday, please don't let it hinder your relationship with God today. Allow the Holy Spirit to do strategic surgery on your heart and emotions so that you can relate to your Heavenly Father in the praise posture He desires. He loves you so much! He knows that when you live with an attitude of gratitude today, you will thrive in His presence tomorrow.

It doesn't matter who you are or what your status in the world is. At some point you will feel like life just isn't fair. You will either waiver in your faith or stand firm and grow closer to God. Your Heavenly Father is praiseworthy, no matter what this imperfect world presents to you. Whether you had "good old days" or not so good ones, know that you must focus on praising God today so that your relationship with Him can flourish tomorrow.

The Fear of God

- Is God perfect or not?
- Can you activate your life song...no matter what?
- Do you have a healthy fear of God?

It can be a challenge to relate to a loving and merciful God while maintaining a healthy fear of Him. If we are only looking at what God can do for us without remembering who He is, our view of Him will be distorted. We get so focused on the humanity of Jesus that we can't see that He really **is** God. It is great to feel comfortable with our Lord and relate to His humanity. After all, He did leave a flawless example that speaks directly to **our** humanity. But we must keep a healthy perspective of our King in order to be able to humble ourselves in a loving posture of praise.

Much of our prayer life consists of making requests to God; the Bible tells us to do that. People everywhere asked everything of Jesus, and He was always gracious to them. I ask everything of Him too. But I have learned that without a healthy fear and reverence of Him, I treat my Lord like a genie in a bottle; my wish is His command. If I am not careful, my demands upon God will outweigh my awe of Him. When that happens, God is suddenly not so perfect and awesome anymore. God merely becomes a peer, and I place Him on my level of understanding.

In Isaiah 55:8, the Bible says *"'For My thoughts are not your thoughts, nor are your ways My ways,' says the Lord."* Sometimes I think I have things figured out and establish unrealistic expectations of God. I assume He is going to answer my prayers a certain way. I think I'm standing in faith...when really I am standing on my own agenda. I can become so narrowly focused in my prayers that I am blinded by my agenda. How tragic!

When that happens, I only see things my way. And when I see it my way, then I lose my healthy reverence of God and develop unhealthy attitudes about Him. This opens the door to anger and resentment. Anger and resentment jeopardize your attitude of praise toward God. Ultimately your relationship with Him will be altered.

You can't hold the God of the universe in high esteem if you are mad at Him. Either God is perfect, or He isn't. If you believe He is perfect, then He doesn't make mistakes.

If God doesn't answer your prayers the way you assumed or within your timing, try not to be angry with Him. Know that He always has the bigger picture in mind and that He is still worthy of praise, no matter how things turn out. Ask the Holy Spirit to show you what He sees and give you what you need to continue to praise God. Then you won't struggle so much with anger. You will live with the revelation that God is God and that you aren't. You will be in awe of your loving, merciful God, and your life song will be a pleasing melody to Him, no matter what.

Count Your Blessings

For most of your life you've been told to count your blessings. This is nothing new to you. Yet there is a sure guarantee that when you take the time to recount the good things that God has done for you, you will enter into an attitude of gratitude toward Him.

"Remember the things I have done in the past. For I alone am God! I am God, and there is none like me" (Isaiah 46: 9 NLT). When the Jewish people prayed, they always began their prayers by remembering who God was and what He did for them. That makes sense to me! When I remember to do that, I always have a better attitude as I enter into prayer. My faith increases as I recount God's goodness. It helps to keep God on the throne where He rightfully belongs.

Let's take this a step further. Think of what your attitude toward God might be like if you are constantly mindful of Him and His goodness. You will fall in love with your Savior over and over again. You will naturally enter into a wonderful awareness of His amazing presence as you contemplate His goodness toward you and others.

God is pleased with your willing soul that contemplates His goodness often. That is how you will develop a thankful heart. It comes with deliberate focus on God's love and goodness.

Your life song becomes a sweet aroma to God. It is a lifestyle of praise and worship to the Love of your Life!

*"Shout for joy to the Lord, all the earth.
Worship the Lord with gladness; come before him with joyful songs.
Know that the Lord is God. It is he who made us,
we are his people, the sheep of his pasture.
Enter his gates with thanksgiving and his courts with praise;
give thanks to him and praise his name.
For the Lord is good and his love endures forever;
his faithfulness continues through all generations."*
(Psalm 100 NIV)

Pause a Moment

You have the awesome privilege of worshiping your Maker, the Creator of the Universe. Embrace your good fortune and praise Him!

Your Heart... His Temple

In the Bible, the temple was the place where God dwelt, and people went there to be closer to Him. It was a sacred structure, a holy place set apart for God. "*Then He went into the temple and began to drive out those who bought and sold in it*" (Luke 19: 45).

Jesus discovered that some parts of the temple were being used in ways that showed no respect for its purpose, ways that dishonored God. He was filled with righteous anger and rid the temple of all that was contrary to its purpose.

"Do you not know that you are the temple of God and that the Spirit of God dwells in you? If anyone defiles the temple of God, God will destroy him. For the temple of God is holy, which temple you are" (1Corinthians 3: 16,17). Remember that when you gave your heart to Jesus and dedicated your life to Him, you became a dwelling place for His Holy Spirit. Your heart actually is the niche where you are closer to God. There is no other like it; it belongs only to you. It is a sacred, holy place set apart for fellowship with God through the Holy Spirit.

It is easy to forget that Christ actually dwells in us through the presence of the Holy Spirit. Living each day mindful of this will keep your heart sacred and holy for God. You won't be as likely to fill your mind and heart with things that pollute them. You will find yourself being more protective of your heart, guarding it day and night. This will help you access the presence of the Living God on a moment to moment basis.

You are never alone...period.
You never have to be destitute...period.

You have constant fellowship with the Holy Spirit. Access the presence of God moment to moment, and watch your temple glow with the glory of God.

The Miraculous

We like to focus on what God does in the world, how He answers prayer, and builds His kingdom on earth. These things help to raise our level of faith. Yet while all that is worthy of praise, we would also do well to concentrate on the relationship we share with God.

One of the greatest miracles of all time is the miracle of being able to know God.

You have been invited to **know** Him who created you and the universe! In the Bible, knowing means more than having knowledge of God and the Scriptures; it implies intimate relationship. Jesus modeled perfect intimacy with the Father so that we could commune with God as well.

Are you responding to your invitation, to the miracle of being able to know God?

"*Today, if you will hear His voice, do not harden your hearts*" (Psalm 95: 7). When you hear the voice of the Holy Spirit, don't doubt or disobey. Doubt and disobedience prevent you from truly knowing your Heavenly Father, and the soft, pliable condition of your heart is severely altered. Instead of doubting, ask Jesus to bring revelation and clarity. You will grow to know the Father just as Jesus did.

Jesus said, "*My Father has entrusted everything to me. No one truly knows the Son except the Father, and no one truly knows the Father except the Son and those to whom the Son chooses to reveal him*" (Matthew 11: 27 NLT).

The relationship you already have with Jesus Christ will certainly help you to understand God more completely. Embrace every revelation from Jesus concerning the Father. You will recognize the voice of God everywhere you go, and He will guide you through your circumstances. Soon you will overcome your weaknesses, and your struggles will diminish as well. It all comes out of relationship with the Holy Spirit. So don't let anything hold you back from complete intimacy with God.

Your Joyful Place

- Where is your joyful place?
- How often do you go to your place of refuge?
- What keeps you from your joyful place?
- Have you ever invited God to visit your special place?

Time is a precious commodity. In our world of busyness and overwhelming schedules, there isn't much time to retreat on a regular basis. Yet each of us in in dire need of rest and relaxation. Unfortunately we tend to ignore that need while we strive for more and more.

Not many of us have a special place designated for rest and relaxation. It's hard enough to keep up with one place to live much less have a vacation home in a dreamy location. Finances keep us from retreating to a far off oasis regularly. Having a joyful place seems more like a dream; it is simply not a reality.

What if your perfect spot wasn't in a physical location? Your place of joy doesn't have to be costly or so far away that you can't get there often. It can be readily accessible and available in an instant.

Your true joyful place is a spiritual matter, a state of being where you converse with God on a regular basis.

God waits for you in that amazing spot where He slips your feet into "rest and relaxation" the moment you enter in. You will be built up, renewed, and filled after the stress of life wears you down. You are treated as an heir to the throne in that happy place designed specially for you. People pay great amounts of money for that kind of pampering. But for you, it is complementary, an extravagant gift from God. Jesus paid a royal price so that you could live so luxuriously.

Everywhere you go, there are pot holes along the way. If you aren't careful, you can slip into a deep one and throw yourself out of alignment from God's will. But if you have been in your joyful place with God, you will probably recognize the voice of the Holy Spirit warning you of the danger ahead. God's Spirit will even give you the insight you need to avoid calamity without much effort. But if you don't take advantage of your personal retreat times with God, you will probably obtain your insight the hard way.

Prayer and fellowship with the Holy Spirit is what you were made for. It pleases God greatly when you communicate with Him on a regular basis. But you are the one who benefits the most from it. You have the King of all kings with you every moment. His lasting fellowship never gets old and stale. Your heart never has to suffer the pain of loneliness or rejection because God is filling your voids.

God tells you He loves you as often as you need to hear it. And it all comes out of prayer and fellowship with Him.

Never stop listening for the voice of God. Always practice, and don't be afraid to make a mistake. Jesus is on your side, and He is cheering you on while He paves the path for you to know the Father more intimately. All you have to do is pursue God, and He will let you catch Him. Sometimes you will catch Him running in the wind, and other times you will run into Him when you least expect it.

Most importantly, don't stop your pursuit of God or the activity of the Holy Spirit in your life. As long as He knows you are available, He will speak to you.

God doesn't stay as silent as we think He does. When we aren't able to tune in to Him, we think He isn't saying anything to us. Sometimes that is the case. But oftentimes God is speaking; we just aren't in a correct posture to hear His voice clearly. We're too busy with life to sit quietly and listen. We expect Him to deliver the goods on our terms, in our timing, and the same way He did it before.

Never think you have the formula for hearing God's voice.

Just when you think you do, He might change things a bit. This helps you stay engaged, pursuing the relationship because of love, not because of what you want from God. Remember that God is love and that love comes first. Everything comes from loving God more than anything else.

The greatest benefit of prayer and fellowship with God is simply enjoying His company.

You will be amazed at how many things fall into place after a good run and frolic with the Holy Spirit in loving intimacy. Many times that is when the clouds part and the sun shines on your day. Don't be afraid to approach your relationship with the Holy Spirit that way. I can assure you that He is waiting for you to discover your joyful place with Him.

He's the Same God

Fellowship with God isn't a new, spiritual invention. It isn't the latest craze or a current event. God has been speaking to His people since the creation of man. Not only was God verbal with His children, He had them doing things out of the ordinary.

God spoke to Noah and instructed him to build an ark. *"Make yourself an ark of gopherwood; make rooms in the ark, and cover it inside and outside with pitch"* (Genesis 6: 14).

God told Abraham to sacrifice his son, Isaac. *"Then He said, 'Take now your son, your only son Isaac, whom you love, and go to the land of Moriah, and offer him there as a burnt offering on one of the mountains of which I shall tell you'"* (Genesis 22: 2).

God commanded Moses to perform signs and wonders before Pharaoh so that the Israelites could be freed from slavery. *"And the Lord said to Moses, 'When you go back to Egypt, see that you do all those wonders before Pharaoh which I have put in our hand'"* (Exodus 4:21).

God commissioned Joshua to cross the Jordan River into the Promised Land. *"Now therefore, arise, go over this Jordan, you and all this people, to the land which I am giving to them...the children of Israel"* (Joshua 1; 2).

In Hebrews 13: 8, the Bible says that God is the same yesterday, today, and forever. The God who spoke to His people in the past is still speaking to His people today. He is speaking words of love, instruction, and encouragement just as He did thousands of years ago. God is speaking to you now through His Holy Spirit.

The Holy Spirit could be whispering words of love and delight to you right now. You might be on a training ground with Him as He fine tunes you for a specific purpose. Perhaps God has been imparting vision and direction to keep you in His will. The list of possibilities is endless, and it is all so exciting.

Be available to fellowship with the Living God, and watch your relationship soar to new heights and places! When you are on God's schedule, He will fill your calendar with divine appointments...and all for His great glory!

> *"They called upon the Lord, and He answered them.*
> *He spoke to them in the cloudy pillar;*
> *They kept His testimonies and the ordinance He gave them."*
> *Psalm 99: 7*

Pause a Moment

You were created to know God and have His companionship. So simply enjoy Him!

Settle the Issues

We've spent plenty of time talking about learning to trust God and depend upon Him for everything. Your journey has probably taken you places where you have had to lean on God in various ways. It's good for you because you won't be able to thrive in God's presence if you don't trust Him for even the smallest details.

Sometimes I think that the Holy Spirit invents ways to get me to practice trusting Him more. It's not always easy, especially when my family is involved. There's nothing like good homeland security and a few ducks in a row! Yet even as I grow and advance on my journey, I sense the Lord testing my willingness to trust Him more and more.

The big questions always come up for me to answer.

- Is God really God...or not?

- Am I going to trust Him even though my ducks aren't lined up...or not?

We have to remember that God cannot be controlled, contained, or manipulated no matter how we think or what we do.

Before you can advance your pursuit of God, you have to come to terms with who God is and who you are in relation to Him.

You must see God as your Father and the One in charge. You also have to be comfortable being a little child in His arms and perfect will. When you settle that issue, you will become "a natural" at dependency upon your Heavenly Father.

If you struggle with control issues, then go back and spend quiet time in your joyful place with God. The Holy Spirit will provide an environment that will help you to settle your issues and get you back on track for the rest of your journey. Don't lose precious time floundering in your struggles. As soon as you realize you aren't making progress, take your issues to the Father quickly for emergency care. And please don't be too proud to admit that you are too proud to trust God. He already knows, so just acknowledge it, and let His Spirit help you.

Remember that Jesus was totally dependent upon the Father and frequently retreated to spend time with Him. That's when the Holy Spirit gives revelation, wisdom, and hope to you. All you need to know is that you need Him; the rest is up to God.

We forget that being as a little child puts most of the responsibility on God. We just need to love and obey Him radically. Sometimes it is easier said than done. God's gift of free will gets in the way, doesn't it? For such a great gift to have, it sure gets us in trouble at times! That's when the timeless Word of God bails us out. When you go to the Bible and read God's spiritual principles for your life, He'll help you tame your free will, use it as a special gift, and cash in on His perfect will for you instead. It's amazing!

Always settle issues before they cause you to settle for less than God's perfect will.

Who Trusts Who?

Learning to trust God comes with an unexpected surprise. Not only do we learn to trust and depend upon God, but we also learn whether or not God can trust **us**! If we go back to all those Bible heroes, we will find a common thread when it came to trusting God.

In order for them to accomplish the will of God, they had to have great faith and trust Him implicitly. But then they learned that God also trusted them.

Can you imagine how those Bible greats felt knowing that God trusted them?

Knowing that God picks you and trusts you is not an opportunity for pride; it's a most humbling feeling. That's when you know you need Him most. You wonder... who trusts who? It turns out to be a mutual agreement that says I know I need God and He knows I depend upon Him, so He entrusts me with His perfect will. What a beautiful agreement between a Father and His child!

Have you ever heard the saying, "God doesn't call the qualified, He qualifies the called?"

Jesus did it the Father's way, totally dependent upon Him. The Holy Spirit is looking for those who will do it the same way that Jesus did. He isn't looking at credentials or ability; the Holy Spirit is looking for a willing heart that is totally dependent upon God. He'll do the training. Then He knows the job is going to get done according to the will of the Father. God knows that arrogance and selfish pride won't be there to contaminate His mission because His willing servant is totally dependent upon Him. Likewise, that humble servant knows that God is pleased and will entrust more later.

▸ What has God entrusted to you, and how are you doing with it?

If you practice trusting God for everything, be assured that He will notice and trust you in return.

You will represent the King as an ambassador of the Kingdom of God, and that is an awesome privilege. Yet it results from being a little child in His arms daily.

It's hard to imagine a little child accomplishing great and mighty things on the Lord's behalf. But God is pleased with His little ones who spend time getting to know and love Him. He knows they will do it His way and in His timing. They trust Him to lead and direct their paths, and He trusts them to accomplish His perfect will.

"Trust in the Lord with all your heart, And lean not on your own understanding; In all your ways acknowledge Him, And He shall direct your paths." (Proverbs 3: 5,6)

Trusting God is a conscious decision to love Him no matter what. Out of unconditional love you will naturally lean on God and depend upon Him for everything. Get to know God, acknowledge His greatness, and learn to live in His presence moment by moment.

In return, God knows that He can depend upon you and trust you with His will. He will guide your path and take good care of you.

Counting the Cost

When you decide to trust God and obey His will, you are making an eternal investment into His kingdom. As we learned earlier, you give up a lot when you decide to depend upon God instead of yourself. But what you leave behind is nothing but rubbish compared to the riches you gain.

Still, we can't diminish the fact that much of what goes out the back door has been with us for a very long time. So long, that it has become a part of us, and it's not easy to set it out for pick-up and removal. Much of what needs to go has been working against us and hindering our relationship with God. It hides in subtle places so that we won't recognize the control is has in our lives.

The Holy Spirit will expose the rubbish in your life if you really want to get it get rid of it. In your pursuit of God, the Holy Spirit will gently bring to light what has been hidden in the darkness. Jesus said, *"For there is nothing hidden which will not be revealed, nor has anything been kept secret but that it should come to light"* (Mark 4: 22).

Your relationship with God has to be so important to you that you are willing to put your agenda aside in eager anticipation of His plan. That means exchanging self seeking independence for dependence upon the perfect will of God. Even though your heart knows it's a good thing to do, your will can put up a good fight. If you stay close to God in a posture of praise and keep your spiritual ears tuned in to the Holy Spirit, your heart will win the fight. Your spirit already desires the great freedom that is in store for you.

Remember...everything that keeps you from trusting God must leave at any cost.

You will struggle to live in the presence of God if you allow stubborn strongholds to govern your spiritual well being. What you have achieved in your own strength doesn't amount to much in the Kingdom of God because it tends to feed your ego and selfish pride. You have to become a nobody so that the Holy Spirit can turn you into somebody for God's eternal purpose. Keep in mind that becoming a nobody doesn't mean you lack good self-esteem or confidence. It simply means that who you are centers around the person of Jesus Christ and that your confidence is in what His Spirit does in your life. It means that in order to realize your full potential, you must be like a little child, totally reliant upon God for everything.

Becoming like a child in order to be reliant upon your Heavenly Father is expensive. It demands relinquishment of your selfish pride and stubborn will. But you receive an enormous return on your investment. Not only will your journey progress within the will of God, but you will also enjoy the roadside perks along the way. Your relationship with God will blossom, and your fellowship with Him will be sweet. When you weigh the cost against the benefits of trusting God, you will make the right choice.

Less Room for Sin

It's easy for sin to go unnoticed because we live in an imperfect world where sin is prevalent. Sin is a part of our human nature; that is why we all need a Savior. Yet because we have been saved by grace through Jesus Christ, sometimes we ignore sin, knowing that we'll always be forgiven. Paul addresses this in Romans 6: 1,2. *"Well then, should we keep on sinning so that God can show us more and more of his wonderful grace? Of course not! Since we have died to sin, how can we continue to live in it?"*

Without placing unreal expectations upon you, I want to encourage you to live each moment under the leadership of the Holy Spirit. Everyone makes mistakes, but those who yield to the promptings of God's Spirit will overcome temptations to sin more easily. Your trust in a Higher Source will help you to do things God's way instead of your own.

Even though we are human and imperfect, The Bible tells us not to sin. *"My dear children, I am writing this to you so that you will not sin. But if anyone does sin, we have an advocate who pleads our case before the Father. He is Jesus Christ, the one who is truly righteous"* (1 John 2 NLT). We don't have a license to fall short knowing Jesus is there for us and that His forgiveness is always available.

Don't live the same way you did before Jesus Christ became your Lord and Savior.

When you live according to the promptings of the Holy Spirit, your countenance is brighter and sin won't be in control of your life. Instead, God has a loving embrace on your life because you've asked Him to lead and guide you gently on your journey. You'll love His presence and leadership so much that sin just isn't as attractive anymore.

It takes radical trust to live in the radical presence of God moment by moment. It's as if you are feeling your way around in a pitch black room. When you reach out for the loving arms of God to see you through, you will find your way. It is much the same with sin. As long as you are reaching out, trusting God to lead and guide you, you will overcome the darkness of sin and its consequences.

Be encouraged to go against the flow and listen to the voice of the Holy Spirit. Pay attention to His promptings, and ask for the ability to overcome temptations.

The Holy Spirit will move in your heart to transform your life so that there really is less room for sin and more room for Jesus. Abide in Jesus Christ, and He will abide in you.

*"I am the vine, you are the branches.
He who abides in Me, and I in him, bears much fruit;
for without Me you can do nothing."*
John 15: 5

Desire God

Throughout our time together, we have talked about how much God desires you. He is crazy about you; after all, He created you. God only sees His perfect masterpiece every time He looks upon you. Your loving Father is God; He has everything, owns it all, and doesn't need a thing. All He really desires is you, your love, and your obedience.

Because we have many needs and concerns, we tend to desire God's performance in our lives more than His presence. Even though He's always there for us, God loves it when we simply desire Him the way He desires us. Just as He sees a beautiful creation when He thinks about us, we ought to see a loving Father every time we think about Him.

Run to your Father out of pure desire instead of frantic need all of the time. How refreshing it must be when that happens to Him! God knows you need Him, but does He know that you desire Him? Can He see your desire for Him grow stronger each day? Does your desire of God outweigh your cares and concerns?

Come to God out of desire, and watch Him meet your needs as well.

Love God

The love of Christ enables you to love the Father. United with Jesus through His Spirit, we can fully express our love to God. It is a love that is unconditional and uninhibited by the cares of the world. It's a love that embraces God for who He is no matter what happens.

Your love for God opens windows that welcome the refreshment of His presence like nothing else can.

When you are focused on God's love, you will sense His presence more and more. It's easier to praise, fellowship, and trust God when you feel Him all around you. It is also easier to love others when your relationship with God is flourishing.

How much you love God can be measured by how well you treat others.

"Or when did we see You sick, or in prison, and come to You? And the King will answer and say to them, 'Assuredly, I say to you, inasmuch as you did it to one of the least of these My brethren, you did it to Me'" (Matthew 25: 39,40). Whether there is an opportunity for unselfish service or an act of compassion, your love for God and your relationship with Him is reflected in how you relate to those around you.

Don't be afraid to reflect the love of Christ beaming within you. It isn't a phony outer front; it is genuine, and you don't have to work at it. If you find yourself having to work hard at loving anyone, then you need to be spending more time on your loving relationship with God. Get away to your joyful place with God and rekindle your love for Him. Then it won't be as difficult to love as you should.

Your love for God shows when you interact with others.

Oftentimes we overlook how we treat or mistreat those we love the most. Do you lose your temper? Are your answers short and curt? Do you ever take your loved ones for granted? Do you ever hurt the ones you love the most? *"Assuredly, I say to you, inasmuch as you did not do it to one of the least of these, you did not do it to Me"* (Matthew 25: 45).

The life of Jesus Christ was founded on love, and Jesus radiated love. He left you a flawless example to follow. You have His loving road map spread before you in the Gospels. You know you are loved by the King of Kings and the Creator of Life. Accept the gracious gift of love that you have been given, and love God back. Then you will be able to love others as Jesus has loved you.

Obey God

You already have a greater desire for God and His character. Your love for Him has taken you deeper into a realm of His presence where everything about Him is available to you. Now it's time to journey even deeper with God. Remember what Jesus said, *"If you love me, you will obey what I command"* (John 14:15 NIV).

Obedience to God comes from intimacy with Him.

You won't be able to obey God out of sheer will; no one does, and you can't either. That's why we need an amazing relationship with our Savior through His Spirit. *"Work hard to show the results of your salvation, obeying God with deep reverence and fear. For God is working in you, giving you the desire and the power to do what pleases Him"* (Philippians 2: 12,13 NLT).

Obedience pleases God. He already knows how hard this is, so God offers to help you. The Holy Spirit gives you the desire to obey God and even empowers you so that you can. What a loving God! While you pursue intimacy with God, His Spirit does all the work.

You will need to cooperate, though. You can't let any of your weaknesses become strongholds. They will keep you from doing what pleases God.

You must stay close to God. Don't allow the ways of an imperfect world to contaminate your picture perfect relationship with God. When temptation comes along, look to your Higher Source so you don't indulge. Send out an "SOS" immediately, and the Holy Spirit will come to your aid. Run to your joyful place as soon as you can, and you will regroup. The Lord strengthens you there so that you won't succumb when you are tempted again.

Be Compassionate and Forgiving

It doesn't matter what your circumstances are, you must forgive...period. Don't take matters into your own hands; let God be your avenger. The Holy Spirit will do a much better job of dealing with the unfairness than you will. If you take charge, then there might be more hurts and trouble.

Remember to ask the Holy Spirit to show you what He sees about your circumstance. God reveals things that bring you to your knees in prayer for the other person. Don't let your hurt or disappointment cause your heart to be hardened. Instead, ask God to protect your heart from every kind of attack. You become a blessing to your offender when you release the offense. *"Blessed is he whose transgression is forgiven"* (Psalm 32: 1).

When you think you have forgiven but still struggle with negative thoughts, check in with God.

The Holy Spirit will reveal the true condition of your heart and help you get over your hurdle. When you are at peace and it surpasses all your understanding, then you know you have forgiven. Oftentimes that is when you are moved with compassion.

Keep in mind that compassion isn't going to make you feel sorrow or pity for your offender. Compassion allows you to feel whatever God wants you to experience at the time. It brings you to an action depending on what the issue is. Compassion is like the finishing touch on the act of forgiveness. The action isn't always toward the offender. God might have something else that is tailored just for you. As long as you are connected to His Spirit, you won't miss the happy ending to what could have been a sad story.

Whenever you struggle to forgive and move with compassion, read the story of Joseph and his brothers in the Bible. It is a dramatic account of forgiveness and compassion. Joseph forgave and was moved with compassion toward his own flesh and blood. It's one thing to be hurt by a friend or acquaintance, but another to be abandoned and betrayed by your most beloved. Joseph lived with salt in his wounds because all the while he was enslaved, he knew he had his jealous brothers to blame. Yet Joseph's love for God was greater than his anger toward his brothers. He was able to forgive because he let God be God. Many years later, Joseph found favor with God and rose to power in Egypt. It was then that his painful past paid him a visit.

But instead of taking revenge, Joseph was moved with compassion toward his brothers and was reconciled to them. Joseph's story is found in the Book of Genesis in chapters 37-47.

> **Pause a Moment**
>
> Walk in forgiveness. It brings peace, and it feels like freedom at its best.

Spiritual Alignment

If you have a genuine desire to please God and obey Him, then you will have to align your value system with His. Your desires must become like God's. The more you allow the Holy Spirit to work in your life, the easier it is maintain that alignment.

"Let love be without hypocrisy. Abhor what is evil. Cling to what is good."
Romans 12: 9

**Learn to love whatever God loves.
Never embrace sin.**

God is so far removed from sin that those who embrace it usually distance themselves from Him. You could be putting your relationship with God in jeopardy even when you ignore sin. Instead, make it your resolve to turn your back on everything that is evil. Your primary desire in life should be to please God. So when you see acts of selfish ambition, pride, and deceit, have nothing to do with them. Your Heavenly Father will reward you greatly when you choose to align yourself with Him and His character.

In our world of few absolutes, many sins have become socially acceptable. As long as the law isn't broken, anything goes. Without absolutes, everything is relative. Sadly, many fall into that trap. If you aren't careful, you can quietly slip into the same mindset that deceives even well meaning Christians. That's why accountability relationships can be very helpful. Others will help you stay aligned with Jesus Christ and point you to the timeless principles of the Bible.

Your ultimate, accountability relationship with God won't suffer or dwindle when you keep yourself aligned with His character. When you desire God, you will experience all He has for you. He holds nothing back from His precious loved ones who seek Him.

**Your spiritual alignment with God will also help you realize
His presence in the moment to moment of your life.**

It is much easier to recognize the Lord when you are looking for Him. If you are basking in His qualities and character, you won't miss Him.

You will love what God loves, and sin will be less and less attractive. Your absolutes are Biblically based, and you are appalled by the sins that the world deems socially acceptable. Your life looks more and more like your Savior's. He desires you, and you desire Him back.

*"May He grant you according to your heart's desire,
and fulfill all your purpose."*
Psalm 20: 4

The Refining Process

Your journey to live with God has seen mountain top adventures, valley lows, and even some rough terrain. You've been on smooth pathways, dirt trails, and a few rocky roads. A life of praise is not a foreign thought anymore because it's becoming a part of you. The training ground you spend so much time on is becoming familiar turf as you pray and listen for the voice of the Holy Spirit. The simplicity of a trusting relationship with God has lessened your load along the way. Now God's marvelous characteristics are being infused into your spirit so that you can align yourself more with Jesus. You are more than equipped to abandon your burdens and bothersome baggage in exchange for God's perfect plan.

Every good gift in God's kingdom is available to you right now. Take advantage of your resources, and enter into the powerful process of abandonment.

The Holy Spirit carries you across the threshold from having a good life to living a powerful one in Christ.

You won't want to go back into the world of mediocrity because you are destined for excellence, living in the presence of God each moment.

When you cross that threshold, you will shed the tainted, outer coat of your fleshly ways. That begins the refining process that Jesus takes you through as you learn to live in His presence and be more like Him. God uses every circumstance and each moment of your life to weave a custom fit garment of peace.

Remember how I used to fret about abandonment? I thought I was going to lose everything. It never occurred to me that I had everything to gain. But when I let go and allow God to gently refine the impurities from my character, I am freed from many burdens. Now I encourage you to engage in radical abandonment and let the process begin. God sees you through every step of the process.

I can't tell you that I've arrived and that the process is complete. The refining process of abandonment is never over because we live in an imperfect world. There will always be opportunity to forgive. Disappointments appear out of nowhere. Pride and selfishness creep in the back door. Damaging thoughts try to flood your memory bank. Unrealistic expectations take can take you down dark alleys. The list is endless.

The good news is that you've already crossed the threshold, and you are wearing your garment of peace.

You know what it is like to let go and find peace because you've had plenty of practice on the field. You won't be carrying a lifetime supply of heavy burdens or bothersome baggage anymore. You already let that go. Whenever something extra sneaks up on you, the Holy Spirit alerts you to it and helps you take it to the cross of Christ. God even helps you turn your back on it and walk away. He is so generous with His time and love for you!

Don't Stress About It

Our society has conditioned us to plow through life, full speed ahead. In doing this we tend to take matters into our own hands. We learn to problem solve, plan, and then project ourselves into the future. The world we live in tells you that nobody is going to look out for you; you must do it yourself. We even attempt the "do it yourself" method in our spirituality.

We place too much stress upon ourselves when we try to understand spiritual matters and deal with life alone. Sometimes we analyze things to death. Then we overexert ourselves to make a plan, build a bridge, and get over it on our own. Some who make it over the bridge are oftentimes out of breath and energy. They did everything they knew to do, but they lost their zeal for life and God in the process. Many sacrifice their relationship with the Living God in an effort to do it themselves.

"Therefore humble yourselves under the mighty hand of God, that He may exalt you in due time, casting all your care upon Him, for He cares for you" (1 Peter 5: 6, 7).

When you practice casting your cares upon Jesus, you admit that you can't do it alone. You place them at the foot of His cross, and He picks them up to act upon your behalf. That doesn't mean you can always sit back and expect magic. You have to cooperate with God. There are times when things happen supernaturally and times when they happen naturally...supernaturally.

God always intervenes, but oftentimes He requires your participation. The real beauty is in how natural it can become when you allow God to take care of things.

- Are you worried about something?
- Is there a mountain too high to climb?
- Is life feeling more unfair than normal?

There's always going to be a challenge. Why not let God accept the challenge on your behalf? It's His job in the first place. He's your Father, He's there for you, and He is more than able.

Here's what you can do. Whenever a challenge comes, talk to God about it. Let Him know your concerns, but then thank Him for being there for you. Admit that you can't do it without Him. You can even remind Him that it isn't going to be resolved if He doesn't intervene. Ask God to help you recognize His voice, and pray for wisdom to understand it. Thank God for taking care of things. Then expect that God is going to bring peace to you and intervene however He chooses.

"For My thoughts are not your thoughts, nor are your ways My ways," says the Lord" (Isaiah 55: 8). Always remember that our ways are not God's ways. So leave the thought process and the outcome to God. Simply rest in His ability and desire to take care of everything. God will let you know what to do; you won't miss it. As long as you are seeking **His** will, it is pretty hard to miss what God is doing or saying.

Protect Your Relationship

Practice leaving matters in God's hands. The peace that comes from your acts of abandonment is priceless. You will be able to describe the light hearted feeling that comes from the release of heavy burdens. It's freedom in a very special form.

Even though we place matters in God's hands, most of us still struggle to keep our own ways and ideas out of the picture. We always have an opinion! Just know that your precious peace and new found freedom are meant to sustain you if things are not going quite like you thought they would after letting go.

Sometimes it gets worse before it gets better. There are times when God has to do a work in your heart before He can change your circumstances. I've learned that there is always a bigger picture that I can't see. God's timing isn't always the same as yours. If the Holy Spirit tells you that your prayer will be answered soon, don't decide when that is. Your unsafe assumptions can cause you to impose false expectations upon God.

False expectations will cause turmoil for you.

When God doesn't meet them, you will be tempted to get angry with Him. We've talked about how dangerous that is. Your relationship with God is at great risk if you allow anger to spoil it.

Remember that Jesus warned us about trials and tribulations. He said they would come our way. What we do with them is critical. Don't allow them to destroy your relationship with God. Never blame God when life presents you with difficulties. God is your bright spot in life, not your thorn, and **never** to blame.

Every relationship with God is tested when life isn't fair. *"Examine yourselves as to whether you are in the faith. Test yourselves. Do you not know yourselves, that Jesus Christ is in you?"* (2 Corinthians 13: 5)

You must protect your relationship at all costs because it is your most prized possession. Everything else is secondary to your new life with God.

In order to unite your heart with God's, stock pile the five ingredients needed to live with Him moment to moment.

You can't overstock praise and thanksgiving; you need a lifetime supply of it. Invest in many lines of communication between you and your Father, and pray without ceasing as the Bible instructs. Let your trust and dependency upon God spill out of the cupboards of your soul. Your childlike attitude with God should blossom to full maturity. Desire all of God's character traits that you can, and load up on them. There are more of them than you can count. Reckless abandonment unto God should be a habit by now. Then your relationship with God will be more secure, unwavering, and untouchable when difficulties come and life doesn't go the way you planned.

"Don't Wrestle; Just Nestle"

While I was writing *Living in His Presence*, I became friends with Ruth Myers. I had read some of the books she authored and greatly admired her relationship with the Lord. More than any other person in the world, I wanted to meet Ruth and be like her. If you've read any of her inspirational books then you might understand my desire. You would undoubtedly sense her deep intimacy with God, as I did. Ruth has spent her lifetime serving God and getting to know Him. I had to get to know this wonderful lady who "knows God."

Whenever we are together, I'm always amazed at her spiritual wisdom and insights. Ruth has an uncanny way of unveiling the heart of Christ so that I can recognize Him better. I could never list all the ways that she has encouraged me in my relationship with God. You and I don't have enough time together for that. But I **would** like to share one thing with you that Ruth said which helped me over the hurdle of abandonment.

Ruth recognized my fears and struggles concerning abandonment. We talked about how difficult it can be to let go unless you have a solid love relationship with God. Ruth told me that God never meant for it to be that hard. Jesus showed us that everything comes out of loving God. She encouraged me to spend more alone time with God. Perhaps I would stop striving so hard and struggle less with abandonment.

Ruth reminded me that Jesus has always been my Victor, still is my Victor, and always will be my Victor. Then she quoted Corrie ten Boom when she said, "Don't wrestle, just nestle!"

Whenever I struggle with **anything**, I try to remember those reassuring words. I can fight my way through life, or I can simply love God with my whole heart, soul, and body. It isn't as hard to let go in abandonment when you grab on to Jesus at the same time. You can hold on to mere rubble, or you can wrap your arms around your Savior and nestle in. It's hard to do both at the same time; you only have two arms. Imagine the heavenly bliss that rests upon your weary soul when you bask in the arms of God knowing that your relationship with Him is secure!

"Therefore, having been justified by faith, we have peace with God through our Lord Jesus Christ, through whom also we have access by faith into this grace in which we stand, and rejoice in hope of the glory of God.

And not only that, but we also glory in tribulations, knowing that tribulation produces perseverance; and perseverance, character; and character, hope.

Now hope does not disappoint, because the love of God has been poured out in our hearts by the Holy Spirit who was given to us."
Romans 5: 1-5

For You

You and I have spent quite a lot of time together. I hope you feel like your time has been well spent. I know I have enjoyed being with you, and I've learned so much. Everything I've shared has come from what the Holy Spirit has taught me over the years through God's Word, personal experience, and the wisdom of so many. I'm sure that you have plenty to share as well. Perhaps someday our paths will cross again.

For now, I encourage you to continue your journey to pursue God and nurture your relationship with Him. Remember that the journey is your goal and that the Holy Spirit will be with you the entire time. You will spend the rest of your life learning to live with God moment to moment. There's no better way to live out your days than in the sweet awareness of God's presence.

You are well equipped for your journey with God. Yet don't be shy about asking the Holy Spirit to help you apply what you've learned so that you will have the best relationship possible. He's there for you whenever you need Him.

The five ingredients you have practiced will help you live by the power of the Holy Spirit instead of in your own strength. Guard them closely so that you won't misplace them. I love how they blend so well together and help me to live with God. Just think of all the wonderful ways they can work together to help you progress on **your** journey! The possibilities are endless, so enjoy exploring them as you live in His presence.

While you live in His presence, the Holy Spirit will share some of God's most intimate secrets with you. Each day is fresh and marks a new adventure with God. You will never be the same; what a joy!

God never changes. He is the God of the Old Testament and the God of the New Covenant. He'll be the same tomorrow as He is today. You don't have to read about Bible heroes of yesterday and wish you could have been there... you are there **now**. You are a Bible hero, walking in triumph, every time you do whatever God asks of you!

Enter into the secret place, the holy place set apart just for you. No one else has a relationship with God like yours. Enjoy it; and spend generous amounts of time with Him. God is always waiting for you, He loves you more than you know, and you are His pleasure.

Live by the Spirit and continue to pursue God.
His personal stamp of approval is already resting upon you.
God bless!

"...having believed, you were sealed with the Holy Spirit of promise, who is the guarantee of our inheritance."
Ephesians 1:13, 14

Twelve-Week Planning Guides

Personal Planning Guide   234

Living Groups   235

Living Groups Planning Guide   236

Secrets in His Presence: Twelve-Week Study
Personal Planning Guide

Week 1 | Prepare to study *Secrets in His Presence*

Read *Living in His Presence* as an overview for your study of *Secrets in His Presence*. As you journey through *Secrets,* spend more time in *Living,* reflecting on the Prayer Poems. Pray, and ask God to prepare your heart and draw you deeper into intimacy with Him.

Consider this: God will take you to spiritual places you've never seen, as you journey through this study.

Week 2 | New Beginning...pages 10-20

Consider this: This is a journey, and the journey is your goal.

Week 3 | Praise and Thanksgiving, First Ingredient...pages 22-46

Consider this: Be kind to yourself if you fail from time to time, and receive God's love and grace.

Week 4 | Prayer and Communication, Second Ingredient...pages 48-64

Consider this: Hearing God's voice should drive you to holiness.

Week 5 | Prayer and Communication, Complete Second Ingredient...pages 64-80

Consider this: Keep practicing, and watch for God to speak in various ways throughout your day.

Week 6 | Trust in God, Third Ingredient...pages 82-99

Consider this: Having great peace can change the course of your life.

Week 7 | Trust in God, Complete Third Ingredient...pages 100-122

Consider this: When worry grips and impatience brews, trusting God is suddenly out of the picture.

Week 8 | Desire for God, Fourth Ingredient...pages 124-150

Consider this: Ingredient Four solidifies your identity in Christ as you begin to share in His nature.

Week 9 | Desire for God, Complete Fourth Ingredient...pages 151-170

Consider this: God's love is bigger than selfishness. It sees others first and looks out for them.

Week 10 | Abandonment, Fifth Ingredient...pages 172-194

Consider this: You must have at least a little, solid history with God before you can "let go" and trust Him.

Week 11 | Abandonment, Complete Fifth Ingredient...pages 195-208

Consider this: Abandonment is a beautiful encounter with God that helps you thrive in His presence.

Week 12 | Blend of Ingredients, pages 210-232

Consider this: "Don't wrestle; just nestle." Run into the arms of your Savior and live!

Living Groups

Living Groups is the name given to groups that gather weekly to study *Secrets in His Presence*. Each group provides a safe environment where members can be honest about their relationship with God as they journey, share, and grow together. This wonderful avenue for spiritual growth and fellowship offers a special safety net of acceptance and transparency which under girds each group. There is a comfort level within Living Groups that is warm and inviting to all who join. Living Groups emerge from church groups, neighborhoods, and workplace settings. They also form amongst family and friends. Many meet one another for the first time when they join to study *Secrets in His Presence*. Soon, relationships develop, and members grow in the Lord together.

Some Living Groups continue to gather after the twelve-week study to remain connected. They fellowship and share in other spiritually, edifying works to nurture their relationship with God and encourage one another. Ideally, new groups sprout from the Living Group after the twelve-week study. New facilitators surface from the group to begin additional studies of *Secrets in His Presence* with more Living Group members. It's as if rows of lights are flickering in the night when new groups sprout and launch.

The unmistakable presence of God, spiritual growth, and sweet fellowship make Living Groups unique.

A Typical Living Group

Living Groups gather weekly for twelve weeks. They can meet anywhere... in a house, church, coffee shop, or even at a park. Group size varies from two to twelve members. This format invites intimacy, transparency, and an opportunity for everyone to share and be heard. Each group has a facilitator who keeps the meeting flowing. Facilitators complete normal, weekly assignments but do not have added preparations each week. They simply attend meetings willing to encourage personal sharing and discussion of the material. The facilitator uses the Planning Guide to foster group discussion and assign the reading for each week. Group members read the weekly assignment, complete Living Work at home, and come to meetings prepared to share. Living Work consists of answering a few reflective questions, applying spiritual principles to everyday life, and prayer. Reading assignments are minimal, about 25 pages per week.

Living Groups always open with prayer. During the meeting, groups share insights and answer discussion questions as outlined in the Planning Guide for each week. The facilitator maintains the flow of the meeting and encourages transparency during discussion. Living Groups always end with prayer for personal needs as they apply to the discussion of the day. Meeting times are approximately 90 minutes to two hours.

By the end of the twelve-week study, groups will have practiced the five ingredients necessary to thrive in an intimate relationship with God. Living Group members will learn to hear God's voice better, discover peace in the midst of the storm, watch as worry and fear melt away, and feel God's presence instead of loneliness.

Secrets in His Presence: Twelve-Week Study
Living Group Planning Guide

 ## Week 1 | Introduction of Living Group format and sharing of expectations

The facilitator and all group members introduce themselves and share briefly about their lives.

Facilitator Notes for discussion with Living Group members

Discuss: Using the Living Group Planning Guide, the facilitator simply assists in group dialogue. Group members complete assignments in *Secrets in His Presence* and come prepared each week to discuss the material. Living Groups may prefer to read *Living in His Presence* prior to studying *Secrets in His Presence* or simultaneously.

Discuss: Living Groups are interactive and Biblically based with practical, life application principles for growing spiritually in intimacy with God. The group will study and practice the five ingredients necessary to thrive in a relationship with God moment by moment. Living Group members will also learn to hear God's voice better, discover peace in the midst of their storms, watch as worry and fear melt away, and feel God's presence instead of loneliness.

Discuss: The unmistakable presence of God, spiritual growth, and sweet fellowship make Living Groups unique. Living Groups foster a safe, comfortable environment where each member is highly valued. Members are encouraged to be transparent and honest about their relationships with God as they journey, share, and grow.

Prayer request: Begin to pray about new Living Groups sprouting from this group after the twelve-week study.

Reading for Week 2: New Beginning, pages 10-20

Consider this: God will take you to spiritual places you've never seen, as you journey through this study.

 ## Week 2 | New Beginning...pages 10-20

Facilitator Notes: The group has read through page 20.

Assign reading for week 3...First Ingredient, pages 22-46.

End with prayer for each other.

The group will discuss some or all of the following questions as time permits.

Reference page 13: What makes you sure that God longs for a loving relationship with each of His children?

Reference pages 13, 14: What keeps you from moving forward in intimacy with God? Identify intimate road blocks that hinder you.

Reference page 15: What do you expect to find when you uncover your hidden treasure?

Reference page 16: We really are like sheep needing 24/7 tending. Without hearing God's voice, in what ways might you go astray?

Reference pages 17, 18: In what ways are we no busier in our culture today then our Bible heroes and those of the past?

Reference Pages 18, 19: God desires your companionship. He doesn't exist solely to answer prayer. Why is this critical to establish?

Reference page 20: What are you most looking forward to as you begin to journey and deepen your relationship with God?

Consider this: This is a journey, and the journey is your goal.

Week 3 | Praise and Thanksgiving, First Ingredient...pages 22-46

Facilitator Notes: The group has read through page 46.

Assign reading for week 4...Begin Second Ingredient, pages 48-64.

End with prayer for each other.

The group will discuss some or all of the following questions as time permits.

Reference pages 24, 25: Why is it critical to establish God's kingship and put Him on the "throne of thrones" in all areas of life?

Reference page 30: What is the benefit of being part of God's life instead of God being part of yours? Discuss Living Application, pg 31.

Reference pages 35, 36: Why is praise in the deeper waters more of a lifestyle of moment to moment thanksgiving toward God? Your posture of praise and attitude of gratitude affects how you handle trials. Why is this true?

Reference pages 37-39: Learning to ponder God takes practice. In what ways do you tend to take God and His greatness for granted?

Reference pages 40-42: What are the benefits of learning to live with an attitude of gratitude toward God?

Reference pages 44, 45: What do you risk when you don't keep your posture of praise toward God?

Consider this: No guilt. Be kind to yourself if you fail from time to time, and receive God's love and grace.

 ## Week 4 | Prayer and Communication, Second Ingredient...pages 48-64

Facilitator Notes: The group has read through page 64.

Assign reading for week 5...Complete Second Ingredient, pages 64-80.

End with prayer for each other.

The group will discuss some or all of the following questions as time permits.

Reference page 48: What does it mean to have true, lasting fellowship with one another and then ultimately with God?

Reference pages 50-53: Why is fellowship with God a key to a vibrant life?

Reference pages 54-56: Why is renewing your mind critical? Keys: ponder God, read Scripture, and choose what is spiritually edifying.

Reference pages 56, 57: In a relationship, God must not be on demand only. Is your communication system for prayer, one or two ways?

Reference pages 58-61: How do you see your prayer life changing if you no longer have an exhausting, endless prayer list?

Reference pages 61, 62: Why is it important to pursue God? Ask, seek, and knock...why are all three necessary?

Reference pages 62-64: You won't know God's thoughts until you ask. How can you enjoy God's companionship in the moment?

Consider this: Hearing from God should drive you to holiness.

Week 5 | Prayer and Communication, Second Ingredient...pages 64-80

Facilitator Notes: The group has read through page 80.

Assign reading for week 6...Begin Third Ingredient, pages 82-99.

End with prayer for each other.

The group will discuss some or all of the following questions as time permits.

Reference pages 64-66: You must learn to pursue God. Why are deliberate quiet times with God so important?

Reference pages 67-69: Recognizing God's voice takes practice. What daily nuts and bolts help you on your practice field? What are the various ways that God speaks to us? Share your experiences listening for His voice.

Reference pages 70, 71: Why must you keep a pure heart and make no false assumptions about hearing from God? Discuss the hindering, red lights.

Reference pages 77, 78: What are the highs and lows of listening for God? Share successes and struggles, strengths and weaknesses.

Reference pages 78-80: What is the value of prayer with confirmation? Why is it dangerous to respond to God if confused? Your spirit must be strong to discern God's will. When do your emotions speak too loud and mask God's voice?

Consider this: Keep practicing, and watch for God to speak in various ways throughout your day.

 # Week 6 | Trust in God, Third Ingredient...pages 82-99

Facilitator Notes: The group has read through page 99.

Assign reading for week 7...Complete Third Ingredient, pages 100-122.

End with prayer for each other.

The group will discuss some or all of the following questions as time permits.

Reference page 86: What does "trust in God" mean? How well do you see your helplessness and embrace God's sovereignty?

Reference pages 87-89: Why is "dependence" a negative word today? And why is dependence critical to live with God in the moment?

Reference pages 89-92: You will keep your posture of praise when you are mindful of the roadside perks from trusting God. Which roadside perks help you keep your posture of praise and give you a healthier trust in God?

Reference pages 93-95: What can happen to your relationship with God when you take a break from your steady pursuit of it?

Reference pages 95-97: How does your life change when you build it upon Biblical principles instead of on the world's system?

Reference pages 98, 99: What is "more or less" Christianity? What are the warning signs and the risks of it?

Consider this: Having great peace can change the course of your life.

Week 7 | Trust in God, Third Ingredient...pages 100-122

Facilitator Notes: The group has read through page 122.

Assign reading for week 8...Begin Fourth Ingredient, pages 124-150.

End with prayer for each other.

The group will discuss some or all of the following questions as time permits.

Reference pages 100-103: Less sin, more direction, and less stress are benefits of trusting God. How will these hidden benefits improve your life?

Reference pages 105-108: Be aware that pride is oftentimes subtle. How do pride and arrogance hinder your efforts to trust in God?

Reference pages 108-110: What are you afraid of when it comes to trusting God?

Reference pages 110-113: What are the personal stumbling blocks that hinder your total dependence upon God? Discuss them.

Reference page 114: How does a trusting relationship with God change the outcome of your day?

Reference pages 116-118: What is the relationship between lack of patience and selfishness?

Reference pages 120-121: How will you take advantage of the Holy Spirit's guidance, so that He can direct your journey better?

Consider this: When worry grips and impatience brews, trusting God is suddenly out of the picture.

 # Week 8 | Desire for God, Fourth Ingredient...pages 124-150

Facilitator Notes: The group has read through page 150.

Assign reading for week 9...Complete Fourth Ingredient, pages 151-170.

End with prayer for each other.

The group will discuss some or all of the following questions as time permits.

Reference pages 126, 127: Why is it that the more time you spend with God, the more His character develops within you?

Reference pages 128, 129: God must become your prized possession. Are His desires, yours... and do you desire Him more? Why can't you desire God's nature until you are passionate about His ways?

Reference pages 130-134: Trustworthy: How does a loving commitment to God make you more trustworthy to others?

Reference pages 135-144: Faithful: Why do loyalty and trustworthiness lead to obedience to God and His will? How did Jesus model this?

Reference pages 144-148: What is the difference between sympathy and compassion? Which does more for God's kingdom, and why?

Reference pages 148-150: How does compassion triumph over judgment? When and how have you experienced victory in this?

Consider this: Ingredient Four solidifies your identity in Christ as you begin to share in His nature.

Week 9 | Desire for God, Fourth Ingredient...pages 151-170

Facilitator Notes: The group has read through page 170.

Assign reading for week 10...Begin Fifth Ingredient, pages 172-194.

End with prayer for each other.

The group will discuss some or all of the following questions as time permits.

Reference page 151: Mercy resembles God's gift of grace to us. What are the similarities between mercy and grace?

Reference page 152: How does withholding genuine forgiveness damage your relationship with God?

Reference pages 153: In what ways does mercy extend forgiveness? How does a relationship with God put forgiveness into motion?

Reference page 154, 155: You know you've truly forgiven if God's lasting peace governs the issue. What is the three step plan to forgive?

Reference page 163: "Battles are fought with blood, but truly they are won with love." What does this mean? How can you apply it to your life?

Reference page 164: Greater Love lives inside of you. What must happen for God's love to be released if yours gets stuck?

Reference pages 167, 168: How much of God do you desire? Which of His attributes do you need more helpings of at the buffet line?

Consider this: God's love is bigger than selfishness. It sees others first and looks out for them.

 Week 10 | Abandonment, Fifth Ingredient...pages 172-194

Facilitator Notes: The group has read through page 194.

Assign reading for week 11...Complete Fifth Ingredient, pages 195-208.

End with prayer for each other.

The group will discuss some or all of the following questions as time permits.

Reference pages 173, 174: "Babies" range from sin and burdens to goals and dreams. Which ones most hinder your relationship with God?

Reference pages 175-177: What is the difference between surrender and abandonment? What will you gain from abandonment?

Reference pages 179-181: How does letting go in peaceful abandonment become a gift to God?

Reference pages 181-186: Why are selfishness and selfish pride so dangerous when learning to live with God in the moment?

Reference pages 186-188: When practicing servant leadership, how can you exercise kingdom rights instead of earthly rights?

Reference pages 189-191: Which of God's attributes from Ingredient 4 is the driving force behind abandonment? Why?

Reference pages 192-194: How heavy are your pockets? What weighs you down enough to hinder your intimate relationship with God?

Consider this: You must have at least a little, solid history with God before you can "let go" and trust Him.

Week 11 | Abandonment, Fifth Ingredient...pages 195-208

Facilitator Notes: The group has read through page 208.

Assign reading for week 12...Blend of Ingredients, pages 210-232.

End with prayer for each other.

The group will discuss some or all of the following questions as time permits.

Reference page 195: How does letting go and placing your cares at the cross of Christ bring peaceful abandonment?

Reference page 196: How can abandonment begin as a desire to do what's right, depend on faith, and finish at the Cross?

Reference pages 197-199: There shouldn't be any regrets with genuine abandonment. Why is abandonment worth it?

Reference pages 199, 200: What is the difference between a mediocre and an excellent relationship with God? Why should you not settle for less than excellence?

Reference pages 201-203: Why can you look forward to abandonment instead of dreading and fearing it? How do you feel about it?

Reference pages 204, 205: What are the life changing perks that come from peaceful abandonment?

Reference page 205: When has abandonment been helpful and not felt like a forceful act of God to control you?

Consider this: Abandonment is a beautiful encounter with God that helps you thrive in His presence.

 # Week 12 | Blend of Ingredients...pages 210-232

Facilitator Notes: The group has read through page 232 and has finished the book.

Finish with questions and comments...Discuss possible Living Groups that will sprout from this group.

End with prayer for each other.

The group will discuss some or all of the following questions as time permits.

Reference pages 211, 212: Does your life song express who you are and your posture of praise to God, moment by moment?

Reference pages 212, 213: How can the past and the future keep you from thriving in God's presence right now?

Reference pages 216, 217: Keep your heart pure and remember that God lives there. Why is God's residency in your heart such a great miracle?

Reference pages 217, 218: Where is your joyful place? How much time do you spend there, and is it as often as possible?

Reference page 219: How do you know that the presence of God is the same today as it was in the Bible?

Reference pages 221, 222: Why is it that when you trust God, He trusts you with His will and purpose as well?

Reference pages 223, 224: How can you make room for more of God and crowd out more of the world's ways in your life?

Consider this: "Don't wrestle; just nestle." Run into the arms of your Savior and live!

www.ingramcontent.com/pod-product-compliance
Lightning Source LLC
Chambersburg PA
CBHW051403070526
44584CB00023B/3271